THE ROBIN HOOD OF EL DORADO

Historians of the Frontier and American West
Richard W. Etulain, Series Editor

THE ROBIN HOOD OF EL DORADO

The Saga of Joaquin Murrieta, Famous Outlaw of California's Age of Gold

WALTER NOBLE BURNS

PUBLISHED IN COOPERATION WITH THE
UNIVERSITY OF NEW MEXICO CENTER FOR THE AMERICAN WEST
UNIVERSITY OF NEW MEXICO PRESS
ALBUQUERQUE

1999 University of New Mexico Press
Paperback Edition.

Library of Congress Cataloging-in-Publication Data

Burns, Water Noble.
The Robin Hood of El Dorado: the saga of Joaquin
Murrieta, famous outlaw of California's age of gold /
Walter Noble Burns.
p. cm.—(Historians of the frontier and American
West)
Originally published: New York : Coward-McCann, Inc.,
c1932.
"Published in cooperation with the University of New
Mexico Center for the American West."
ISBN 0-8263-2155-0 (pbk. : alk. paper)
1. Murrieta, Joaquin, d. 1853.
2. Outlaws—California—Biography.
3. Mexican—California—Biography.
4. Frontier and pioneer life—California.
5. California—History—1850–1950.
I. Title.
II. Series.
F865.M96B87 1999
979.40'4'092—dc21
[B] 99-26428
CIP

To That pal of Mine:

My Wife

CONTENTS

FOREWORD

TO THE THE PAPERBACK EDITION

The historical Joaquin Murrieta has inspired scores of novelists, historians, and poets to create and recreate his life. Since Murrieta's exit from California in 1853, each generation has resurrected him to tell his story anew from a contemporary point of view. The novelistic history of Walter Noble Burns, an eastern-born and -bred newspaperman, tried to recapture the romance of the Old West, a West that had long passed out of existence when *The Robin Hood of El Dorado* was first published in 1932. The United States needed heroes during the darkest days of the Great Depression, and Burns's book described a more glorious and adventurous time and place, gold rush California, when a poor Mexican fought heroically against tremendous odds. During the 1930s, Hollywood films and musical extravaganzas helped a suffering public escape the hopelessness of unemployment and poverty. Burns's *The Robin Hood of El Dorado*, a lavish, romantic, and gripping tale of gallant heroism, unspeakable cruelty, and horrendous violence, betrayed youthful innocence and avenging spirit. The Murrieta story allowed the general public to flee for a few hours the drab and depressing realities of industrial America into a distant, imagined past and, simultaneously, to identify with the hero's quest for justice and revenge.

The author, Walter Noble Burns, was born in Lebanon, Kentucky, in 1872. He was the son of Colonel Thomas Edgar Burns, a Civil War veteran. As a child, young Walter listened to the tales of Civil War battles and the heroism of soldiers, including his father. The family moved to Louisville where Walter attended high school. Unable financially to attend college, Burns secured an apprenticeship as a reporter on the *Louisville Evening Post.* His talent for words and description led him to a career in journalism. Thirsting for adventure, Burns decided to join a whaling ship bound for the South Pacific. The crew set sail from San Francisco in 1890 and went to the South Seas and later the Bering Sea and Arctic Ocean. This experience became the basis for Burns's first book, *A Year With a Whaler* (1913). After returning home from his voyage, he continued his work as a reporter until the outbreak of the Spanish American War in 1898, when he joined a Kentucky contingent and served in the battles around Puerto Rico. When he returned from the war, he married Rose Marie Hoke and then worked his way west, serving as a reporter successively for the *St. Louis Post Dispatch*, *Kansas City Times*, *Denver Republic*, and *San Francisco Examiner.* While working for the *Examiner*, Burns first learned of the story of Joaquin Murrieta and had a chance to visit many of the sites mentioned in his later work. Perhaps he even collected a few stories told by surviving gold miners. In 1910 Burns moved east to Chicago to become an editor of the *Chicago Inter-Ocean.* Eventually his experience earned him a position as editor of the prestigious *Chicago Tribune* in 1918. Late in his career as a journalist and editor, Burns began writing fictional histories about the American West. Published in 1926, his *The Saga of Billy the Kid* was followed by *Tombstone: An Iliad of the Southwest* in 1927 and then by *The One Way Ride* in 1931. *The Robin Hood of El Dorado*, Burns's last book, appeared in 1932, the same year that he died.

How are we to interpret this "historical" romance

published seventy years ago? To begin with, Burns was following a venerable tradition of retelling historical stories in a journalistic style, a vivid and emotional language that would appeal to the working masses. *The Robin Hood of El Dorado* was not an academic study but a popular history, and, as such, it tried to recreate the mood, dialogue, and thoughts of Murrieta and his compatriots. Burns did a great deal of research for this book, collecting hundreds of oral reminiscences of old-timers, some of whom claimed to have known Murrieta. Burns seems to have collected the stories without much skepticism about their historical truth. At times in his narrative, Burns reminds his readers that he has consulted living sources for this history and that it is not just a product of his imagination. Yet, imagination is what moves every page and brings the characters to life. The colorful dialog and emotional turmoil jump from every page and are the creative fiction of Burns the journalist. Occasionally, however, he interrupts the narrative to give us local history lessons on the gold rush mining camps, as he does in the stories of the "Hanging trees" of Amador County or in a brief description of the society and culture of Los Angeles in the 1850s. These historical asides are vivid word pictures drawn from the facts as he encountered them. No professional historian, Burns did not bother with citations or bibliographies of sources for his local histories.

The entertainment value of Burns's work is self-evident, although sophisticated audiences conditioned by Hollywood films and TV may not readily identify with the overdrawn and sometimes exaggerated prose. Nevertheless, *The Robin Hood of El Dorado* reflects the evolving history of ideas regarding Joaquin Murrieta and Mexicans in the United States as well as recreating gold rush California.

This brings us to Burns's imagining of the character of Murrieta in particular and Mexicans in general. Given the context of the 1930s and the general acceptance of racial stereotypes about Mexicans, Burns's portrait of Murrieta and his compatriots was generally positive, if not perhaps overly romantic. Burns depicted Anglo miners as rough and brutal racists, and their fictitious dialog communicates a deep contempt for all Mexicans, but Murrieta is portrayed as a handsome, intelligent, and polite young man. He stoically endures a whipping for a crime that he never committed, all the while swallowing his rage. When Anglos murder his wife and brother, Murrieta systematically kills them in revenge—a motive that Burns seems to applaud. In Burns's hands, Murrieta's lieutenant, Three Fingered Jack, however, is a psychotic, ruthless gunman who kills for the mere joy of it. Generally, Burns's description of Mexican culture and life gave human personality to a people who lacked visibility and even historical recognition within California. When Burns's book appeared in 1932, the police and immigration officials in California were enthusiastically deporting hundreds of thousands of Mexicans, claiming that they were unworthy to reside in the Golden State. *The Robin Hood of El Dorado* created a new and alternative image for Mexicans, one that was not well known.

Walter Noble Burns's history was the first twentieth-century journalistic effort to retell the story of Joaquin Murrieta for a popular audience. Undoubtedly his work drew from the classic 1854 novelistic history by the Cherokee Indian, John Rollin Ridge, *The Life and Adventures of Joaquín Murieta, The Celebrated California Bandit.* Although a fictional account, this work was the standard historical source well into the twentieth century. Burns followed much of Ridge's story line, while adding details drawn from oral interviews and legends. Burns mentioned that he had read the account of Murrieta by Ireneo Paz, the mother of the famous Mexican poet-philosopher, Octavio Paz. In 1904 she published a literary history of Murrieta entitled, *Vida y adventuras del mas célebre bandido sonorense, Joaquín Murrieta: Sus grandes proezas en California.*

Her work was brought out in an English translation in the United States in 1925. In fact the later work may have been even more influential in shaping Burns's narrative. *The Robin Hood of El Dorado* would stand as the most popular interpretation of Murrieta until 1995, when James Varley published *The Legend of Joaquín Murrieta: California's Gold Rush Bandit*, a work that uses Burns as a source. The most recent fictionalized historical view of Joaquin is a lurid adventure tale by Don Gwaltney, *The Bandit Joaquín: An Orphaned Mexican's Search for Revenge in the California Gold Rush* (1997).

Of course, Joaquin Murrieta is today an important hero to hundreds of thousands of Chicanos and Mexican Americans. Murrieta stands for the resistance against Anglo American cultural and economic domination. In revolutionary Cuba and pre-Peristroika Russia, Murrieta appeared in textbooks and in life-size statues as an example of Third World peoples' revolt against Western imperialism. World-famous poet Pablo Neruda saw in Murrieta the struggle of Latin American people to be free of North American hegemony. One of the first Chicano Movement poems, written by Rudolfo "Corky" Gonzales in 1968, was entitled "I Am Joaquín." Later it was the text of the first Chicano movie. Perhaps Joaquin Murrieta's appeal to the imagination arises from the many mysteries surrounding his life and death, and from his status as an underdog who suffered injustices and fought against impossible odds. This Mexican who lived in gold rush California has inspired a generation of Chicano activists who see him as a victim of Anglo racism and as an avenger of the rights of the Spanish-speaking peoples in the United States. In this way, Murrieta is a hero to the Chicano Movement as well as to those in Latin America and Europe who are critical of North American aggression and colonialism.

As unlikely as it may seem, Walter Noble Burns's *The Robin Hood of El Dorado* was a steppingstone towards this modernization of Murrieta's significance. The book, reprinted by the

University of New Mexico Press, stands on its own as an interpretation of Murrieta as genuine American folk hero.

Richard Griswold del Castillo
Department of Chicana and Chicano Studies
San Diego State University

THE ROBIN HOOD OF EL DORADO

THE ROBIN HOOD OF EL DORADO

CHAPTER I.

JUST ANOTHER MEXICAN.

THE old man in overalls and checked cotton shirt sitting in a rocking chair on the front porch fanned himself with his battered straw hat and looked out over the little valley. The high hills were dark with pine and live oak and here and there on their lower benches were four or five farm houses gray with weather and half hidden among orchard trees and roses and oleanders in full bloom. Wood's Creek winding through a level flat sang a pleasant tune among willows and alders.

"This is all that's left of Saw Mill Flat," said the old timer waving his straw hat at the landscape. "Back in the early fifties when these California hills was swarmin' with gold hunters, it was a roarin' camp with more'n a thousand people and a main street a quarter of a mile long lined with saloons and gamblin' houses. They say the fellers that come in the first rush picked up gold like hickory nuts along Wood's Creek and later on a miner was out o' luck who couldn't wash out $300 and $400 a day in gold dust. I often wonder what become of all that gold. My dad was one o' them miners, but he died pore and all he left was this here two-by-four farm. The rest o' the people in Saw Mill Flat—there ain't no more'n fifteen or twenty—ain't got no more'n me. And I reckon you'll find it that a-way all up and down the Mother Lode. The Forty-Niners dipped up a fortune casual-like from some nameless creek in a tin washpan but their children have had to scratch mighty hard for a livin'.

"There was a couple o' saw-mills here in the early days and that's how come the camp got its name. But Saw Mill Flat ain't heard the whine of a buzz-saw for nigh on seventy years. The camp wasn't as tough as Sonora a mile or so off over that ridge yonder or as wild and woolly as Columbia four miles up that other way but it was a hard town with the saloons and gamblin' games wide open day and night and the fiddles goin' in the fandango house from dark till sun-up. Judgin' by the old tales, you might think them miners of early times worked all day up to their hips in muck and water and then drank whiskey and danced with Mexican gals and bucked the tiger all night. The camp didn't have a man for breakfast every mornin' but there was considerable cuttin' and shootin' and killin' and a hangin' now and then. You hear a lot about the honesty in the mines in them gold rush days and how the miners used to leave their gold dust layin' around in their cabins in kettles and tin cans and buckskin sacks. Well, maybe that was true but the honesty of Saw Mill Flat wouldn't 'a' stood no sech test and the feller who took them kind of chances was a fool. Thieves was thick as fleas, and with a bottle of whiskey worth its weight in gold, there was plenty o' low-down cusses who'd slit your throat for the price of a dram. Hardly a night passed some sluice boxes wasn't robbed.

"I was born in Saw Mill Flat and never was more'n sixty miles away from it in my life. But I can't remember the old wild days. All I know about 'em is what my father and mother and the old timers 've told me. You see I'm only seventy-five years old. Like most of the old people of these parts I'm what you call a second generation Forty-Niner. But if I never seen the town when it was alive, I seen it die. I ain't given to sentiment, bein' raised rough, but I'm here to tell you, stranger, it ain't pretty to see a town die. I felt like a mourner at a funeral standin' by an open grave listenin' to the clods thumpin' down on the coffin. By the time I was old enough to remember anything, the gold here petered out, the miners struck out for new diggin's and the saloonkeepers and gamblers and Mexican dance gals closed up shop and hit the out-trail. The town was left lifeless all of a sudden and seemed like it might 'a' died with its boots on with a bullet between the eyes. But its corpse was still here with no undertaker to bury it and, as the years went by, it crumbled into dust before my eyes. Some of the buildings was tore down for the lumber; others fell into wrack and ruin and almost before I knowed it, all was gone and where they'd stood was only chaparral and thickets of young pine.

"When I was a lad, the old place seemed like it was haunted. When I looked into the windows, splashed over with rain and dirt, I kinder thought I might see ghosts clinkin' glasses at the old bars or whirlin' round the dusty floor of the old fandango house. That palatial dancin' establishment, made out o' pine boards with a plank stretched across a couple o' barrels for a bar, stood right out yonder where that jackrabbit is scratching hisself with his off-hind foot and where you see that robin wrastlin' with a worm, Joaquin Murrieta * dealt monte in Ed. Parson's saloon. Nowadays as I set here on the front porch and look out over the empty valley, I somctimes

* There is a great diversity of opinion as to the correct spelling of the famous outlaw's name. It has been spelled Murieta, Murrieta, Murietta, Murrietta and Muriete. Ridge in his life of the bandit spells it Murieta. Bancroft spells it the same way. This spelling is used by the U. S. Congressional Library at Washington in cataloguing the name and by the California State Library at Sacramento. As the name of a town in Southern California the U. S. Post Office authorities have adopted Murietta. Ireneo Paz, whose life of the outlaw has been translated from the Spanish by Frances P. Belle, spells it Murrieta. This spelling was pronounced correct by Don Antonio Coronel, once mayor of Los Angeles, who knew the family, and it is the spelling that was used by Rosa, Herminia and Anita Murrieta, who formerly lived in Los Angeles and were the daughters of Joaquin's brother Antonio.

rub my eyes and wonder if the old hell-roarin' gold camp of Saw Mill Flat wasn't just a dream after all."

The old man mentioned Joaquin Murrieta's name casually. A tablet by the red dirt road that winds through the valley corroborates his statement. "Joaquin Murrieta dealt monte here," the tablet reads. So it is here in Saw Mill Flat we first pick up the trail of that famous young outlaw, knightliest of highwaymen, most romantic of cut-throats, who to avenge a tragic personal injury became the most remorseless of killers and wrote his name in letters of blood across California's Age of Gold.

"See that big pine tree over there on the hill across the creek?" remarked the old timer. "Just about there Joaquin Murrieta lived in a little adobe house with his wife Rosita. A grape vine they say Joaquin and Rosita planted used to wind about the trunk o' the tree. It's done gone now but many's the bunch o' grapes I et off it when I was a boy. You can still see some low ridges grown over with weeds where the house used to stand. Them's what's left o' the 'dobe walls melted down to nothin', you might say, by the rains of eighty years. And if you look close you can make out the line of a ditch runnin' past what used to be the front door. That was the *asequia* that watered Joaquin's little vegetable patch."

It is difficult to imagine that this little valley, peaceful and beautiful, brimming with sunshine and filled with the clean smell of pines, was ever the scene of outrage and murder. But here in this cabin on the hillside occurred the tragedy that changed Joaquin Murrieta from a normal young man, living happily with a wife whom he loved and who loved him, into a murderous demon who tracked those who had wronged him to their death with a sustained passion of vengeance that knew no mercy. And the old pine tree that casts its shadow over the ruins of his home marks the starting point of a career as lurid as a madman's dream.

A handsome young fellow with black eyes and black hair but with a face of ivory pallor such as you might have expected if his hair had been golden and his eyes blue. Of medium height, well set up, athletic. An *hidalgo* touch in his grave dignity, his punctilious politeness and his air of proud reserve. A calm thoughtful countenance that indicated a coolly poised character. Quiet, frank, unpretentious. Honest. Known as a square gambler and a square man. Not averse to a glass of wine. Considered a good dancer. A lively, agreeable companion. Some humor and laughter in him. Even tempered. Never known to have had a fight or a quarrel. A far remove from the traditional adventurer type. Finding his greatest pleasure in quiet domesticity. His interest centered in his wife and his home.

That was the Joaquin Murrieta that Saw Mill Flat knew. All the old timers, who knew him and who disagreed on many of the details of his career, were in unanimous agreement on this estimate of his original character. All declared that in these early years before he turned a corner of the road and by an accident of fate stumbled upon life-wrecking tragedy, there was nothing in his appearance or conduct to suggest even vaguely any dangerous or criminal possibilities. Yet beneath the calm exterior of this every-day young man were slumbering whirlwinds and in the still depths of his commonplace soul volcanoes of passion were smouldering. Doubtless if he had been left in the grooves of ordinary routine, he would have lived a humdrum, blameless life and been forgotten before the first daisies bloomed on his grave. But when a catastrophe of seismic proportions jarred him from his peaceful foundations, this unassuming youth became a devil who rode through blood to his horse's bridle and sank all scruples of conscience and every kindly impulse in the depths of a frozen heart. One can imagine no stranger or more revolutionary metamorphosis. But with his wild, tempestuous future unguessed, this human hieroglyph, that no one could read, aroused no curiosity and went unregarded by the men who elbowed him on the street or crowded nightly about his monte table. Few knew or cared anything about him. He was a nobody lost in the hurly-burly of the mining camp. To Saw Mill Flat, Joaquin Murrieta was just another Mexican.

Listen now to the quaint tale of the love affairs of Joaquin and Rosita. At the Real de Bayareca between Arispe and Hermosillo in one of the great valleys into which the Sierra Madres divide the state of Sonora in the northwest corner of Mexico, Joaquin Murrieta and Rosita Carmel Feliz were born. Their families were of old pioneer stock and boasted pure Castilian descent though doubtless, as is commonly the case in Mexico, their ancestral lines had been tinctured at one time or another with a drop or two of Yaqui or ancient Aztec blood. The valley had been settled by the Spaniards soon after the Conquest; Cortez had visited it; from it Coronado had set out on his romantic quest for the Seven Cities of Cibola; and it is possible the forebears of Joaquin and Rosita had marched as mail-clad soldiers under the banners of the old Conquistadores. From babyhood, the boy and girl grew up together. They were educated at the convent school, went to mass every morning at the old church in the plaza, danced together at the fandangos. When Joaquin was eighteen and Rosita sixteen, they fell in love. Or perhaps they had been sweethearts all their lives.

Just here, Don Jose Gonzales steps unexpectedly from the wings into the little drama. Don Jose was old and very rich. His *hacienda* was measured in square miles rather than acres; he owned cattle and horses by the tens of thousands; he lived like a grandee among his servants and retainers and had once been a familiar figure at the court of the Emperor Augustin Iturbide. By chance one morning, Don Jose saw Rosita on her way to church. Very sweet and pretty she looked as she stepped daintily along with her rosary and missal in her hand. Never, thought the old hidalgo, had he seen a girl so beautiful. He had long felt the need of a wife to solace his declining years. But not for him a frumpy old dowager painted and powdered to hide her wrinkles. His wife must be young and comely. Here was the very girl of his dreams ready to his hand. He had but to reach out and pluck her as he might a rose. What mattered it that Don Jose was old enough to be her father? His vast wealth would tilt the scales in his favor. Did not every pretty darling have her price? Were not all women for sale?

When Don Jose opened diplomatic negotiations with Ramon Feliz, Rosita's father, that worthy man was elated at the prospect of such a dazzling alliance. Of course he would arrange the affair at once. He had but to speak to Rosita and that would settle it. Don Jose could rest assured of that. How Rosita felt about it was a matter of no moment. She was very young and needed paternal guidance in the selection of a husband. She was a dutiful daughter and her father's word was her law. So between Papa Ramon and Don Jose, Rosita's future seemed pretty definitely determined.

Ramon Feliz now walked among the clouds. All his life he had been very poor. As a packer, or what might be called less euphemistically a mule skinner, he earned a meager living carrying provisions by mule train to the silver mines in the mountains. He had grown gray driving mules over the mountain trails, fighting with them, dodging their heels, lashing them, swearing at them. Mules, nothing but mules, as long as he could remember. In the new life opening for him, the hee-haw of nightmare mules would fill his ears no more. Don Jose was no niggard; he would provide handsomely for his father-in-law; and the old mule-skinner dreamed of the happy days when he would loll in the cool patio of his home, gorging himself on costly viands and tossing off bumpers of sparkling wine. The dear God, it seemed, had at last been good to him.

Ramon returned one day from what he supposed was his last trip to the mountains and his farewell forever to those terrible mules. As he entered his home from the street, his mind was in a whirl with the glitter and pomp of the approaching wedding of Rosita and Don Jose. He pictured to himself the crowded church, the bridal procession, the solemn ceremony at the altar. How the people would stare and crane their necks. What a beautiful bride Rosita would be in her shimmering white gown and billowing veil. Walking through the hallway, still under the spell of his happy dream, Ramon stepped out into the patio . . . and saw Rosita in Joaquin's arms!

"*Nombre de Dios!* Rosita! What does this mean? Joaquin, you young scoundrel, how dare you make love to my daughter? Do you not know she is promised in marriage to the great Don Jose Gonzales? Has a beggarly rascal like you the effrontery to aspire to her hand? Out of my house! Begone! Never darken my door again."

That night the thunder of horses' hoofs aroused the dwellers along the valley road from their slumbers. In the moonlight they saw two riders sweeping past at breakneck speed. One was Rosita, the other Joaquin. They were married next morning in Arispe.

For the young lovers, the Camino del Diablo and

Hell's Home Stretch, those tragic roads across the deserts of Arizona and southern California strewn with the bones of so many men and women in the days of the gold rush, became a honeymoon trail. On their journey to the California mines, they stopped frequently here and there for an indefinite length of time to replenish their funds. In Los Angeles, Joaquin worked as a horse trainer with a Mexican *maroma* or circus. At San Juan Bautista and San Jose he dealt monte. On the ranch of the famous Dr. John Marsh in the Mount Diablo country, he was employed as a bronco buster. In Stockton, according to tradition, he opened a store stocked with goods bought on credit at the exorbitant prices of the period and lost money in the venture. Near the mining town of Sonora he panned for gold. He lived for a while at Martinez, where to-day they will show you the site of his cabin, and mined among the gulches of Yankee Hill. Next we find him settled at Saw Mill Flat where he is supposed to have arrived in the spring of 1850. The journey from Mexico must have taken a year or more. When he left his native village, he could not speak a word of English. When he arrived in the California hills, he spoke the language almost without trace of foreign accent.

Rosita was a modest girl for all her roving life with her vaquero-gambler husband. She was, however, no cloistered spirit, no madonna, but a lively little minx, gay, sparkling, bubbling over with happiness; a vital part of the world about her, full of interest in everything in it, reacting with quick sympathy to its joys and sorrows, tears just back of her smiles; a woman of the earth as unaffected as a woodland creature. The vividness of the tropics was in her dark beauty. Her eyes were Mexico. All the languorous charm, mystery, romance, of that ancient Spanish land were in them. In a flowered mantilla with a crimson blossom in her hair, she would have been such a figure as one might imagine dancing a fandango to the click of castanets or leaning from a latticed balcony to drop a rose to a cavalier strumming a guitar in the moonlight.

Small wonder men stared at her when she went abroad in Saw Mill Flat. Women were not numerous in the camp. Pretty women were rare. But Mexican women were not above suspicion; the camp judged them by the free and easy standards of dance hall wenches. The glances that followed Rosita were for the most part the tributes of clean-minded men to beauty abloom with health. But not all the glances were of that kind. Among the men who jostled one another on Saw Mill Flat's crowded street were many of refinement and scholarly attainments. But there were also bad eggs. The luck of gold rush days was uncertain. It made some men rich overnight. It left others stranded vagabonds. But in the rough mining camps, the lucky and unlucky, the good and bad, dressed alike. A lawyer was hardly to be distinguished from a horse-thief or a preacher from a stage robber. The bartender in a tough dram shop might have been a judge in the East. A musician scraping a fiddle in a fandango house possibly had been a college professor back home. The boarding house waiter or saloon roustabout once might have strutted proudly as a society beau and made love to dainty belles in crinolines and corkscrew curls. It was not easy to read character through a red flannel shirt and patched pants stuffed into heavy boots were a poor clew to a man's past.

But Rosita walked serenely among them all, unmindful alike of admiration of the better sort or the burning glances of drunken satyrs. She was as chaste as a lily. No whisper of scandal had ever touched her. For her there was only one man in the world and that was her husband. Other men meant nothing to her.

Joaquin, Rosita and Frank Wilson, a friend who lived on an adjoining claim, sat in the front room of the Murrieta home—the adobe of three rooms under the old pine tree on the hill. The afternoon was waning. Cool shadows filled the valley. Miners were busy at their long toms along the creek. Saw Mill Flat was quiet, awaiting the night's revelry. The walls of the room were neatly whitewashed; the floor was of clean, hard earth. On a little bracket stood a painted plaster image of the Virgin. Beneath it hung a crucifix. On a table lay Joaquin's bowie knife in a leather sheath. Rosita sat in a corner idly plucking the strings of a guitar. A door at the rear opened into a bedroom. Behind the bedroom was the kitchen.*

"They tell me," remarked Wilson, "those five fellows working the claim next to yours have struck it pretty rich."

"I heard so," replied Joaquin.

"But it seems to me they are trenching over on your ground."

"They are. And they are using water from my *asequia* to do their sluicing. I went out and spoke to them about it."

"What did they say?"

"They got ugly and told me they would dig where they pleased. I wanted no quarrel and walked away."

"I think they are bad men," declared Rosita.

"What do you know about them?" asked Joaquin.

"Two of them tried to flirt with me on the street. One caught me by the arm and called me '*querida.*' The other

* My account of this affair is based on a story supposed to have been told originally by Frank Wilson. It was corroborated with some difference in details by Lewis Page, a resident of Saw Mill Flat at the time, who told it to his daughter, Miss Marian Page, still living a half mile or so from the scene of the occurrence.

asked me to slip out some night and meet him. I had a hard time getting rid of them."

"Why didn't you tell me of this?"

Rosita shrugged. "I didn't want you to get mixed up in a fight. It was nothing. I think they were drunk."

"Well," said Wilson, "are you going to let these rowdies rob you of the gold in your claim without doing anything about it?"

"I hardly know what to do. If trouble started, some one might get killed."

"I think I can take care of this for you," Wilson answered. "There's some law in this country. I'll go into town right away and consult an attorney. He'll find a way to stop them."

Soon after Wilson had gone, the five American miners, fresh from the ditches, their clothes splotched with wet mud, marched into the house, boldly, noisily, with the air of swashbucklers. They were plainly bent on trouble. Rosita looked up in alarm. Joaquin arose.

"Well?"

"We're here to tell you, you've got to pull your freight out o' these here diggin's," blurted out the leader, a huge, glowering savage, in a loud, menacing voice.

"Who says so?"

"We say so."

"Who are you?"

"We're good American citizens—that's who we are and that's who you ain't. This here's a white man's camp and no greasers wanted."

"I don't know about that."

"We're tellin' you."

"There are plenty of Mexicans in Saw Mill Flat."

"They're thick as flies at hog killin' time. They've come crowdin' in here like they was as good as white folks and they've took up some of the best claims on the creek. But we're goin' to serve notice on 'em to pack up and clear out and waste no time about it. California belongs to the U. S. of America. The Mexican war done settled that. California's ourn. And the gold in these California hills is ourn. America for Americans and to hell with furriners. These here greasers pannin' out our gold air thievin' varmints. They're robbin' us American miners of what American soldiers fit and bled fer. Them's the facts put fair and square."

"There's no law barring Mexicans from this country and no law against their mining here. Mexicans have as much right to dig for gold in California as you have." *

"Well, we don't allow to git into no argyment with you. We ain't no lawyers. But we know our rights and, by gosh, we're goin' to have what belongs to us. We're sick o' bein' robbed by a lot o' low-down greaser thieves and we ain't a-goin' to stand it no longer."

"I still have faith in the American government. I think it will do justice to the Mexicans in these mines and see that their rights are protected."

"You and Uncle Sam kin settle that betwixt you. But we're takin' over this property right now. This claim is jumped."

"This claim is mine and you and your bullies won't run me off of it."

"We'll run you off or shoot you off."

"You'll jump my claim if you have to murder me, will you?"

"That's jest what we'll do."

"Kill me and your own countrymen will hang you on the tallest pine in Saw Mill Flat. And you know it. There may be mighty little law in these diggings but there's miners' fair play."

* The California law taxing foreign miners $20 a month was not passed until the summer of 1850. It was repealed in March 1851.

"Git them fool notions out o' your head. It ain't no crime to kill a greaser but we don't aim to take no chances on stretchin' hemp. You light out peaceable and nobody's goin' to lay a finger on you. But git balky and you shore air liable to go out in a pine box."

"I will stay right here on this claim."

"No, you won't," roared the ruffian white with rage. "You dig out o' here or thar'll be hell a-poppin'. Git goin' and keep on movin' and don't you never show hide nor hair in these diggin's agin. Thar's the trail right out yonder. You hit it and hit it quick."

But Joaquin was not to be intimidated by bluster and big talk.

"You can't bulldoze me," he said quietly. "I'm not a rabbit to run every time a cur dog barks. I'm a Mexican but I'm a man. Make no mistake about that. You're wasting time. Go on about your business and leave me to mine. You'll never get this claim unless you pay me for it."

"Well now that's a right bright idee. Fair enough, says I. You're a smarter feller than I took you fer. We'll pay you. Shore we'll pay you. Here's cash down on the spot."

His heavy fist crashed into Joaquin's face. Joaquin fell to his knees but was up in a flash and sprang for his bowie knife on the table. Against such odds, cold steel was his only hope.

"Look out, boys. Don't let him git that knife. Tear into him. Beat the daylights out o' him."

The five men leaped upon Joaquin with flying fists. Strong young athlete as he was, he had as much show against this swarm of hardy villains as a jack-rabbit cornered by a pack of wolves. Their rushing attack drove him fighting desperately back and forth across the room.

"My knife, Rosita. Quick. Get me my knife."

Rosita snatched the bowie from the table. But with Joaquin in the center of the furiously swirling battle, she could not reach him. But in that terrific moment, the gentle girl turned tigress. If Joaquin could not have the knife, she would use it. She would help him if she died in the attempt. Springing at the leader, she aimed a thrust at his heart. Brave Rosita! But her heroism was in vain. The giant seized her wrist, and twisting the knife from her hand, pinioned her in his arms against the wall. "You little wild cat," he snarled.

Beneath the bludgeoning of iron fists, Joaquin went down time after time, scrambling to his feet only to be felled again. As he sprawled on the floor, the murderous knaves kicked him in the face, the head, the body, driving in the blows from their ponderous boots with all their might and main until, battered and mangled, he lay insensible, a pool of blood spreading slowly about him.

Held against the wall by the miscreant who had wrenched the knife from her, Rosita, pale with horror, watched her husband battling for his life and saw him stretched on the floor limp and apparently lifeless. Her sense of helplessness drove her to the verge of frenzy. She screamed hysterically. She cried to the saints for some miracle of deliverance. She called down the curse of heaven on the pitiless brutes. It was a heart-breaking tragedy through which she was passing—an ordeal of torture like the agonies of a martyr being burned at the stake.

Now that the hurly-burly was over, the ruffians, with brazen ribaldry, looked her over critically like gutter voluptuaries appraising the charms of some nymph of the brothels.

"As purty a piece of calico as I've set my eyes on sence I left the Missouri."

"Fer a Mexican wench, she's shore a humdinger. Take a look at that figger. Kinder neat, ain't it?"

"I'll bet she could love a feller to death. She ain't got them black eyes fer nothin'."

"Tried to kill me, eh?" purred the scoundrel who still held her in his arms. "Naughty baby."

"Let me go," cried Rosita.

"What you want to kill a good friend like me fer? You ain't fergot me, have you—me and my pard over thar? We're the fellers who met you on the street and tried to fix things up with you. But pretty baby turned us down cold."

"Holy Virgin protect me!"

"But this is another time, honey. Quit your squirmin'. It won't do you no good. We've got you dead to rights this pop."

"Help me, help me, Mother of God!"

"Come on, baby."

The relentless blackguard dragged the screaming, writhing, fighting girl into the back room. The others crowded in after him. The door slammed behind them.

When Wilson returned from his call on the lawyer, the cabin was silent. The five miners had disappeared. Joaquin still lay insensible. Dashing water in his face, Wilson revived him.

"Rosita? Where is Rosita?"

Joaquin staggered into the back room. There on the bed lay his wife, as white and still as if she were dead, her clothes torn and disheveled. He caught her in his arms. *"Querida! Mi querida!"* Back and forth he carried her as if she were a baby, covering her face with kisses, crooning to her over and over, "My darling! My poor little darling!"

Perhaps in the dark spaces where her spirit wandered, she heard his voice calling her back from the brink of the grave. Her eyes opened as if in resurrection. They lighted with happiness as she saw his face close to hers.

"Joaquin!"

All her love for him thrilled in her voice. Her arms stole about his neck.

Again she sank into unconsciousness. Placing her tenderly upon the couch, Joaquin watched her with anxious gaze. Once more her eyes opened.

"I am cold," she murmured. "It is growing dark. Put your arms about me, Joaquin."

Folding her to his breast, Joaquin could feel the beating of her heart against his own. It was like the weak fluttering of young wings. It grew fainter—and fainter—and ceased.

With bowed head Joaquin stood in a daze looking on his dead wife, unable to understand the sudden, crushing tragedy, unwilling to believe it. Wilson took him by the arm and drew him gently away. But Joaquin shook him off. A transforming change came over him. His face twisted in a grimace of savage ferocity and his black eyes burned with maniacal fury. He trembled from head to heel as he shook his fists aloft and his husky voice was like the menacing snarl of a wild beast at bay.

"By the blood of Christ, I will make them pay for this! I will kill them if I have to follow them to the hinges of hell! I will have their hearts' blood as sure as there is a God in heaven!"

A flock of buzzards wheeled high above a lonely gulch in the Stanislaus river hills a few miles from Columbia. What rare tidbit had these sable-plumed epicures spied upon which to satiate their dainty appetites? Somewhere in the green, still wilderness beneath them, a banquet of death had been spread and slowly, majestically, in vast spirals, they descended to the feast. On weighed pinions, they sank in narrowing circles below the rim of the hills, below the tree tops—lower—lower—lower—

Months later some prospectors looking for gold in the wild ravine stumbled upon five skeletons. The ghastly relics, lying about the ashes of an old camp fire, had been washed by the rains and bleached by the sun until they were as white as polished marble. Creeping vines half covered them. Wild flowers bloomed among the gleaming bones. No one knew who these dead men had been and the skeletons of mystery were buried together in a nameless grave. But there was one clew remaining as to the cause of their death. Through each of the five skulls was a neat, round hole made by a bullet.

CHAPTER II.

THE MARK OF THE LARIAT.

MURPHY'S DIGGINGS, famous in the Joaquin Murrieta legend, was as lawless and tumultuous a gold camp in old days as the mining country knew. To-day it is an idyllically peaceful little village. Its cottage homes are embowered among orchard trees and hollyhocks. The bell of the little church on the hill sounds its peaceful summons to worship every Sabbath morning. The main street with its gray, weather-beaten buildings is a tunnel of coolness formed by long rows of ancient elm trees that arch above it. Nothing ever happens there. When the gold gave out, the old town rolled over and went to sleep and has been slumbering ever since. In a little graveyard in the outskirts, the rude forefathers of the hamlet sleep under the live oaks and pines and it is a toss-up which is the livelier place, the village or the cemetery.

Murphy's Diggings is one of a group of old-time camps whose very names are redolent of the Big Stampede and the trails of Forty-Nine. Within a few miles are Poverty Flat, Dead Man's Gulch, Poker Flat, Murderer's Bar, You Bet, Gouge Eye, Whiskey Slide, Hell's Delight, Devil's Elbow, Rawhide, Rattlesnake Gulch, Poorman's Flat, Hangman's Bar, Hungry Camp, Gospel Gulch, Git-up-and-Git, and Big Oak Flat. Picturesque names they are;—crude poetry shot through with the romance of wild times; crusted with raw gold dust and baptized in blood and thunder; washed out of a swirling mountain stream with a rocker in some purple gorge or pried from the crevices of gray rocks with a jackknife; full-length novels and dramas in two words.

But when the age of culture dawned and pick and shovel miners put on boiled shirts and blacked their shoes and took a bath every Saturday night, nomenclature grew more refined. There was Fiddletown. Judge Purrington of the Fiddletown bar raged inwardly every time he went to San Francisco and had to sign "Fiddletown" on a hotel register. The crude name, he felt, stamped him as a simple-minded hick from the tall timber. Old camps around Fiddletown were still known as Suckertown, Hogtown, Helltown and Shirt Tail; which was all very well for such backwoods settlements. But Fiddletown went to church and Sunday school and had board floors in its homes and an elegant hotel with real glass in the windows. So at a mass meeting of citizens, which was profoundly stirred by the judge's eloquent indignation, the name of Fiddletown was changed to Oleta. You will find Oleta still on the map but you will look in vain for Fiddletown outside the pages of Bret Harte. Then there was Freezeout. You might think that name as romantic as any mining town would want. But no. Mr. Thomas Brown, the village highbrow, had found a more polite name in Bulwer's "Last Days of Pompeii." It was Ione. So the town was known thereafter as Ione, though doubtless three-fourths of its inhabitants had a vague idea that Ione was some new-fangled kind of medicine; and the scholarly Mr. Brown, who of course should have been shot, was greatly applauded by his more elegant fellow citizens. Jimtown of old days assumed the smug name of Jamestown. American Camp became Columbia. Bottileas (Place of Bottles—empty beer and whiskey bottles) was rechristened Jackson, and Hangtown, where the hang tree stood on the main street, settled down to a dignified future as Placerville.

The country of Bret Harte and Mark Twain is all around Murphy's Diggings. At Tuttletown—there are only two houses left in Tuttletown, one of them empty—the old stone store in which Bret Harte clerked is still standing; and as you wander through the dilapidated old ghost towns of the hills, you half expect to meet some of the characters that live so vividly in his stories,—John Oakhurst, beau ideal of gamblers, Mother Shipton, the Duchess and Uncle Billy of "The Outcasts of Poker Flat"; Col. Starbottle of "An Episode of Fiddletown" and "The Iliad of Sandy Bar"; Old Kentuck of "The Luck of Roaring Camp"; the Rose of Tuolomne, M'liss, Brown of Calaveras and Truthful James of Table Mountain, known in real life, incidentally, as "Lying Jim" Townsend. Across the road at Second Garrote a giant oak stretches a gnarled limb on which half a dozen men have been hanged and almost within its shadow is the house in which lived the two men whose classic friendship Bret Harte immortalized in "Tennessee's Pardner."

Mark Twain's cabin on Jackass Hill, happily restored, is just as it was when he lived there in the sixties with Jim Gillis as his mining partner and missed a fortune by one pail of water. A cold rain was falling one day as they worked on their claim, Twain carrying water, Gillis panning dirt.

"I won't carry any more water, Jim," said Twain. "I'm cold and wet to the skin and I'm going to the cabin and keep warm by a fire."

"Just one more pail," pleaded Gillis. "I'm getting nice color in this dirt."

"Not another drop. I'm freezing."

That settled it. On a page torn from his notebook, Gillis wrote a thirty-day claim notice and stuck it on a stick beside the pan of dirt. Then in a few days he moved to other parts and Twain went to San Francisco. The rain kept up and washed away the dirt in the pan and laid bare a handful of nuggets—pure gold. Lewis Page and a Swede from Saw Mill Flat, prospecting that way, chanced to stumble upon the pan with its glittering contents and settled down in camp to wait until the notice should expire. The minute the thirty days were up, they went to work on the claim and took out $20,000 in gold.

It was in his cabin on Jackass Hill that Mark Twain wrote his humorous classic "The Jumping Frog of Calaveras." They say Ross Coon, a bartender in Angel's Camp, told him that yarn; and in a glass case in the Calaveras hotel is preserved what they say is the mummy of the great Dan'l Webster, the original jumping frog of the story. Jim Smiley, you remember, who owned this wonderful frog, boasted it could outjump any frog in Calaveras county. And then along came a sad-faced stranger and matched up a common, garden-variety of frog against Jim Smiley's champion for a forty dollar bet; and when Smiley said, "One, two, three," the stranger's frog went hopping off as lively as you please while Dan'l Webster remained squatting at the starting line "as solid as a church," the guileful stranger having secretly filled the beast to the neck with quail shot.

The fame of Angel's Camp seems to rest more on a fictitious frog than on the $100,000,000 in real gold taken from its placers. Every year in May the little town holds a Jumping Frog Jubilee. Frogs by the hundreds from the Pacific coast, the Middle West, the South, New England—some from Europe—take part in the contests. They are tremendous frogs, some a foot long, and their owners train and groom them as if they were thoroughbred race horses being prepared for the Preakness or the Kentucky Derby. The contests are staged on the main street; each frog is given three jumps from taw; the events last three days and are witnessed by twenty or thirty thousand people; and the results are flashed by wire to newspapers all over the United States. A Stockton frog won the tournament two years in succession and when it was taken back to its home town after its second victory, it was met by the mayor and a delegation of distinguished citizens who escorted it through cheering crowds in a sort of Roman triumph to the city hall where a reception was held in its honor. The defeated frogs are usually set at liberty and the marshy lowlands about Angel's Camp now have a population of thousands of gargantuan frogs whose nightly chorus is like the deep-mouthed bellowing of a herd of bulls.

Some of the richest gold country in California lay about Murphy's Diggings. Miners were swarming over it soon after Marshall discovered gold in the race of Sutter's saw-mill at Coloma; and tales of the wonderful strikes of those Arabian Nights times still linger in the hills. Not far from Murphy's Diggings was the Sheep Ranch mine where Senator George Hearst once worked with pick and shovel and from which he took an immense fortune that was bequeathed to his son William Randolph Hearst. At Whiskey Slide, Andy Karney, staggering drunk, stumbled into a deep prospect hole and slept there all night. When he awoke next morning, he found that his overnight floundering efforts to climb out had exposed a gold vein. Digging with a pocket knife, he filled a quart can with nuggets and in two weeks took out $70,000. At Columbia, a man named Holden pulled up a weed in his garden and found a $5,000 nugget tangled in its roots. A gambler at Shaw's Flat on his way home stumbled over an $8,500 nugget and six months later pawned a pair of sleeve buttons made from it for food.

J. H. Carson died practically penniless in Stockton

after discovering one of the richest quartz ledges in the world on Carson Hill. The fame of the discovery brought so many miners swarming in that a ferry across the Stanislaus river two miles to the south took in $10,000 in six weeks. Jim Perkins, who had been mining three years and had never had more than $200 in gold at one time, found on his Carson Hill claim the second largest gold nugget in world history. The nugget weighed 2,576 ounces or 214 pounds troy and was sold for $44,000. The Morgan mine yielded $2,000,000 in two years and five hundred men made fortunes on the scene of Carson's discovery.

A woman near Murphy's Diggings on her way to church picked up a four pound nugget and dropped it into the contribution box. Near San Andreas, a miner dug $1,000 from a crevice in an hour with his pocket-knife. At Mokelumne Hill, two brothers cleaned up $80,000 in two weeks. The cabin of a miner named Wayne was destroyed by fire in Angel's Camp and he lost everything including a large sum in gold and silver coins. Sluicing the ground, he recovered all his money and found enough nuggets to pay for a new cabin and leave him $1,000 profit on the fire.

On Carson's Creek, a miner died and a crowd of his friends assembled about the open grave for the obsequies. While the preacher was praying, a miner with head bowed solemnly, saw a nugget sticking out of the dirt thrown from the grave and, reaching out a furtive hand, dropped it into his pocket. "O Lord" intoned the parson, "forgive the sins of our departed brother—What was that you picked up, Bill?—and receive his soul into Thy Kingdom —A nugget?—Amen. This funeral's adjourned. I'm staking my claim right at this grave." It turned out to be a rich claim. The deceased was buried somewhere else.*

* It may be interesting to mention that Albert A. Michelson, the distinguished scientist of the University of Chicago, awarded the Nobel prize

A wave of civic righteousness was sweeping Murphy's Diggings when Joaquin Murrieta arrived there soon after his tragic experience in Saw Mill Flat. Flush times had had their inevitable consequences. The camp was afflicted with too much prosperity. With $100 a day to be washed out in the gulches and liquor plentiful, the town thought less of law enforcement than of pleasantly hilarious ways of shooting its money at the birds. Hard characters had drifted in, handy with their shooting irons, bold in nefarious enterprises. The good old days were swiftly passing; the criminal element seemed in a fair way to gain the upper hand. Sluice boxes were rifled; horses were stolen; drunken men staggering to their cabins at night were waylaid and robbed; if an honest toper fell asleep on a beer keg he was pretty sure to find his pockets empty when he woke up; and miners in from the placers for an evening of quiet enjoyment indulged in the innocent pastime of shooting out the lights at serious personal risk. Such conditions were giving the town's reputation a black eye. The time had come for drastic reform and the camp bestirred itself to prove to the world that Murphy's Diggings stood for law and order.

A vigilance committee was organized. Composed of miners, saloonkeepers and gamblers, it held its meetings in a barroom and embarked at once upon its campaign of ridding the town of undesirables. It operated under a Draconian code. Its penalties were severe; it wasted no time in halfway measures. But before inflicting punishment, it gave every suspect charged with crime a fair trial, with presiding judge, prosecutor and de-

for his experiments to determine the speed of light, went to school as a boy in Murphy's Diggings where Sam Michelson, his father, kept a store for many years. Pauline Michelson, a sister of the scientist, grew up in the camp and Miriam Michelson, another sister, author of "The Bishop's Carriage" and other novels, was born there. From Murphy's Diggings, the Michelson family moved to Virginia City, Nevada.

fending counsel. Witnesses were examined; the defendant was permitted to tell his side of the case; arguments were made by opposing counsel; all the formalities of court procedure were scrupulously observed. Then the prisoner was taken out and hanged.

An interesting little note has come down that is a testimonial to the effectiveness of Murphy's Diggings' moral uplift. It was written by a thief, doubtless while the vigilantes were selecting a good tree, and read:

"Dear friend I take the opportunity of writing these few lines to you hoping to find you in good health me and Charley is sentence to be hung today at 5 o'clock for a robery goodbye give my best respect to Frank and Sam and Church John Bucroft."

No more is known of John Bucroft. This polite little note of farewell announcing his approaching death is the only evidence that he ever lived.*

While the campaign of reform was in full swing, a stranger rode into Murphy's Diggings as the Stranglers were making preparations for a hanging. He saw some men smoking cigars and engaged in casual talk under a tree. They seemed unconcerned, a little listless. The only indication of the job they had in hand was a noose dangling from a limb. One of the men had hold of the other end of the rope and was dusting his boots off with it. A pale, thoughtful looking youth stood apart from the crowd. Perhaps he was too timid to take part in the execution or had moral scruples against lynchings. "Who are they going to hang?" asked the stranger stepping up to him. The young man seemed embarrassed. "I believe it's me," he said.

A few miles out on the trail to Angel's, a prosperous Mexican mining camp had sprung up. John Williams and Hugh O'Neill, Murphy's Diggings gamblers, moved in

* This note is preserved in the Chamber of Commerce at San Andreas.

and opened a monte bank. They had an uninterrupted run of good luck from the start and every night when the game closed down, the bank was big winner. Suspecting the two gamblers were operating a brace game with waxed cards, the Mexicans stabbed Williams in the back one evening while he was dealing and he fell dead across the layout. O'Neill, who had been sitting lookout, grabbed a buckskin bag containing the firm's bank roll of $3,000 and, escaping from the angry crowd, hit the trail back to Murphy's Diggings. The Stranglers decided the affair called for a hanging and rode over next morning in a body. They found the camp quiet; all the Mexicans who had taken part in the row had disappeared; no one apparently knew anything about the murder. So the men from Murphy's Diggings took a drink.

While they stood at the bar, the ugliest Mexican they had ever seen wandered in. One glance at his gargoyle face convinced the raiders he was the murderer, and seizing the astonished Mexican, they attempted to browbeat him into a confession. But he had nothing to confess; he had killed no one. They looped a rope about his neck and, hustling him out to a tree, strung him up. When he ceased to kick they let him down and revived him. He still protested his innocence. They hoisted him and let him down again. Still no confession. A third time they shot him into the air. But this up and down business was growing monotonous and they were thirsty. They would take one drink and then lower him and see what he had to say. They adjourned to the bar. Over their liquor, they grew pleasantly garrulous and for the time forgot the man dangling just outside the door. When they recovered from their absent-minded lapse the Mexican was dead. They didn't go out and investigate. They knew he was dead. No man could hang by the neck all that while and not be dead. So they left him hanging and continued their potations.

In Murphy's Diggings as in Saw Mill Flat, Joaquin Murrieta was just another Mexican. Few people in the camp knew anything about him or had ever heard of him. Locked in his breast alone was the secret of the vengeance he had taken upon the men who had outraged and killed his wife. The five skeletons in the Stanislaus river hills had remained undiscovered. When finally they were found, no one had any idea who these men had been or whose hand had sent them to their death and unless Joaquin himself revealed it—as he afterwards did—there seemed little likelihood the identity of the avenger would ever be known. Still ambitious for a modest success in honest industry and with youth and health in his favor, Joaquin settled down quietly in Murphy's Diggings, hoping to forget the past and wishing to be forgotten.

During the time he lived in the camp, he ran a monte game in partnership with Bill Byrnes in the latter's saloon. A strange, cold character was Bill Byrnes, gambler, fighter, adventurer, who had followed the frontier from the Missouri river to the California gold mines. He enters the story here for one brief interval, not to be heard of again until as a member of Harry Love's Rangers he helped trail Murrieta to his death and was credited by many with having killed him. Three miles from town Jesus Murrieta, an elder brother, who had been in California two years before Joaquin left his native village in Sonora, lived in a small Mexican camp where he worked as a miner on his own placer claim. Joaquin kept in close touch with Jesus and made frequent trips to his cabin to see him. There was no one in this land of strangers to whom he was so warmly attached as his brother.

Borrowing his brother's mule, Joaquin started off for Los Muertos, six miles beyond Angel's Camp, to visit

Joaquin Romero, a Yaqui Indian whom he had known in Mexico and who had harbored him after he had disappeared from Saw Mill Flat. As he ambled along on his mule, he met Bill Lang near Vallecito. Lang lived in Murphy's Diggings and was a miner. He was a hard-drinking, unscrupulous, loud-mouthed swashbuckler, later to die with his boots on, and had a certain prestige as a bad man among the rowdies and tough customers of the gold camp. He had frequently bucked Joaquin's monte game and Joaquin knew him well.

"Como le va, caballero," said Joaquin in casual greeting as the two met in the trail.

Lang glared at him savagely. "Pull up there. What're you doin' on my mule?"

Joaquin, astonished, thought for a moment he might be joking but Lang's menacing mien undeceived him. "This is my brother's mule," Joaquin replied. "I borrowed it from him."

"I reckon you borrowed it off o' me by the light o' the moon," growled Lang. "My mule was stole t'other night and that's my mule."

"You're mistaken. My brother bought this mule."

"Who'd he buy it from?"

"I don't know but he told me he bought it and my brother is an honest man."

"I reckon I had oughter know my own mule. I ain't no ways blind and that's my mule shore and sartin. Climb down."

"What kind of a fool do you take me for?"

"If you don't give that mule up, I'll have you took up fer a hoss thief."

"Look here, Lang," Joaquin answered quietly. "You know me and you know I'm not going to run away. I'll have my brother in Murphy's Diggings tomorrow morning. You meet us there and he'll prove to you this mule belongs to him." *

Joaquin and his brother waited in Murphy's Diggings next morning to keep the appointment. It lacked two hours of noon. The main street was empty; overnight revelers were still asleep and miners had gone off to their claims. Tied to a nearby post, the mule was lazily switching flies in the sunshine.

It was not long before Lang stepped out of a saloon. "Thar's them greasers now." Others who had been drinking with him boiled out into the street and gathered about the two Mexicans. There was no mistaking the temper of the crowd, which numbered twenty men. They were half-drunk, ugly and ready for trouble.

"Well," said Lang in a loud menacing voice, looking at Joaquin, "what have you got to say about that mule today?"

"Here's my brother. I've brought him in to meet you. He'll explain all about it."

"And he's got a sight of explainin' to do." Lang turned to Jesus. "What lie have you cooked up to save your thievin' hide?"

"I speak the truth, señor," replied Jesus alarmed at Lang's boisterous tone. "The mule belongs to me."

The crowd looked the animal over. They knew it of old. "That's your mule, Bill. Ain't no doubt about it."

"Of course it's my mule. This hoss thief stole it."

"I am no thief," protested Jesus. "I bought that mule and very well you know it, Señor Lang." He pointed his

* The story of Joaquin's tragic experience in Murphy's Diggings and of his subsequent revenge was told to me with names and details by Frank Marshall, who lives at Pleasant Valley, near Sonora. Mr. Marshall was the second white child born in Murphy's Diggings and had the story from his father, Ben F. Marshall, who was sheriff of Calaveras county from 1851 to 1854 and died in 1886. Ben Marshall located in Murphy's Diggings in 1850 and served as constable and deputy sheriff before he succeeded John Hannon as sheriff.

finger accusingly. "You yourself are the man who sold me that mule and took my money for it."

At this startling revelation all eyes were bent upon Lang. It looked as if he were the one who had the explaining to do. But Lang only blustered with noisier bravado.

"You're a liar and a hoss thief," he bawled. "You stole that mule; you can't lie out of it; and you're goin' to stretch hemp. We're plumb sick of havin' our stock lifted by you sneakin' greasers. Git a rope, fellers."

Sam Green, Bill Bickell, Ben Marshall and Bill Byrnes, hearing the uproar, came hurrying to the scene. Green and Bickell were saloonkeepers. Marshall, who afterwards became sheriff of Calaveras county, ran a butcher shop and also served as a constable.

"What's up boys?" asked Green.

"Nothin' to git het up about," Lang answered. "We're fixin' to hang a couple o' greaser hoss thieves—that's all."

Joaquin, tersely and quickly, explained the quarrel to the four newcomers. "They've got no cause to hang us. We've done nothing."

"Don't be in a sweat, boys," warned Marshall. "Don't do nothin' you'll be sorry for. I'll lock these Mexicans in the calaboose and hold 'em till Sheriff Hannon gits back from Mokelumne Hill. We don't want no more Strangler committees operatin' in these diggin's. We've done had a bellyful o' the brand o' justice they dish out. These men are entitled to a fair trial in a law court. Let a jury decide their case."

"You've stacked the cards agin these boys," declared Green hotly. "You've rung in a cold deck on 'em. Be men. Give 'em a run for their money. Give 'em a square deal."

"I'd trust Joaquin with my last dollar," spoke up Byrnes. "He's an honest boy."

But the protests were of no avail. The crowd seized the

two Mexicans and, with Lang leading the way, hustled them off to a live oak tree at the edge of town.

But the pleas in behalf of the Mexicans had had some weight. After much wrangling, the crowd decided to hang only Jesus and let Joaquin off with thirty-nine lashes on the bare back. As a constable, Marshall made a last effort to prevent the outrage and in the name of the law ordered the crowd to disperse.

"You fellers ain't got a thing agin neither one o' these Mexicans," shouted Green. "If thar's been any lyin' done, I'll bet Bill Lang done it. I wouldn't believe that cut-throat on oath."

"Keep your mouth out o' this," Lang bellowed, "or we'll hang you too."

"I can't figure out what Joaquin's done to be whipped for," urged Byrnes.

"He'll git thirty-nine lashes jest the same," fumed Lang. "I'll lay 'em on myself."

The noose was made tight about the neck of Jesus and the loose end of the rope thrown over a limb of the live oak. Stripped to the waist, Joaquin was bound to the trunk of the same tree.

"All ready? Let her rip."

Jesus shot into the air. For a few moments, his body twisted with violent contortions. Wave-like spasms of shivering, as if from icy coldness, swept over him. Gradually the convulsive writhings ceased and his limp form dangled motionless. With eyes uplifted to the ghastly spectacle, Joaquin watched his brother die.

Sleeves rolled up, a rope in his hand, Lang stepped into position for the flogging. The crowd roared approval.

"Bear down, old hoss. Pour it into him. Blister him good."

A strong man was Bill Lang, cruel, merciless. Whirling the rope, he brought it down viciously across Joaquin's back. Another full-armed swing. "I'll beat you black and blue, you mangy hoss thief." Three, four, five. "Fetched the blood that time." Nine, ten, eleven. "I'll cut you into mince meat." He worked himself into a frenzy. He danced about like a wild man. Sweat rolled down his face. He panted hoarsely. But the blows rained with undiminished vigor. Thirty-seven, thirty-eight. He paused. "Here's the last one. I'll make it a jim-dandy." The rope swished about his head twice, three times, and ripped with slashing force across the mangled, blood-smeared flesh. Thirty-nine. "Thar now. I reckon you won't steal no more mules around these diggin's."

Joaquin took his punishment with the stoicism of an Indian. He spoke not a word. His grim, set face gave no sign of suffering. No groan or writhings betrayed his agony. Only his eyes gave a hint of what was passing in his mind and the expression of his eyes was not of pain but of burning, unutterable hatred.

The crowd went back into town and lined up at a bar for refreshments.

"Did you take notice of that greaser's eyes while Bill was lacin' him?" asked one, pouring out his drink. "I never seen sech tiger eyes in a man's head before. They glistened like coals of fire. They looked like seven devils, hoppin' mad, was dancin' in 'em. And he kept them eyes rovin' round the crowd from one to t'other of us like he was fixin' us in his mind."

"Well you can gamble the bank roll on it, pard," roared Bill Lang jovially, raising his whiskey glass, "that greaser won't never fergit none of us to his dyin' day."

"He shore looked bad. Wouldn't surprise me none ef he laid fer some of us. Better keep your eyes about you, Bill."

"Who, me? I ain't botherin' my head about him. He won't never do nothin' to nobody. What that greaser'd better do is make himself scarce mighty quick. Ef he hangs round these diggin's, he'll wake up some fine morning and find hisself twisting in the breeze at the end of a rope."

Some Mexican friends cut Joaquin's bonds, applied an unguent to his wounds and helped him into his clothes. Lowering the body of Jesus from the tree, they drove off with it into the hills where, in some secret spot, they buried it. Joaquin stood like a statue carved out of stone as his dead brother, wrapped in a serape, was lowered into the grave. When the burial was over, he turned and walked away in silence. But it was ominous, jungle silence—the silence of a tiger ready for the kill.

Murphy's Diggings gossiped over the lynching for weeks at bars and card tables, hashing and rehashing every detail until the subject was worn threadbare. Soon the affair was forgotten and the silence of oblivion closed slowly about it. Murphy's Diggings was a live camp and had other things to think about.

Bill Lang lounged in the door of a saloon and puffed at a cigar. A miner leading a burro came in from the hills and halted in the main street. Something on the burro's back caught the curious eyes of the idlers. With casual interest, Lang stepped out and joined the little crowd that began to gather. The thing on the burro's back was a dead man who had been found in the chaparral a few miles out along the trail to Angel's Camp. As Lang looked more closely, his jaw dropped and his eyes bulged. The dead man had been one of the twenty who had hanged Jesus and flogged Joaquin. The body was covered with stab wounds; the ears had been sliced off close to the head; and about the neck was a deep red scar made by the noose of a rawhide lariat. Evidently the man had been lassoed, dragged into a thicket and horribly tortured before he was murdered. "Well, I'll be damned," said Bill Lang.

In the next few weeks the bodies of four other murdered men were found here and there in the hills. All had been members of the lynching party. All had been tortured and stabbed to death and about each throat was the mark of the lariat.

A doctor—his name is lost—was riding back to Murphy's Diggings from a professional call over in Cucumber Gulch. The sun had set, dusk was falling and the hills were dark and shadowy against the glowing sky. Suddenly he heard a clatter of hoofs behind him and turned to see a grim, spectral figure sitting as still as death bolt upright in his saddle and riding toward him like a demon. The terrified physician put spurs to his horse. But even in the desperate crisis of a life and death race, it occurred to him there was something vaguely familiar about his ghostly pursuer. Across his mind flashed a vision of a young Mexican dealing monte in Bill Byrnes' saloon and in his ears echoed a well-known voice,—"Make your game, gentlemen. Come down with your money. Ten of diamonds in the door. The game is made. All ready."

But the death's-head hobgoblin was drawing nearer. The drumming thunder of his horse's hoofs grew louder. A lariat swished through the air. Bending forward in an instinctive dodging movement, the doctor missed death by inches, the flying loop knocking off his hat which it struck with the solid thud of a bullet. Still with undiminished swiftness, the remorseless apparition came on. Bullets began to whine. But the evening lights of Murphy's Diggings gleaming close ahead seemed to have the effect of a spell of exorcism. The demon horseman vanished like a ghost at cockcrow, and the doctor, scared half out of his wits but safe and sound, rode into town.

Joaquin Murrieta! So it was he who was sweeping the hills like a whirlwind of death. The doctor had recognized him and had lived to tell the tale. No doubt remained as to the assassin's identity or his motives. Burning with a sense of injustice and outrage, it was evident Joaquin had doomed his enemies to death. But the doctor's adventure seemed to indicate that the scope of his vengeance had been widened and all Americans had come under the ban of his hatred. With death, like a lurking panther, waiting in ambush along every trail, Murphy's Diggings fell into a panic. Miners trembled in their boots when they went out into the gulches to work their claims. Only the bravest dared set foot beyond the limits of town. Few cared to risk the dangers of travel and highways were practically deserted.

Terror gripped the hearts of Bill Lang and his Stranglers. Five of the twenty already had paid the penalty for their brutal crime. Who would be next? At what moment would the hurtling loop of death fall about the neck of another victim? Which one, today or tomorrow, would be dragged with wild beast ferocity to torture and death in a wayside thicket? Fiends themselves, they had now to face the vengeance of a more remorseless fiend. With skeleton hands forever groping and clutching for them, they at last sought safety in flight. One by one they stole away from Murphy's Diggings and scattered to the four winds. Not one remained behind.

A merchant of vengeance deals in a strange commodity but Joaquin was handling that line exclusively and he put his business on an efficiency basis. He had certain bills to collect, certain deals to close. If a debtor tried to evade payment, he brought that debtor to time; the rising young business man was not to be cheated. He kept a careful check on every item on his ledger. His books must balance.

Two of the fugitives, who had joined the exodus from Murphy's Diggings, moved out of the hills into the San Joaquin valley. They felt safe at last. Danger was far behind them. The lone avenger would never find them there. But the noose of the fatal reata suddenly squared their accounts. One was killed near Knight's Ferry, the other near Stockton.

Within six days along a six mile stretch of trail near Marysville far to the north of Murphy's Diggings, six men were dragged from their saddles with a lasso and hacked to death with a knife. To mark his handiwork, Joaquin, according to an old story, cut an M, the initial letter of his surname, on the forehead of each of these six men with his dagger.

Missouri Bill, one of Bill Lang's hanging party, killed one man and shot two others while drunk in Vallecito. Ben Marshall, who had succeeded John Hannon as sheriff of Calaveras county, captured him in Placerville. Brought to Murphy's Diggings, Missouri Bill broke jail. A week later, he was found dead with the mark of a lariat about his throat between Middle Bar and Jackson.

Jack McGinnis, another of the Stranglers, was known as Three Fingered Jack McGinnis. He had several notches on his gun and had established a reputation as a desperado. Joaquin trailed him to Aurora, Nevada, where he arrived just in time to see McGinnis, who had recently been convicted of murder, drop into eternity through the trap-door of a gallows.

Long after Joaquin had launched upon his career of banditry, he was camped with his band on the Merced river. Manuel Garcia, the famous Three Fingered Jack of the Murrieta story, reported four miners with packs on their backs traveling along the opposite bank. "If they do not molest us, let them pass," said Joaquin. But when he had taken a good look at them, his face contorted with rage and, seizing his rifle, he dropped three dead in their tracks and brought the fourth to the ground badly wounded. The wounded man raised himself on his arm and stared across the stream to see if by chance he might discover some clew to the motive for this ruthless attack. "You scum of hell," shouted Joaquin, "do you recognize me? I am Joaquin Murrieta." Raising his rifle, he fired three shots and the man fell back dead. Then at Joaquin's command, Three Fingered Jack waded across the river and cut the throats of the four men from ear to ear. "Those men," said Joaquin in explanation, "were in the gang that hanged my brother in Murphy's Diggings."

Of the men who had wronged him, Joaquin hated Bill Lang most bitterly of all and Lang was the one man above all others he wished to kill. Joaquin hung on Lang's trail for months at a time waiting and watching for an opportunity to murder him. But strangely enough Lang escaped his vengeance and died at the hands of another man. When Sam Green met Lang on the street in Mokelumne Hill, Green who had been drinking, denounced him in every opprobrious term he could lay his tongue to for the part Lang had played in the lynching bee at Murphy's Diggings.

"You cowardly hound," raged Green, "them Murrieta boys never had nothin' to do with stealin' that mule o' yourn and you knowed it. Jesus paid you fer the mule and you tried to whipsaw the deal and git it back fer nothin' by trumpin' up the charge he stole it off o' you. You got up that lynchin' party to cover up your own lies and crookedness; and you hung one o' them Mexicans and beat the other half to death fer nothin'. You're a born scoundrel, you never was no good, and you'd orter been hung long ago. I've always had a notion I'd kill you some day and I reckon this is about as good a chance as I'll ever git."

Whereupon Green hauled out his six-shooter and killed him. Green was tried in the District court before Judge Charles N. Creaner; a jury found him guilty and he was hanged at Mokelumne Hill July 31, 1852. Sheriff Ben Marshall, who with Green had tried to save Jesus and Joaquin from Lang's merciless crew, officiated at the execution of his old friend and sprang the death-trap. Green's death warrant is still preserved among the records of Calaveras county at San Andreas. Joaquin, old timers say, wept when he heard of Lang's death, not for sorrow but because an unkind fate had robbed him of the pleasure of cutting his heart out.

So ends the tale of Joaquin's vengeance—a vengeance patient, relentless and complete. Five men had been concerned in the attack on his wife at Saw Mill Flat. He had killed them all. Twenty had taken part in the outrage at Murphy's Diggings. He had slain eighteen of them, one had been shot by another man and one hanged by law. Of the twenty-five men who had wronged him, he was credited with having killed twenty-three with his own hand. And nearly a score of these atrocious murders traced back to a mule. Humph!

Joaquin Murrieta was no longer just another Mexican. His name, unknown a little while before, had become a synonym for terror. His ruthless exploits as a tiger man were told in cabins and around camp fires from one end of the mining country to the other. Fame had come to him with the flaming suddenness of a red sunrise.

CHAPTER III.

ROBIN HOOD AND HIS MERRY MEN.

TIME as it lengthens weaves strange illusions. A murderer of to-day is a villain who is rushed to the electric chair. A wholesale killer of eighty years ago is a hero of romance. Joaquin Murrieta was one of the most ruthless bandits that ever lived. His career was crimson with blood and his trails were littered with corpses. But time has dropped a sentimental veil of poetry about him. Myth and fable have enveloped him with the rose and purple of a mountain seen from afar off. The murderous robber has become a picturesque figure of fantasy, high-souled, as chivalrous as he is brave, riding forth merrily with a plume in his hat and a roguish sparkle in his eye to a thousand madcap adventures. He makes love with the gallantry of a cavalier. He flings away his gold at the gambling table with princely abandon. He is a protector of women. He robs the rich and gives freely to the poor. He feasts, he dances, he toasts his merry men in bumpers of wine, he takes his ease under the greenwood tree. He is the Robin Hood of El Dorado. The live oaks, digger pines and manzanita thickets of the Sierra foothills are his Sherwood Forest; and Three Fingered Jack, Claudio, Gonzalez, Valenzuela,—as atrocious knaves as ever cut a throat—lack only jerkins of Lincoln green, long bows and cloth-yard arrows to be the Little John, Allan-a-Dale, Will Scarlet and Friar Tuck of his roystering crew.

Murrieta's outlaw career is a chapter of only three

pages, each page a year. It is believed to have begun toward the close of 1850, though the exact date is dubious. It ended definitely with a bullet for its period on July 25, 1853. He was twenty years old when he became an outlaw. He was twenty-three when he was killed. But he made those three crowded years one of the most lurid chapters in criminal history. California rang with his crimes. Daring robberies and murders followed upon each other's heels in a sequence of startling rapidity and an unknown Mexican youth became one of the most famous figures of his day.

The Age of Gold was his background,—a background of storybook romance. The Sierra foothills, an empty wilderness a short time before, had become a bonanza land swarming with fifty thousand miners. It was a time of tumult and excitement when men were mad for gold and law had been forgotten. Fortunes were being made overnight. Tin wash pans became magic vessels in which men dipped up riches. The stroke of a pick might mean wealth. The starving adventurer of to-day was a plutocrat to-morrow. The poor devil who awoke in the morning wondering where his next meal was coming from went to bed a millionaire. The flush period of easy money was a veritable invitation to a bold criminal and Murrieta rose to the golden opportunity and enriched himself in campaigns of pillage.

The youthful outlaw was unquestionably a criminal genius. Bancroft, who recognizes a Napoleonic spark in him, says, "Bonaparte would have been no more out of place on the Salinas plains than Murrieta at Toulon." Proof of a masterly and brilliant mind lay in the fact that veteran chiefs of marauding bands already notorious for their desperate exploits allied themselves under the leadership of this youth just out of his teens. Much of his success was due to his marvelous skill in organization.

He molded his robber band into a semi-military machine. It had its headquarters, general staff, field forces and an army of spies and secret agents. His captains and subordinates were oath-bound to obey him. His word was law. For disobedience or any sign of rebellion, the penalty was death. His crimes were mapped out in as careful detail as the battle plans of a general. He did nothing impulsively but acted only after mature deliberation. His secret agents kept him supplied with up-to-date information—mining camps in which treasure was hoarded; miners who were leaving the hills with gold dust; wagon trains coming up from the valley settlements with cargoes of rich merchandise; the likeliest place for an attack, possible dangers to be encountered, the safest trails to follow. With such a fund of facts at his command, he was enabled to deliver his strategic blows quickly and decisively.

To Americans, who hated him, Murrieta was only a robber and a murderer. To the Spaniards and Mexicans of California, who admired him, he was a revolutionist and the champion of their race. The strength of his outlaw organization, the audacity and rapidity of its movements and the success of its operations, gave the young leader in their eyes the prestige of a military hero. They called him El Patrio and looked upon him, not as a bandit, but as the leader of a revolt against American domination, engaged in righteous war against the injustice and oppression of the Yankee invaders. Murrieta undoubtedly had some such exalted idea of his status and, with complacent egotism, viewed himself as an insurrectionist actuated by motives of patriotism and destined to be the liberator of his people. Toward the end of his career, he boasted that he could muster two thousand men, and with this force he planned to launch a campaign of wholesale massacre against the despised gringo race in a desperate attempt to reëstablish the supremacy of Mexico over California. Quixotic as the scheme may have been, it was seriously entertained by many California Spaniards of distinguished lineage who imagined the redoubtable young chieftain might yet restore their lost glories and free them from American sovereignty. The fascinating dream seemed less chimerical in those disordered times than it does to-day. With a smaller army Cortez had embarked upon the conquest of Mexico, Pizarro had overthrown the empire of the Incas, and Simon Bolívar had begun the war that delivered half the South American continent from the rule of Spain.

California Spaniards and Mexicans had different causes for hating the Americans but both hated them with equal fervor. The Spaniards, who had been the original lords of California and now lived in faded splendor on their ancestral estates along the coast, had seen their beloved country pass into the possession of an alien people as a conquered province, and nursed a bitter enmity against the Yankees who, since the discovery of gold, had burst upon the land in ruthless hordes, as voracious as vultures, to rob, swindle, bulldoze and impoverish them. The Mexicans, who poured into California during the gold rush, were still inflamed with the anti-American prejudices engendered during the Mexican war. Their attitude towards Americans was hostile from the first and in return, the Americans regarded them as secret enemies and treated them with frank contempt.

When the news of the gold discovery went round the world, the Mexicans were the first foreigners to reach the new El Dorado. While the Americans swarmed into the hills along the American, Feather, Bear and Yuba rivers in the region adjacent to Coloma where Marshall had discovered gold in the race of Sutter's saw mill on January 24, 1848, the Mexicans invaded the country to the south, equally rich and known later as the land of the Mother Lode, and their camp fires were soon burning along the Tuolomne, Calaveras, Mokelumne and Consumnes rivers. Sonora and Hornitos, that became important and populous towns, were settled by Mexicans. The Mexican pioneers were better miners than the Americans. The first Americans in the gold fields knew nothing of mining while many of the Mexicans were experts who had had practical experience in Mexico. To the Mexicans, the Americans were indebted for the *batea,* or wooden bowl for washing out gold, and for the *arrastra,* a contrivance equipped with a water wheel that came into common use and greatly facilitated placer operations.

When American gold hunters spread southward from the Coloma country, they were filled with resentment to find thousands of Mexicans in possession of some of the richest claims of the Mother Lode. As California had fallen into American hands as spoils of war, the American miners were imbued with the idea that the gold of California was rightfully theirs and theirs only. But as selfishly human as the idea may have been, it was legally without justification. According to the constitution and laws of the United States, Mexicans and all other foreigners had as much right to mine in California as Americans themselves. But the legality of the position of the Mexicans had no effect in mitigating American hostility towards them. The feeling between the two races grew more and more embittered. Many clashes occurred. The Mexicans fought to maintain themselves in the country that they had pioneered. The Americans sought in lawless ways to drive them out.

The tense situation culminated in the summer of 1850 in the enactment by the state Legislature of a law imposing a tax of twenty dollars a month on all foreign miners. Such a tax in what was then the richest gold fields in world history, might seem, in the retrospect, insignificant. But to many foreign miners it was in effect an edict of banishment. They could not afford to pay it, and their inability to make money at mining under such a light impost is an illuminating side light upon the bonanza days of the gold stampede. Gold was plentiful but the prices of all necessities were sky high and it took a fair mining claim to pay a miner's expenses. Flour at first sold at $800 a barrel and was considered cheap when it fell to $400. Bacon and ham, sugar and coffee retailed at $4 a pound and eggs at $3 apiece. A pick and shovel cost $10 each, a tin pan $5, a butcher knife $30, a pair of boots $40, a pair of long boots $100, a pair of blankets $40, a pair of pants $35, a clay pipe $2, and candles to light the cabin $12 a dozen. Moreover, there were periods during the year when the miners were forced to remain idle while their overhead continued. In rainy seasons there was too much water for mining and in dry seasons too little. Add to these necessary expenses, the expenses of drinking and gambling, which were the customary diversions of the country, and it will be seen that without a stroke of luck, gold mining was far from being a certain road to riches. Bancroft says, "There were few miners who had $1,000 laid by at the end of the first two years in California." For the fortunate few, the gold fields were El Dorado. For the vast majority, they were hell.

The foreign miners tax did little, if any, good and a vast amount of harm. Foreigners left the country in droves. Some camps were entirely deserted. Others were almost depopulated. With markets reduced to the vanishing point, merchants, who had freighted supplies into the mines at enormous expense, faced ruin. Such a protest went up from business men confronted with bankruptcy and from towns that had been almost wiped off the map, that the law was repealed in March, 1851. But for the short time it was in force, the law had fanned to white heat the animosity between Americans and Mexicans. What had been bad had been made worse and the repeal of the law had no effect in ameliorating the deep-seated, inter-racial enmity. It was in such an atmosphere of hatred that Murrieta turned outlaw and in such turbulent conditions he achieved his murderous fame.

As an outlaw, Murrieta retained many of the finer instincts that distinguished him as an honest man. He was intensely loyal and his gratitude was proverbial. No kindness shown him was ever forgotten. More than one man owed his life to some casual courtesy that had all but slipped his mind but was still vivid in Murrieta's grateful memory. He had the magnanimity of a generous soul and at times spared a life when it endangered his own to show mercy. He had the instinctive flair of a Latin temperament for melodrama. Some of his murders were marked by pure theatricalism such as might have been expected from an actor reaching for a sensational climax before a spell-bound audience; and he sometimes risked his life in staging a startling adventure merely for the thrill of achieving a spectacular effect.

Murrieta never killed merely for the pleasure of killing and, after he had glutted his vengeance on the men concerned in the outrages at Saw Mill Flat and Murphy's Diggings, his attitude toward murder, it might seem, became rather aloof and impersonal. He kept death in stock as a merchant keeps canned beans on his shelves for which he may have a call at any minute. But except as a means to an end, murder meant nothing to him. A good cigar perhaps meant more. If killing became necessary, he killed without emotion of any kind and got the matter over with as little fuss as possible. He killed a man who was dangerous to him or who had injured or betrayed him as he killed a mosquito that annoyed him.

The distinction between men and mosquitoes was hardly worth considering and he killed both insects with the same indifference.

Toward the end of his career, however, Murrieta became consciencelessly murderous. His long schooling in bloodshed had made him utterly callous. He had ruled so long with a tyrannical hand over his followers and had imposed his iron will upon so many men and communities that he became filled with vainglorious pride in his own prowess and invulnerability. In his early period, he slipped often into a church and confessed his sins to a padre. But in his later years we hear nothing of any lingering religious impulses and he relieved his soul no more of its dark secrets in the confessional. As time went on he had occasion to hate a number of men and women who had betrayed him or done him a wrong which he considered unforgivable. Some of these he murdered cruelly; others he pursued with relentless malevolence. One or two of his threats have come down in their exact language and give a glimpse of a man as coldly deadly as a rattlesnake. It was his deadliness as much as his dominant mentality that enabled him to control the turbulent spirits he gathered about him. All his followers feared him as they might the devil and he kept Three Fingered Jack, the most murderous ruffian in his band, in cowed subjection.

As suspiciously like a joke as it may sound, Murrieta was adept in disguising himself. Disguises nowadays are regarded as the claptrap of dime novels. Wigs, false beards and mustaches are laughed at by modern detectives and criminals. But stories of indisputable authenticity have come down that go to show Murrieta could disguise himself so cleverly that his most intimate friends could not recognize him. In make-up, he ventured into places where he would have been shot instantly if his identity had been known; and masquerading as a priest, a ragged peon, a gray bearded old man, or a woman, he often eluded capture or death or learned the secrets of the men who were hunting him. Hawkshaw the Detective, it might seem, had nothing on him.

He was rated as a good shot with both six-shooter and rifle and was famous for his dexterity in throwing a knife. To amuse his friends, he would stick an ace of cards against a tree and from a distance of ten or twelve paces drive his knife through the center of the ace and half up to the hilt in the trunk of the tree. Under fire many times, he escaped injury so often and in such seemingly miraculous fashion, a story was bruited that he wore bullet-proof armor under his clothes. According to this tale, he paid a Frenchman $1000 to procure him a coat of chain mail from France. When it arrived he ordered the Frenchman to put it on. Greatly alarmed, the Frenchman refused. "If you put it on," said Joaquin, "my bullets may not harm you but if you do not put it on, I will surely kill you." Between possible injury and certain death, the Frenchman chose the former alternative. Standing off, Joaquin emptied his six-shooter at him and when the armor stood the test, paid the Frenchman $1000. This quaint yarn, it may be added, was not generally credited.

He was perfection itself as a horseman. No more accomplished rider is conceivable. No cowboy of the Texas plains, gaucho of the Argentine pampas, or Bedouin of the Arabian deserts could have surpassed him. Of all feats and tricks of equestrianism, he was a past master. He seemed, like a centaur, a part of his horse. He was an expert at riding without saddle or bridle, guiding his mount with his voice and the pressure of his knees and frequently hanging precariously along the animal's side while at full speed, like an Indian shielding himself from hostile arrows. He loved horses and horses loved him and obeyed him as if with human intelligence. He rarely hitched his horse. The animal was trained to stand with the bridle reins dragging the ground and thus was ready for instant flight in an emergency. He rode the best horses that it was possible to steal in California and took great pride in caparisoning them in sumptuous style. His massive Mexican saddle with high pommel and cantle was always a work of art, made of the finest leather and stitched in fancy designs while both saddle and head-stall were elaborately ornamented with silver. With his skill as a horseman went skill with the lasso. He swung a noosed rope with remarkable accuracy and many of the men he killed he first lassoed and dragged from their saddles.

If old chroniclers can be relied on, Joaquin was vain of his personal appearance and usually dressed in gaudy vaquero style. Plumed sombrero, shirt of some gay color, gold-laced jacket, pantaloons strung with silver discs along the outer seams; a red silk sash bristling with derringers and dragoon revolvers; half boots of the finest leather, the handle of a bowie knife projecting from the top of the right boot; heavily roweled spurs as big as saucers; and, as the completing detail, a fringed silk-lined cloak or bright colored serape draped about his shoulders. Such a costume, one must admit, was rather flamboyant for one who, it might be assumed, wished to remain incognito or inconspicuous, but so the items are set down in the old records.

Two perfectly authentic daguerreotype portraits of Murrieta are extant however that give an entirely different idea of him. One is owned by Frank Marshall of Pleasant Valley, son of Ben Marshall, sheriff of Calaveras county in old days, and the other by Mrs. Eva Keyes Barney of Angel's Camp. The Marshall portrait was taken in Sonora, according to Frank Marshall, when Joaquin was twenty years old and was still an honest man and was presented by Murrieta to Ben Marshall in appreciation of his efforts to save Joaquin and his brother from Bill Lang's crowd in Murphy's Diggings. Mrs. Barney's picture was taken after Murrieta had become an outlaw, but further than that, Mrs. Barney, for reasons of her own, refuses to reveal its history. Marshall values his pictures at $500; Mrs. Barney hers at $1000.

In the Marshall picture, Joaquin is hatless. His straight black hair, parted on the side, falls in a heavy mass about his ears. His smooth-shaven face has a serious, somewhat somber expression; his rather sullen eyes are set beneath level brows; his nose is straight, mouth full-lipped, jaws rounded, chin strong. His dress is the ordinary American dress of the times,—dark sack coat, pants of the same cloth, checked vest of light material, a generous expanse of shirt front, roll collar, a wide bow tie the straight ends of which extend out over his coat lapels.

In Mrs. Barney's picture, Joaquin wears a wide-brimmed, low-crowned, black felt hat with no plume, dark coat and pants, a low-cut vest evidently of black velvet and his collar and tie are of the same kind as in the Marshall portrait. His face is slightly leaner and perhaps a little harder with the same unsmiling sullen expression. A thread of a mustache—the kind known to-day as an eyebrow mustache—lies as straight as a string across his upper lip, and a little string-like goatee extends from his mouth almost to the point of his chin. In both pictures Joaquin is seated and no weapons are in sight in either. The Murrieta of the Marshall picture looks youthful and innocuous; the Murrieta of Mrs. Barney's portrait is plainly a dangerous man.

A number of other pictures of Joaquin made by California artists of early days are in existence but all are fanciful sketches and have no value as portraits. A copy of one is on exhibit with one of Joaquin's spurs in the rotunda of the state capitol building at Sacramento. It shows Joaquin with long curly hair tumbling about his neck, a curly mustache, thick lips, fierce glaring eyes and an expression of scowling savagery. It obviously represents the best the artist's imagination could do in visualizing a ferocious bandit.

One other picture besides the daguerreotypes, however, is worth considering. This is an oil painting now in possession of Mrs. J. A. Phillips of Los Angeles, daughter of the late Major Horace Bell, a Forty-Niner, and author of "On the Old West Coast" and "Reminiscences of a Ranger." In the summer of 1853, not long before he was killed, Joaquin, according to Major Bell, was raiding through the Santa Clara valley on a horse stealing expedition. While camped near San Jose, he was attacked by a sheriff's posse and barely escaped with his life, leaving his horse and his hat in the hands of his pursuers. After this adventure he took refuge in Carmel Mission near Monterey, the second oldest of the Mission establishments founded by Father Junipero Serra. While he was in hiding there, a young priest persuaded him to sit for his portrait. Soon after Joaquin had been slain by Harry Love's Rangers, the young padre sent the portrait to an American woman in Los Angeles, explaining in a letter the circumstances under which it had been painted and asking her to see that it was delivered to Joaquin's brother, Antonio, or to some other member of his family. The woman, it seems, was unable to carry out the priest's request and when she died thirty years later, Major Bell, as administrator of her estate, found the portrait and the priest's letter among her effects. The edges of the canvas had been eaten off by mice, the colors had faded, and the picture was woefully dilapidated. Recognizing the historic value of his find, Major Bell took it to an artist and had it retouched and restored to its original condition.

Around Joaquin's head, as the picture portrays him, a red sash is bound like a turban and about his shoulders is a manga or poncho of the same vivid color. A black mustache droops beyond the corners of his full, softly curved, sensuous lips; his rather large nose has a ripple in its outline; his sensitive nostrils suggest the quick palpitant breathing of a wild animal; and beneath sharply oblique eyebrows, his eyes flare wide, much white showing about the iris. Those great, flaring black eyes light up the face weirdly. They are the eyes of a hunted man, alert, apprehensive, vigilantly on guard. There is a hint of menace, of savage cruelty, in them but they are eyes that seem to sense death; ghosts lurk in their somber depths; they are unmistakably horror-haunted. The portrait is rather crudely done but tremendously thrilling. This is Murrieta in the last phase of his madly tempestuous career. A few weeks after the portrait had been painted, he was trailed to his death in his last wild covert.

Best known among the brigands of Murrieta's band were Three Fingered Jack Garcia, Joaquin Valenzuela, Claudio, Reyes Feliz, Pedro Gonzalez, Luis Vulvia, Manuel Sevalio, Luis Guerra, Juan Senate, Pancho Daniel, Fernando Fuentes, Juan Cardoza, Florencio Cruz, Juan Sanchez, Rafael Quintano, Antonio Lopez, Jose Maria Ochova, Pedro Valera and Juan Borilda. Murrieta's outlaw force at the peak of his career numbered from eighty to a hundred men. These were divided into several companies commanded by his captains acting under his directions. Murrieta himself rarely rode with more than twenty men at his back and usually with not more than half that number. He kept Three Fingered Jack, Claudio and Reyes Feliz almost always with him.

When Domingo Hernandez, the great robber, used to come riding into Monterey in the old days with a string of human ears dangling from the pommel of his saddle, a barefoot urchin with a shock of touseled black hair would gaze at him with unbounded admiration. What joyous shudders thrilled the gamin as he stood with his finger in his mouth at the door of some tavern on the old plaza and watched the ogre drain bottle after bottle of wine and roar with laughter as he recounted his hair-raising exploits on the Soledad Mission road. This jovial monster, who hoarded human ears as a miser hoards gold, would murder a traveler on the highway not so much for the money his pockets might contain as for his ears. He was a connoisseur in ears, preferring large ears, so he said, and he sometimes spared the life of a wayfarer whose ears were too small to meet his aesthetic approval.

To his small admirer, never was such a hero as this Hernandez. But one day when the rollicking brigand jogged into Santa Cruz with his string of ears at his saddle bow, the citizens seized him and hanged him on a tree in the public square. This tragedy was a cruel blow to the tatterdemalion hero worshiper who could not understand how the Santa Cruz people could have been so rude to such a wonderful man.

The name of the Monterey urchin was Manuel Garcia, and not many years went by before the horrors of his own infamies threw into the shade those of the monster he had taken for his model. He was first heard of in the rebellion of Generals Jose Castro and Juan Alvarado against Governor Micheltorena in 1844. The only casualty of the insurrection, it seems, was a mule, but one of the half dozen shots fired during the war chanced to tear off one finger of young Garcia's right hand and he was known thereafter as Three Fingered Jack.

He first came into wide notoriety during the Bear Flag episode in 1846. When the American filibusters had taken Sonoma, two of the party named Cowie and

Fowler were ordered on some mission to Bodega. Near Petaluma creek they were captured by a force of Spanish Californians and turned over to Three Fingered Jack and Juan Padilla for execution. According to Three Fingered Jack's own boastful story, nothing could have exceeded in fiendishness the slow tortures to which the two Americans were subjected. Bound naked to trees, knives and stones were thrown at them, pieces of flesh were cut from their bodies, the skin was stripped from their arms and shoulders and Three Fingered Jack finally ended the devil's saturnalia by slashing them to death with his knife.

Three Fingered Jack played the heavy villain in the Murrieta drama. He was of medium height, broad shouldered and as strong as an ox. Bandy legged, with thick, orang-outang arms swinging almost to his knees, and hands like hickory-cured hams, he was an ungainly looking brute but as quick and agile as a panther. His head was massive and his black hair, coarse as a horse's mane, fell about his bull neck in tangled elf-locks; a heavy mustache as black as ink half-hid a thick-lipped, swinish mouth, his furtive black eyes glittered under rugged, beetling brows, and his swarthy face was pitted with small-pox scars and looked as if it might have been cut out of a rock with a dull chisel.

One might have expected such a man, whose lowering ugliness would have insured him a triumph as a villain on any stage, to be a morose, sullen, ill-tempered knave ready to carve up any man who batted an eye at him. But for all his bloodthirsty ferocity, Three Fingered Jack was, as fiends go, about the most rollicking, jovial, carefree fiend that ever lived. He turned murder into a lark and committed the most diabolical crimes as if they were the merriest pranks in the world. If his heart was black, it was light also. His atrocities did not affect his good humor; he walked among the writhing bodies of dying victims with the complacency of a smiling housewife at her chores; he robbed and tortured and murdered and was happy. The fortunate man whose throat he failed to cut was likely to find him a charming companion. When the bottle was passing he was the jolliest of comrades; he told stories, cracked jokes, the gusto of genuine enjoyment was in his deep-throated laughter. He was a very devil among the girls. At the fandangos, the prettiest senoritas made eyes at him from behind their fans and spread their most alluring wiles to take him captive.

Chinamen were his favorite prey and he slaughtered them by the dozen with an immense knife, fashioned like a bowie, which, it is said, he himself had made. He never shot them; he always cut their throats, and, so the old stories say, he had a dexterous way of taking them by their pigtails and jerking their heads back to give him a free swing at their necks. When the outlaws raided a camp and left a number of dead Chinamen in their wake, it was always easy to tell those Three Fingered Jack had slain;—the slashed throat was his trade mark. He slew from an uncontrollable impulse and his savage thirst for blood was undoubtedly a form of madness. Murrieta, whose hands were not stainless, was often disgusted with his orgies of slaughter but protested in vain. Three Fingered Jack was at times ashamed of his murderous excesses and when he caught the disapproving eye of his chief upon him, he would hang his head sheepishly like a small boy detected in mischief.

"I can hardly keep from killing Chinamen," Three Fingered Jack confessed to Murrieta. "Every time I see one I have a yen to murder him. I was born a devil. I have had a mania for torturing and killing as long as I can remember. Blood has the same intoxicating effect on me that brandy has on other men. I love the sight and smell of it. If it came to a pinch I think I might enjoy drinking it. I kill Chinamen because they are easy to kill and I can satisfy my craving for blood by killing them whenever I please. I am drunk with pleasure when I cut their throats. I am happy when I hear my knife blade strike against their backbones."

The mining country was dotted with Chinese camps. If American miners could not pan out a hundred dollars a day, they became disgruntled and hit the trail for richer fields. When the Americans moved out, the Chinamen moved in and with Oriental patience and untiring industry worked and reworked the abandoned claims. Incidentally, it may be said, they not infrequently struck it rich along the streams the Americans had deserted and grew affluent on the white man's leavings. Hardly a Chinese camp but was prosperous, hardly a pig-tailed heathen's cabin in which gold dust was not hidden in odd nooks and crannies. Peaceful by instinct and tradition and readily terrorized in a hurly-burly land of strangers and sudden death, the Chinese were defenseless against attacks by robbers and their hoarded wealth was like an invitation to hardy knaves to come and take it. Murrieta was not blind to such easy pickings. He held Chinamen as little better than livestock and made no bones about popping them off whenever a little judicious slaughter helped him steal their gold.

Files of old newspapers preserved in the State Library at Sacramento are full of items about Murrieta's merciless war upon the Chinese. At the Big Bar of the Consumnes, six Chinamen were murdered and their camp robbed of $6,000. At Dry Creek, $4,000 was stolen and three Chinamen killed. A sheriff's posse, coming upon Murrieta and four of his gang at Forman's ranch near San Andreas fired into them and the outlaws rode off at full speed. Three miles farther on, the posse riding hard in pursuit, struck a Chinese camp in which three Chinamen were dead and five dying. As he breathed his last, one of the Chinamen gasped that the cabins had been robbed of $3,000. Swooping upon the camp like hawks from the sky, the bandits had paused in their flight not more than five minutes for this incidental slaughter.

Surprising a camp at Moccasin Creek at the foot of Priest's Grade on the Big Oak Flat trail, the robbers made off with $8,000, leaving twelve Chinamen, bound hand and foot, hanging in a row by their queues from the rafter of a cabin. The victims of this hilarious joke were cut down after the bandits had departed by one of their countrymen who had hidden in a cellar and, though suspended by their pigtails for at least half an hour, they seemed none the worse for their harrowing experience.

Two of Murrieta's outlaws attempted to rob a Chinese camp near Chile Gulch but were seized and bound by the Chinamen. With their prisoners swinging like shoats from bamboo poles carried on their shoulders, the Chinamen set off for Mokelumne Hill to have them tried before a magistrate. But remarked one of the Celestials, "Me know magistlate and he no likee China boy belly well." So fearing a miscarriage of justice, they threw the two thieves, weighted with stones, into the Mokelumne river. Score one for the heathen Chinee.

At Bostwick's Bar on the Stanislaus river, in a raid on a Chinese camp that netted Murrieta and his men $5,000, Three Fingered Jack slit the throats of seven Chinamen, cut off their tongues and gouged out their eyes with the point of his bowie knife. While the robbers were refreshing themselves a few hours later in a saloon in Angel's Camp, Three Fingered Jack, unrolling a bandana handkerchief on the bar, displayed the ghastly trophies of the tragedy and grinned gleefully when the bartender blanched with horror.

Two hundred Chinamen had established a camp two miles from San Andreas on the Calaveras river. Pans and rockers had taken rich toll from the river sands and much gold was cached in their canvas huts. Like a cyclone, Murrieta with five of his robber crew burst upon this peaceful village, and with pigtails flying, the Chinamen scattered in all directions. The horsemen quickly rounded them up and brought them back into camp, driving them at pistol's point, dragging them bouncing over the ground at the end of reatas. When the prisoners had been drawn up in a row, Murrieta and Valenzuela passed along the line, robbing them of all the money their pockets contained and pouches of gold dust tucked away in mysterious folds of their flowing garments. Threatening them with death if they did not point out the secret places in which their wealth was stored, the bandits searched the houses and soon had collected a loot of $30,000 in coin and gold dust. Jubilant at their rich haul, the robbers rested from their labors in the shade of a live oak and feasted on sardines and crackers stolen from the camp commissary. All but Three Fingered Jack. Soon he appeared roaring curses at a tandem team of eight terrified Chinamen tied together by their queues, their hands bound behind them.

"What are you up to now, Three Fingers?" laughed Joaquin. "What crazy business is this?"

"Let me eat," said Three Fingered Jack. "I'm as hungry as a wolf."

He fell with huge relish upon the sardines and crackers. Having gorged himself, he rolled a cigarette and puffed luxuriously. At length he arose with a yawn. Sauntering over to the Chinamen, he drew his huge home-made bowie knife and, slapping its blade back and forth across the palm of his hand like one sharpening a razor on a strop, he smiled like a cherub.

"What are you about, fellow?" shouted Joaquin in sudden alarm.

It was all over in seconds and eight Chinamen lay writhing on the ground, their throats slashed from ear to ear.

Three Fingered Jack strolled back to the shade of the live oak and stretched himself out lazily on the grass, knees up, hands locked under his head. He looked very comfortable. "By San Miguel," he said, smacking his lips, "those were fine sardines."

It has been estimated that from first to last at least three hundred Chinamen—some estimates run as high as five hundred—died like sheep before wolves in Murrieta's savage campaigns. Thirty were killed within one month in Calaveras county alone.

Joaquin Valenzuela, another of Murrieta's famous captains, was an accomplished scoundrel, subtle, crafty and versatile, who had been trained in villainy under the famous Padre Jurata, a priest who became one of the most daring and picturesque robbers in Mexico. With the erudition of a scholar, the urbanity of a courtier, the face of a saint and the heart of a demon, Padre Jurata at the close of the Mexican war with the United States died for his crimes between a line of rifles and an adobe wall like the brigand of romance that he was. Valenzuela was thirty-five years old when he threw in his fortunes with Murrieta and had been the leader of a band of robbers in California for several years. A tall, cadaverous man with lank black hair and a face that looked like a death's head except for burning black eyes, he was also known as Joaquin Carrillo, Joaquin Ocomorenia, and Joaquin Bottilier. The crimes he committed under his four names were often confused with the exploits of Murrieta and many believed five Joaquins were operating as the chiefs of five independent gangs.

Luis Vulvia, like Valenzuela, was a veteran brigand who had won his degree cum laude as a bachelor of banditry under Vincente Gomez, known in his day as the Fra Diavalo of Mexico. Gomez, who was noted for his cruelty, hated Spaniards or Gachupines as they were contemptuously called, and the atrocious indignities he practiced upon all members of the despised race who fell into his hands won him the name of El Capador, for the meaning of which any who may be interested are respectfully referred to a Spanish dictionary. He had a way of sewing his Spanish prisoners in fresh ox hides and leaving them on the desert to die in agony as the hides slowly contracted under the heat of a blazing sun. Even his ruffianly followers protested against such abominable outrages and denounced him as a bloodthirsty monster.

"Bloodthirsty?" expostulated Gomez with great resentment. "Show me a man with such refined artistry in torture who puts out a life with less bloodshed."

After the Mexican war, in which he commanded a company of *guerilleros,* Gomez settled in California where he conducted himself with such scrupulous rectitude as a decent, law-abiding citizen that one of his former lieutenants named Ramirez who finally drove a dagger into his heart narrowly escaped lynching at the hands of Gomez's enraged neighbors.

Claudio, whose surname has not survived, bore a striking resemblance to Murrieta and was frequently mistaken for him. He was sometimes referred to as Claudio Murrieta and the belief was widespread among Californians that he was Joaquin's brother. Claudio was a handsome young rogue, resourceful and cunning. He was one of Murrieta's best trusted lieutenants and most intimate friends and took part in many of his young leader's most desperate adventures.

Pedro Gonzalez was chiefly remarkable for his daring as a horse thief, and ranches from Shasta to San Diego suffered from his depredations. Murrieta had unbounded confidence in his honesty and on more than one occasion entrusted him to deliver large sums of money to secret emissaries in Mexico. Aside from his honesty, this noted young horse thief had few exceptional qualities. He was, however, an efficient routine journeyman and could always be depended upon to do a job of robbery or murder in good workmanly style. He was the first of Murrieta's band to fall before the marksmanship of Harry Love when that relentless Nemesis had taken the trail against the outlaws.

Reyes Feliz, hardly more than a boy, was a younger brother of the unfortunate Rosita who met death in Saw Mill Flat. He strongly resembled his sister; he had her dark, dreaming eyes and more than a suggestion of her cameo beauty. Joaquin loved the comely youth like a brother and kept him under the protection of his eagle wings. Reyes Feliz was not murderous or rapacious and was perhaps at heart an honest, decent lad; but his sister's tragic fate embittered him against all Americans and he plunged with fanatical fervor into a life of outlawry as affording him an opportunity to avenge her death. He was only eighteen years old when his life ended at a rope's end in Los Angeles.

So these *caballeros* went gayly riding in search of the bullet or noose that was waiting for them somewhere in the world and sooner or later all of them found one or the other.

CHAPTER IV.

DESIRE UNDER THE DIGGER PINES.

WITH many dashing outlaws to play Little John, Friar Tuck, George-a-Green, and Midge the Miller's Son to our Robin Hood of El Dorado, where was his Maid Marian? Hiding doubtless behind a digger pine. But one blast wound upon the bugle horn and she would step into view, as roguish and beautiful as any lass that ever trolled a roundelay or tripped a morris-dance in the pleasant shades of Sherwood Forest. There were in fact many Maid Marians, one for each gallant rogue of the merry crew. The sweethearts of Joaquin alone, to whom in succession he paid the homage of his troubadour heart, were numerous enough to furnish a heroine for a dozen ballads of love and derring-do.

The first of the many charmers to take Rosita's place in his affections was Clarita Valero of his native village in Sonora. Clarita, so the story goes, loved him in secret when she was a little girl and, just before he ran off with Rosita Feliz, she slipped a gold ring on his finger as a talisman and token of her regard. When he went back to his boyhood home after he had become an outlaw on the only visit he ever made, he still wore the ring and Clarita, believing it proved his love for her, confessed her adoration and was made happy by being taken with him to California. She shared his fortunes for a year or more and returned to Sonora only on his promise to rejoin her there after one more raid. The promise may have been Joaquin's way of ending an affair of which he had wearied but at least his death left it unfulfilled and Clarita, who undoubtedly loved him deeply, is said to have remained loyal to his memory until she died as a lonely and heart-broken old woman.

But the handsome brigand had fallen into the habit of loose gallantries and he was not long in finding another light o' love. For a brief period he was devoted to Dolores Garcia of Santa Cruz and when she had been bowed into outer darkness, he fell under the spell of Maria Ana Benites, whom he met at a dance at Mission San Gabriel near Los Angeles. Maria was different from the enchantresses that had gone before. There was nothing of the clinging vine or timid violet about her. She was a saucy baggage who took life as she found it and her lovers, one after another, as she might pluck blackberries from a bush. But when the fascinating Joaquin crooked his finger, the bewitched and bewitching little beauty went gulloping gayly northward with him over the Tehachapis and across the burning levels of the San Joaquin valley to the hills of gold. For a time she lived blissfully with her lover at Hornitos and at the band's places of rendezvous none danced a fandango with such alluring grace or tossed off wine with such charming abandon. All raved over her. What a girl she was! Ah, that Joaquin was a lucky dog. But at last the romance palled upon her fickle fancy and she ran away with a good looking young gambler named Tom Baker and went to live with him in a secluded nook in the hills about the booming gold camp of Mariposa.

Wild with jealous rage when he learned the little sorceress had played him false, Joaquin trailed her to her hiding place and, in a blazing fusillade, emptied every shot in his six-shooter into her body. While she lay apparently lifeless on the floor, he set fire to the cabin and left her with flames crackling and swirling about her. But strangely enough Maria survived not only the bullets and the conflagration but Joaquin himself. She lived twenty years after Joaquin's death in San Jose where she used to exhibit with great pride the scars that remained as souvenirs of Murrieta's mad infatuation and madder revenge.

Antonia Molinera now steps boldly to the center of the stage. Not so caressingly lovely as Clarita, nor so piquantly pretty as Maria Ana, nor yet so softly alluring as Dolores but more fascinating than them all. The mother of this proud beauty kept a little bake shop patronized by peons on a back street in the old pueblo of San Jose, made her own meal on a metate and served very good tamales, enchiladas and frijoles with tortillas. But when Antonia swept into a fandango house in her lacy and beribboned finery with a gorgeous silk mantilla draped with careless grace over one ivory shoulder, she was the picture of a high-born lady and might have passed for the daughter of some rich hidalgo. Nor did she lack sophistication. More than once she had been to San Francisco, now grown from the poky little village of Yerba Buena into a roaring metropolis of forty thousand people. There she had coquetted with the flashy gallants of the gambling palaces and sporty saloons, and her fling at the mad gaieties of city life had given her the poise and aplomb of a woman of the world.

Antonia, or La Molinera—the Little Miller—as she was called, did not fall into Joaquin's arms at his first burning glance and whispered word. She was too wise to be swept off her feet so easily. She was the dealer in this game and, if the young coxcomb who fancied himself irresistible, really wanted her, he must play his cards patiently like a shrewd gambler and wait for the breaks. To Joaquin who had always had his way with women, this was a new experience. The cool way the little minx had of holding him at arm's length and laughing at him put him on his mettle. He would teach her to play with him. He arrived one night, riding one horse and leading another, in front of a fandango house where Antonia was dancing. He called her out. "Get on that horse," he said, dropping a hand to the butt of his derringer. Without protest and as if it were a matter of course, she obeyed and they rode off together. So the cave man dragged the captive maiden off to his den in the mountains. His conquest was complete. Her coldness changed to passion. Never were such adoring and happy lovers.

Now travelers along the trails in the mining country opened their eyes in wonder as the outlaw chief went flashing past with a comely girl in a man's costume riding at his side. Dressed like a Spanish *caballero*—bolero jacket, gaudy sash, belled and slashed pantaloons—and looking for all the world like a handsome boy, La Molinera became Joaquin's constant companion on his less adventurous journeys. There was a new sparkle to her beauty. Her life in the open, new interests, new scenes, the sunshine, the invigorating air of the pine woods, gave her eyes a brighter sparkle and her cheeks a deeper bloom. She looked as radiantly healthy as a wild flower.

Then Pancho Daniel sauntered insouciantly into the picture. Pancho Daniel was not rated among the outlaws as any great pumpkins. He had done nothing to entitle him to distinction. A good, average robber—that was the best to be said of him. Very good looking—yes. Young, well-groomed, inclining to stoutness, something of a fop; drawlingly languid, coolly indifferent; a smooth olive face with great heavy-lidded eyes half-veiled by long black lashes; a cigarette usually hanging carelessly from a corner of his mouth. He had a wise, contemptuous look. His air of easy superiority seemed to proclaim, "I am Pancho Daniel."

After joyous days with Joaquin in Hornitos, La Molinera threw her arms about his neck, gave him a tender farewell kiss and, sobbing softly as she passed out the door, set off for San Jose to visit her mother. Joaquin was deeply moved at the sad parting and waited impatiently for her return. The day set for her arrival came but she did not appear. A week slipped by but still no La Molinera. What could have happened? Joaquin jumped on his horse and rode hard for San Jose. He found Señora Molinera standing in the door of her little bake shop.

"Antonia?" A look of blank surprise overspread the fat motherly face of Señora Molinera. "I have not seen Antonia. She has not been in San Jose."

Well!

Filled with foreboding, fear clutching at his heart—fear for the woman he loved—Joaquin spurred back along the trail La Molinera had followed out of the mountains. Some terrible accident must have befallen her. She might be lying dead somewhere beside the road. In Stockton, he met Claudio and Valenzuela. Had they seen La Molinera? They blinked at each other with a hang-dog look and did not answer. Possibly they had not heard the question. Had they seen La Molinera? Yes, they had seen her. Where? In a tavern taking a glass of wine. Alone? No, not alone. With whom then? Claudio fidgeted uncomfortably, Valenzuela rubbed his chin in embarrassment. A woman or a man? It was a man—yes, it was a man. What man? Well, it was Pancho Daniel. Pancho Daniel and La Molinera had ridden out of town together and waved them good-bye as they took the trail for Pacheco Pass.

Pancho Daniel! Who would have believed it? The terrible Murrieta—the killer at whose frown men trembled—robbed and betrayed by a fat fop. Pancho had had no more fear of him than of a rabbit. It had been child's play for La Molinera to pull the wool over his eyes. He had been as happy as an infant while two snakes were wrapping him in their coils. From start to finish, he had been a blind, hopeless fool—betrayed by the woman he loved, betrayed by his friend. The silken baseness of the sly Pancho, the smiling treachery of the false-hearted La Molinera,—it was sickening. But as sure as fate he would square accounts with both of them. Let them enjoy themselves while life remained. They would be a long time dead.

But Joaquin could find no trace of the two runaways and it was not until four or five months after their disappearance that information reached him they were living in Los Angeles. At that time the hills were up in arms against the outlaws and Murrieta, hard pressed as he was, could not go to Los Angeles to visit death upon the two traitors. But he sent Pedro Vergara as his emissary of vengeance.

"Pancho Daniel and La Molinera must die," Murrieta said to Vergara. "Give me your oath you will kill them both."

"I swear it," replied Vergara solemnly.

"Very well. But remember if you break faith with me I will kill you on sight."

Vergara was a heavy, stolid, bear-like man and a knife scar that began on his forehead, jumped one eye and ended on his cheek, added to his brutal ugliness. He had killed a number of men in cold blood and his favorite weapon was a dirk.

When Vergara arrived in Los Angeles, he by chance met La Molinera on the street.

"Why Pedro," she cried, her face beaming with pleasure, "I'm so glad to see you. You must come home with me. We'll have a drink together for old time's sake. My wine is excellent."

Luck seemed playing into Vergara's hand. La Molinera was, in effect, cordially inviting her appointed assassin to come and kill her.

"Esta buena," replied Vergara. "I'm dry enough to drink a gallon."

With merry talk, she escorted him to her home in the outskirts and ushered him inside.

"Sit down, my dear Pedro," she said, "and I will bring you a glass of the best wine you ever tasted."

As she swished out of the room to fetch the wine, it seemed to Pedro she could hardly have brought him to a likelier spot for his design. He and his intended victim were alone together in a house isolated from its neighbors and there was small chance her cries would bring rescuers to her aid. A very nice place for a murder, Pedro reflected. In a moment La Molinera returned and stood within convenient reach of him, smiling as she poured out the wine. Pedro dropped his hand to his dagger.

"Did you know, Pedro, that Pancho Daniel and I have played quits?" she said. "That is a fact that I am wasting no tears over. He was only a passing fancy. When I came to know him well, I saw what a poor fish he was. He is out of my life. I hope I never see the conceited donkey again. Yes,"—she kised her fingers tips gayly—"I have said good-bye to Pancho Daniel forever."

It occurred to Pedro as he fingered his dirk that he had never seen La Molinera looking more beautiful.

"Now I'm a widow, Pedro," she laughed, holding the wine glass out to him. "I'll have to find myself another beau."

Pedro clutched the handle of his knife firmly. He was

wasting precious moments. Now was as good a time as any to kill her and get it over with.

"You know I always liked you, Pedro. You are such a handsome, dashing looking man and you are so brave."

Pedro's grip on his dagger relaxed slightly.

"But perhaps you already have a sweetheart?"

Pedro resented the tenderness of her eyes that seemed somehow weaving a spell about him. He was not to be turned from his purpose. He was oath-bound to kill this woman and he proposed to do it. His hand closed more tightly on his weapon and he drew the blade stealthily half out of its sheath. He was ready for the fatal lunge.

"I think, Pedro—dear old Pedro—I could very easily learn to love you," purred La Molinera, smiling her softest smile.

Pedro's knife dropped back into its scabbard with a sharp little click. Perhaps after all it would not be a bad idea to postpone this murder for a while. La Molinera, with the wisdom of a veteran campaigner, sensed her moment of victory. Setting the wine glass on a table, she coolly plumped herself down on Pedro's lap, threw her arms about his neck and kissed him.

Pedro and La Molinera lived quite happily together and Pedro settled down to honest work on Palos Verdes rancho where Wilmington now stands.

When Murrieta learned how Pedro had proved false to his oath in such shameless fashion, he was infuriated and rushed Juan Borilda off to Los Angeles to kill him. But as a minister of vengeance, Borilda turned out to be a more ridiculous fiasco than Vergara. No sooner had he arrived in the City of the Angels than he got drunk in the dives in Nigger Alley. This was foolish. Then, full of bad whiskey, he strutted about and boasted of his murderous mission. This was fatal. Borilda was found a little later sprawled in a back street with his throat cut and it was supposed the man he had been sent to kill had killed him. Vergara reached the end of his trail several years later in Yuma where, after he had murdered a man named Porter, he was surrounded by a company of United States regulars and shot to death.

Pancho Daniel, banned from Murrieta's band, had achieved paradoxical distinction as an outlaw outlawed by outlaws, and with sheriffs searching for him and Murrieta's spies plotting to murder him, he was kept rather busy. He found his niche, however, when he joined the Manila gang headed by Juan Flores. The Manilas were robbers with a strong leaning toward melodrama. They were bound together by an oath of blood. They had secret grips, pass words and countersigns. They posted sentinels about their camps who halted all who approached. *"Quien vive?"* was the challenge. *"Isla,"* was the reply. *"Que gente?" "Manila."* They took their melodramatic nonsense seriously and once shot one of their number who gave the wrong countersign. Among the Manilas, Pancho Daniel, with his prestige as one of the famous Murrieta's veteran buccaneers, soon became a big fellow.

The Manilas rode forth on a foray to San Juan Capistrano. With Juan Flores, the leader, were Pancho Daniel, Jesus Espinosa, Pedro Lopez, Juan Soto, Juan Valenzuela, Diego Navarro, Andres Fontes, Juan Silva, Francisco Ardillero, Chino Varelas and One-Eyed Piquiniño. In the old Mission town, they robbed the shop of Michael Kraszewski and shot the clerk. Then they plundered the store of George Flughardt whom they murdered. Having ordered Flughardt's wife to serve them with supper, they sat at table with bantering talk and laughter and ate with gusto while their victim lay in his blood on the floor.

When the news reached Los Angeles, Sheriff J. R.

Barton and Deputies William H. Little, Charles J. Baker, Charles F. Daley, Frank Alexander and Alfred Hardy started after the murderers. At Jose Sepulveda's rancho, the sheriff was warned that he might meet with disaster if he attacked the robbers with such a small force. But the sheriff regarded the Manilas as a gang of cheap thieves and had no fear of their prowess. Twelve miles from San Juan Capistrano a man was sighted galloping. Little and Baker gave chase. As they rode through a gap in the hills, they were killed from ambush. Sheriff Barton with the three others rushed to the rescue. A second volley from the chaparral stretched Barton and Daley dead in the road. Hardy and Alexander escaped.

The murder of the sheriff and his three deputies moved Los Angeles to decisive action. Andres Pico took the field with fifty men, Bethel Cooper with twenty-six, Tomas Sanchez with twenty-five, James Thompson, who succeeded Barton as sheriff, with thirty. It was to be war to the death against the Manilas. Spies located Flores, Espinosa, Lopez, Silva and Ardillero in camp in the Cañada de la Horca. Andres Pico attacked them at dawn. The bandits rode to the top of a mountain. Beyond them was a precipice. Believing them cornered, the posse closed in. Flores, Espinosa and Lopez spurred their horses over the rim of the wall and slid down fifty feet to a ledge. There they abandoned their animals. Clutching bushes, getting a toe hold now and then on narrow benches, they went slipping and tumbling to the bottom of the gorge five hundred feet below. Climbing another mountain rampart, they left pursuit behind. Ardillero and Silva feared to risk their necks in such reckless fashion and were captured. The other three were taken a few days later. They had taken refuge in a cave but when Pico's company of fifty charged them, they surrendered.

The five prisoners were taken to the ranch of Teodocio

Yorba. Bound and under guard, Flores, Espinosa and Lopez, in some way, managed to escape. To prevent the possibility of their doing likewise, Silva and Ardillero were hanged.

A seedy Mexican on a sorry pony was riding through Simi pass. He was unarmed. There was nothing suspicious in his appearance. He looked a harmless son of poverty. But two of Thompson's troopers halted him. His name was Sanchez, he said, and he lived at San Fernando Mission and he was looking for some horses that had broken out of his corral. That was plausible. The troopers were about to let him pass on when Thompson rode up and recognized him. The disreputable looking Sanchez turned out to be the redoubtable Juan Flores.

While Flores lay in jail in Los Angeles, a citizens' court sat upon his case and condemned him to be hanged on Fort Hill. Flores made no plea. It was what he had expected and he took the matter coolly. He was a handsome fellow only twenty-two. He had been a fine dancer and a favorite among the dance hall girls. He tricked himself out for the gallows as if he were going to a fandango. He was a debonnaire figure as he stood on the death trap in black coat, flowered vest and white pants with a rose in his button-hole. But no black eyed senorita tripped a measure with him to rhythmic music. He danced alone and he danced on air.

Jesus Espinosa was captured and hanged in Santa Barbara. Pedro Lopez was taken prisoner in San Gabriel with Juan Valenzuela and Diego Navarro. When they were led to a live oak, it was found that the ropes looped about their necks were too short to go over a bough. This was disappointing. So the three men were shot. Just prior to their execution, Juan Soto, wounded in the leg by a bullet, took refuge in a swamp. The marsh grasses were set on fire and, as Soto with his clothes blazing, rushed out through the smoke and flames, he died under a six-shooter volley. Of the remaining members of the Manila gang, Pancho Daniel escaped to San Jose; the life of Chino Varelas was spared on account of his youth; one fled across the border into Lower California where he met death in a political feud; the others were hunted down by the pursuing posses and slain. The curtain had fallen upon the hectic Manila melodrama but it was a good show while it lasted.

Governor Johnson offered a reward of $2,500 for Pancho Daniel. The citizens of Los Angeles announced an additional reward of $1,500. Pancho Daniel's worthless head suddenly had become valuable. But for two years he enjoyed his freedom. Finally he was taken near San Jose and returned to Los Angeles. There at dawn one morning, two hundred citizens pounced upon the old jailer as he emerged from the jail with a basket on his arm to do his marketing. Having taken his keys from him, they went in and unlocked the door of Pancho Daniel's cell. The outlaw met them in silence with a grave bow. He had only a few minutes to live and knew it but he seemed as placid as if he were receiving a summons to breakfast and marched out of the jail with a certain dignity in the midst of his captors. They hanged him to the cross-beam of the jail yard gate as the sun was coming up and they did their work so smoothly and quietly that the morning slumbers of the worthy burghers of the neighborhood were not disturbed.

So, with a rope around his neck, Pancho Daniel passes out of the story and we shall hear no more of this robber Lothario. He was an unctuous, treacherous rogue, cool, wise, resourceful and as cunning as a fox. But whatever else he may have been, Pancho Daniel was no coward. He lived without conscience but he died without fear.

But meanwhile what of La Molinera?—La Molinera,

the bright, the jocund, the ever-charming, pirouetting through life to dance tunes, reveling in sunshine, bathing in rainbows, true to herself if true to no one else, winsomely false, joyously shameless, a Greek spirit in a Mexican mantilla. Who would have suspected this moth-like creature could harbor hatred and revenge? But dainty La Molinera betrayed Murrieta to his death and paid him back with a hatred as deep as his own.

Picture, if you please, the village of San Juan Bautista peaceful in the moonlight. Captain Harry Love and his Rangers on the hunt for Murrieta are camped near the dilapidated, gray old Mission church. The captain is sleeping soundly in his blankets. A Mexican boy touches him on the shoulder. The captain rubs his eyes, blinks drowsily. What the devil does this *muchacho* want with him at midnight? A woman with secret information wishes to see him at once. She is waiting for him in an adobe at the edge of town. Will the captain come? Love is not so sure about it. Who is this woman? The lad shakes his head,—she is a stranger to him. This mysterious business may be a trap. But Love is a brave man. He answers the summons. As he enters the house, a woman, her face muffled in a rebosa, rises to meet him.

"I have come many miles," she says, "across mountains and deserts to aid you. Joaquin Murrieta hates me. He has tried desperately to have me murdered. If he remains alive, he will kill me. He has sworn it and he will keep his word. Why this is so you need not know. But I am not moved by fear alone. A deeper motive is my own consuming hatred. I know where he now is. Head eastward across the mountains through Priest's valley. When you come out into the San Joaquin valley, turn south. The Arroya Cantova is his hiding place. There, if you travel swiftly, you will find him. My name would mean nothing to you. The only thing important is that you kill him."

The woman was La Molinera—the butterfly turned rattlesnake—and Murrieta was killed as a result of her information. With this last betrayal, she makes her final bow. We may fancy her, with her old blithe spirit, smiling and blowing a kiss from her fingertips to her audience that has thrilled to her beauty, her mad adventures, her loves, and treacheries. The curtain falls, the lights go out, the show is over. She steps daintily out the stage door and the night swallows her—the deep darkness of oblivion. No one to-day knows what became of La Molinera, who betrayed her lover with an embrace and cheated death with a kiss—the gay, light-hearted, heartless Little Miller.

Mariquita Vasquez was the sweetheart of Pedro Gonzales, the honest horsethief, who was a handsome fellow and of considerable prestige as a squire of dames. Mariquita was a solid chunk of a girl, very pretty and very jealous, with cheeks of dusky rose, smoky black eyes and a cryptic smile that might be a signal of fair weather ahead or might indicate a thunder squall three points off the weather bow. When Mariquita smiled, even though no danger threatened, it was always the part of wisdom for her lover to watch his step and for any love pirate, who might be maneuvering trickily to lay him aboard, to clew down her topsails and stand by for a blow. Throughout his affair with her, Gonzales had smooth sailing and when he was killed by Harry Love, Mariquita was heartbroken for three weeks. Then she forgot him and gave herself into the keeping of Juan Cardoza. But this good looking young bandit had old-school notions about women. He insisted on being boss and when Mariquita, in a jealous tantrum, made a vicious pass at him with a dagger, he laid the little lady coolly across his knees and gave her a sound spanking. Mariquita seemed quite subdued after this and was a model of tender affection. Noting the effect of the chastisement, Cardoza swelled about among his comrades, declaring the only way to tame a balky woman was to man-handle her and, said he, if you gave her a black eye now and then it only made her love you all the more. When Mariquita heard of his boastful talk, her old cryptic smile lifted one corner of her pretty mouth.

Mariquita never appeared in happier mood than when she and Cardoza set out from Arroya Cantova for Los Angeles. As they rode side by side laughing and talking over Tejon Pass, they seemed to be having a grand time. But all the while Mariquita was watching her lover like a hawk out of the tail of her eye and when he turned his head, doubtless to admire the purple beauty of the deep gorge along the edge of which they were riding, she slipped a dagger from her bosom and buried it to the hilt in his back. Cardoza's horse, rearing in fright, backed off the thousand-foot precipice and steed and rider went plunging to death.

Riding back to the Arroya Cantova, Mariquita reported Cardoza's death as an accident and wept and wailed in paroxysms of ostentatious grief. But in a few days, Manuel Savolio dried her tears and she rode off happily with him to Hornitos. Savolio seemed as adept a lover as he was a brigand and the little tigress remained true to him until the end of his life. The fact that Cardoza had been murdered might never have come to light if Murrieta and several of his companions, searching for the body to bury it, had not found Mariquita's dagger still sticking in his back.

Jesusita Espinosa, a dainty little trick with a delicate face and looking every inch the lady, got along famously for a while with Luis Guerra. But Guerra was an uncouth ruffian who drank heavily and beat her occasionally, and the refined Jesusita came to abhor the brute. At Arroya Cantova one morning when Guerra was called for breakfast he did not respond and an investigation revealed him lying dead on his blankets as if in peaceful slumber. No wounds were found on his body and it was supposed he had died from the effects of an overnight debauch. It came out later, however, that Jesusita, with medieval cunning, had melted some lead used for molding bullets and poured some of the molten metal into one of Guerra's ears while he slept.

Having rid herself of her distasteful lover, Jesusita laid herself out to win Three Fingered Jack whom she had admired for a long time. But that captivating person showed no sign of being at all impressed by her blandishments. Jesusita, who in the past had found men such easy game that she felt almost ashamed to play at love with one of the simpering fools, was unable to understand how Three Fingered Jack could resist her fascinations. She had imagined that one who reveled in blood and found his greatest pleasure in cutting throats would jump at the chance to have as his paramour a murderess who by her recent crime had proved herself a monster and in every way worthy of the man she sought to win. Three Fingered Jack's cold aloofness led her to suspect her approach had been a trifle too subtle and she took occasion—in the most refined and ladylike way—to unpack her heart to Three Fingers in so many words. But that fastidious cut-throat threw up his hands in holy horror. He take to his bosom a woman with murder in her heart, a vampire, a midnight assassin, a depraved and inhuman wretch! No, a thousand times no! So Jesusita took Isidoro Conejo for her sweetheart and lived happily with him ever afterward.

Among the madly hectic love affairs of the outlaw

band, the boy and girl romance of Reyes Feliz and his Carmelita seemed a Paul and Virginia idyll. Feliz rode one day into the outlaw camp on the American river with Carmelita seated behind him and, swinging her to the ground, announced abruptly, "Here's my wife." It was a genuine love match and to the end Carmelita who, prior to the elopement, had been the wife of a Mexican packer, was—without benefit of clergy—everything a wife should be. With robbers and demireps as her companions and debauchery all around her, she remained an honest woman. She and Reyes were wrapped up in each other and after every raid and adventure in which he took part, Reyes hurried back, like a child to its mother, to the shelter of Carmelita's arms.

But their happiness was not to last always and this simple-hearted, true-love affair was destined to a pathetic and tragic conclusion. When they were living at Mission San Gabriel, Reyes was clawed and bitten by a grizzly bear while on a hunting trip and lay for a time near death, and it was only the tender ministrations of Carmelita, who stayed by his side night and day for six weeks, that finally saved his life. Shortly after his recovery, Feliz was captured and met death on the gallows and the tragedy broke Carmelita's heart. "Every night I hear him calling me," she said to the old Mexican woman with whom she made her home. And when the disconsolate girl could bear her burden no longer, she drove a dagger into her heart and went to join her lover.

In a wild and uninhabited region where the Coast Range mountains wall in the San Joaquin valley on the west near the present town of Coalinga, Murrieta and his outlaws had their principal rendezvous and refuge in Arroya Cantova, as it was known in those days but is now on the map officially at Cantua Arroya. It was not so much an arroya as a small bottle-neck valley opening through a short narrow cañon from the Coast Range into the great valley of the San Joaquin river. It was about four miles long with precipitous sides. Pines, live oaks and cottonwoods, free from underbrush, gave the place the appearance of a well-kept park and Cantova Creek, fed by springs, hummed a drowsy tune as its clear, cold waters lapped around lichened boulders and broke over gravel bars. In this snug retreat far from the reach of law, the robbers found shelter after their forays, assembled the horses stolen from all over the state before driving them to market in Mexico, and divided their loot. And here with wild game, liquors and provisions in abundance, they rested and feasted and caroused among their women.

Arroya Cantova became in after years the hiding place of the noted bandit, Tiburcio Vasquez, who succeeded Murrieta as the terror of California and who reached the end of his rope—a rope with a hangman's noose in it—in 1875 at San Jose. The valley to-day is just as it was when Murrieta and his wild followers found haven among its peaceful groves and three miles from the cañon's mouth, Murrieta and Three Fingered Jack met death. By the superstitious the valley is believed to be haunted and few care to venture into it after dark. Chance travelers, who have camped there at night, have told weird tales of being awakened by the music of invisible guitars and of seeing shadowy figures dancing in the moonlight. From one end of the valley to the other are innumerable old pits and trenches left by treasure hunters, who through the years have come in endless procession and dug for the fabulous wealth in gold the famous brigand is supposed to have buried. But all have departed empty handed and, if Murrieta ever concealed any treasure there, it still lies in its mysterious hiding place somewhere under the pines and live oaks of his old wilderness sanctuary.

CHAPTER V.

THE HILLS OF GOLD.

JOAQUIN MURRIETA in his robber operations ranged at one time or another over the greater part of California, but in the mining country, the principal stage setting of his exploits, was that part of the Sierra Nevada foothills known as the Mother Lode. This region was tremendously rich in gold and was roughly one hundred and seventy-five miles long by seventy-five or eighty miles wide and extended along the western flank of the mountains from Placerville on the north to Mariposa on the south. It was usually called the Southern mines to distinguish it from the Northern mines in the area about the American, Feather and Yuba rivers where gold was discovered and which was the scene of the first gold rush. As gold fields, the two districts were perhaps equally rich, but the northern country was more ruggedly mountainous than the southern, with more precipitous ridges and deeper gorges and cañons. Though Bear Mountain and Table Mountain were outstanding ranges in the southern district, the region as a whole was foothill country pure and simple, tumultuous and heavily timbered in certain portions but in others as open and gently rolling as a pastoral landscape and diversified by many beautiful valleys filled with groves of live oaks and cottonwoods. The principal gold camps of the Mother Lode were so close to the western edges of the hills that they were easily accessible from Stockton and Sacramento in the San Joaquin and Sacramento valleys, and were so far from the Sierra Nevada mountains that from hardly one of them could those towering ranges be seen. The principal rivers of the country, all famous in gold-rush history, were the Calaveras, Stanislaus, Tuolomne, Mokelumne, and Consumnes, and the richest and most populous gold camps were Sonora, Columbia, Angel's Camp, Murphy's Diggings, San Andreas, Mokelumne Hill, Jackson, Placerville, Hornitos and Mariposa.

At the risk of breaking the continuity of the Murrieta saga, let us at this point glance for a brief interval at life and conditions in the Mother Lode, which in Murrieta's day was swarming with miners and dotted with towns riotous with drinking, gambling and every form of dissipation—a bonanza land of adventure, romance and overnight fortunes where life moved swiftly and death was sudden. The stories in this chapter do not touch upon the personal experiences of the young outlaw chieftain, but they will serve perhaps to orientate him in his immediate environment and picture as vividly as possible the human drama that formed his romantic and colorful background. They are, if you please, nuggets of romance, rich in human interest, picked up in the old gold camps and still to be heard by winter firesides from one end of Murrieta's old stamping grounds to the other. Some are classics in the legends of the gold stampede and some are as essentially dramatic as any tale that Bret Harte ever wrote. They are stories of an era unique in American annals when reality was romance and life was melodrama. Murrieta's exploits could have been possible in no other conditions of society and to understand his career it is necessary to have a clear idea of the rushing, surging, turbulent life of the country in which he rose to lawless fame.

Sonora in the heart of this picturesque region was one

of the most important towns of the Mother Lode. Close to the western edge of the hills and only fifty or sixty miles from Stockton, it was a distributing center for supplies coming up by wagon train from the San Joaquin valley. To-day it is a busy place of three thousand five hundred people and considerable wealth. Its pleasant homes cover the hills. Its paved streets are crowded with motor cars. Prosperous business houses line its main street. Its girls wear smart clothes. Its men go about with creased trousers. The talk is of world affairs—Wall street, the government, international relations. Nothing, or next to nothing, remains to recall the days when it was a town of one long winding street, saloons, gambling houses and dance halls.

It came into existence in 1848. At its peak it had a population of five thousand. Its first church was built in 1850, its first school in 1852. The Sonora Herald, first newspaper in the California mines, was established in 1850. Its press had been brought around Cape Horn from New York on a sailing ship. Its first issue was printed on July 4 on brown wrapping paper and its pages were nine by thirteen inches in size. Single copies sold for fifty cents. A year's subscription was twenty dollars and advertising rates were four dollars for six lines.

The "Grand Opening" of the Phoenix theater in the rear of Ward's saloon on New Year's Night, 1851, was a red-letter event. The Chapmans and their troupe of actors, who had won acclaim in other camps, were escorted to town from Columbia by a procession of a thousand red-shirted miners. The play produced before a packed house was "the celebrated comedy in three acts entitled 'The Serious Family.'" An opening address "written by a Gentleman of the City" was delivered from the stage by Miss Caroline Chapman. "A full orchestra of acknowledged musical talent" was provided. At times the clatter of silver dollars rained upon the boards from a wildly enthusiastic audience almost drowned out the actors' lines. After a thrilling climax the stage would be cluttered with buckskin pouches full of gold dust. Dancing and singing filled in the intermissions and the evening's entertainment closed with "the favorite farce of 'The Rough Diamond.'" "Prices of admission: Parquette $1. Dress Circle $2." Doors opened at 6; the curtain rose at 7. The Chapman Company held the theater for eight nights and presented "Paul Pry," "The Honeymoon" and "She Stoops to Conquer." Several years later Edwin Booth and Lotta Crabtree appeared on a professional tour in the gold camps.

The Sonora Herald's first big story was printed in the third issue. Pablo Martinez, Dionisia Ochoa, Gabino Jesus, and Ruiz Molina had been brought to Sonora as prisoners by Sheriff George Work from Green Flat, nine miles out. They had been caught in the act of burning two dead bodies in their tent house. A mob seized the prisoners who were rescued by the sheriff while the ropes were around their necks. The surrounding country was aroused by what was regarded as an atrocious crime. Two thousand armed men from neighboring mining camps, rode in and joined the mob. A night attack on the jail was beaten off by the sheriff and his men. Drunken rioters marched through the streets firing at every Mexican they met. Several Mexicans were shot and hundreds fled to the hills. The tumults continued for a week. When order finally was restored the prisoners were brought to trial and acquitted. They declared that, following a mortuary custom common among the Mexicans, they had been burning the bodies of two of their countrymen who had died a natural death and an investigation proved the truth of their statement.

The raging mob that howled for the lives of these four

Mexicans was not in keeping with the customary spirit of the mining country. A passion for justice was a dominant trait among the miners. With little law to protect their lives and property, they became their own law. Criminals had flocked to the mines in vast numbers from every part of the world. Robberies were of constant occurrence. More than four thousand murders were committed in California between 1849 and 1854 inclusive.* Vigilance committees and mobs dealt with these conditions. But the men who attempted lawlessly to maintain a semblance of law acted deliberately and with cool judgment. The judicial poise of these mobs is the more surprising when it is remembered that the men of the California mines in the wild days of the gold stampede were in the prime of young manhood when the blood runs hot—four-fifths of them were between eighteen and thirty-five—and were without the moral restraints of home and conventionalized society. Lynch courts became an institution. Criminals were given a fair trial under forms of law and the just temper of these mob courts is proved by the fact that many men tried before them were acquitted and set free. The mobs that weighed evidence in early California established a new precedent in mob psychology. They were perhaps the most remarkable mobs in the history of the world and their verdicts were unique examples of raw human justice.

Dave Hill was known in many camps as a jovial, roystering ne'er-do-well and no one took the trouble to inquire where the money came from that he squandered at bars and monte tables. For a long time he passed as an

* Helper in his "Land of Gold" gives the following figures on casualties between 1849 and 1854 inclusive: Murders 4,200; killed by Indians en route to California across the plains 1,600; perished by want and accident and killed by Indians in California 5,300; wrecked and lost at sea en route 2,200; suicides 1,400; became insane through hardships 1,700.

honest man. But travelers who had been robbed on the highways and drivers of stage coaches that had been held up in lonely gulches began to whisper that the man who had stepped from the brush with a red bandana over his face and a shotgun at his shoulder had looked suspiciously like Hill. The daring robbery of Bemas & Co.'s store in Campo Seco exposed Hill as a veteran criminal. He was trailed to Sonora, arrested and brought back. A lynch court went into session near a convenient tree. Hill confessed the crime and was sentenced to death. With the rope around his neck, he made a plea for his life.

"You all know me, boys," said Hill. "You've had many a drink with me. This is a purty rough deal you're givin' me. I've been a thief all my life but I've never yet shed blood. I've let many a feller off with his life when a colder-blooded man than me would ha' killed him. That ought to count in my favor. I've showed mercy and it looks to me like you fellers might stretch a pint and show me a little mercy."

That was manly talk and it touched some hidden chords somewhere. Nobody spoke for a while.

"I move," said somebody, "we don't hang him but give him a hundred lashes and turn him out of camp."

Some approved, some opposed, this idea. A vote was taken. The count of hands showed an equal division. While Hill's fate teetered in the balance, Sheriff Work arrived unattended. He pledged his honor, if the mob would surrender him, Hill should be tried at the first session of the district court. Those in favor of the hanging strenuously objected to this proposal but the sheriff's argument prevailed in the end and he drove off in a wagon with the prisoner for Sonora.

But the news of Hill's escape from the noose traveled faster than the sheriff. Two men of Sonora—Edwards and Linoberg—went through the streets ringing dinner bells. The citizens assembled in front of Holden's store. Edwards mounted a dry-goods box.

"Courts are farces," he shouted. "Thieves are turned loose. Murderers whittle their way out of jail. It's time to put a stop to such things. The only way to get justice is to take it with our own hands. Hill had a fair trial. He confessed his crime. This country should rid itself of such a man. We owe it to ourselves as good citizens who stand for law and order to put a halter around his neck."

It was night when Sheriff Work drove into Sonora and saw the mob in the glare of a bonfire milling in the street. He had saved Hill's life once that day. Could he save it again? As the mob came rushing toward him yelling, the sheriff and the prisoner jumped from the wagon and, darting into an arroya, ran for a short distance hidden from their pursuers. As they scrambled up the farther bank, escape seemed certain. The jail loomed just ahead in the darkness. Once its iron doors clanged behind them, they would be safe. "We win again," chuckled the sheriff as he mounted the jail steps. Hill laughed out loud. From the shadows of the doorway stepped a man named Cheatham. He shoved a six-shooter under the sheriff's nose.

"Let that fellow go," he said, "or I'll kill you."

The mob stormed around. The sheriff was overpowered. Five minutes later, Hill was swinging from an oak tree back of the El Dorado hotel.

"The crowd was deeply impressed," commented the Sonora Herald. "All were satisfied with the righteousness and necessity of the punishment. All through the city, the rowdies, men who live sumptuously and yet do not work, men who are marked and against whom there are more than suspicions of guilt, were solemn and subdued. Two or three might be seen in groups in various places talking softly and evidently alarmed for their own safety. We say keep the halter ready and use it whenever a known criminal is caught, be he American or foreigner. We glory in the fact that American justice is dealt out to all alike."

The Sonora vigilance committee was charged by the citizens with being too soft hearted at times. Having sentenced a Mexican to receive a hundred and fifty lashes, it tied him to a tree and started in on him with stirrup leather. The Mexican took his medicine in stoical silence, chewing on the end of a cigar as the blows brought blood. Taking pity on him, the committee permitted him to rest after every twenty-five lashes and in one interval took him to a saloon and bought him a drink. After branding the letters H.T. (Horse Thief) on the hips of three other miscreants, the committee raised a purse for them. A fellow who stole $5,000 worth of gold dust from a miner did not fare so well. The committee gave him one hundred lashes on the bare back, shaved his head, cut off his ears, and kicked him out of camp. The incorrigible scamp stole a mule and rode to Murphy's Diggings. There he was pulled out of his saddle and sentenced by a miners' court to be flogged again. But when the miners saw his back covered with lacerations from his former beating, they set him free, not from compassion, as they explained, but because they could not find room on his back to lay another stripe.

Peter Nicholas stabbed John Parote to death in Columbia. A mob seized him and dragged him to a tree. As he was about to be swung up, Sheriff Solomon and his deputies arrived. With them was James W. Coffroth, a young lawyer, whose grandson of the same name is today noted in connection with the turf, baseball and the prize ring and is one of the principal owners of the race track and palatial gambling establishment at Agua Caliente. Well named was this wise Sheriff Solomon who saw his duty and went for it there and then.

"You make a speech, Jim," said Sheriff Solomon to Lawyer Coffroth. "I'll do the rest."

While Coffroth held the crowd spell-bound in an eloquent appeal for forbearance and respect for law, the sheriff and his deputies, edging quietly through the crowd, formed a ring around Nicholas. When the lawyer had finished his address, Sheriff Solomon spoke. "Gentlemen," he said, "you are all good men, your intentions are honorable, and I hate to disappoint you. But this man is going to have a fair trial by law. He is going to the Sonora jail right now and I am going to take him." Before the crowd knew what was happening, Nicholas was lifted into a saddle and he and the sheriff went galloping out of town. Three months later, Nicholas was tried and sentenced to the gallows.

California at that time was excited over the selection of a permanent site for the state capital. Sacramento, Monterey, San Jose, Vallejo, Benicia and Columbia were candidates for the honor and the cities were deluging the Legislature with petitions setting forth their individual advantages. Columbia's petition, with a long preamble, was drawn up and placed on a counter in a store to be signed by the citizens. Twelve thousand had affixed their names to it when Horace Bull, lawyer for Nicholas, who had exhausted all the technicalities of law to save his client's neck, had an inspiration. Stepping to the counter as if to attach his signature, he slyly slipped the underlying sheets containing the names into his pocket and, leaving the preamble in plain view on the counter to mask his skullduggery, hurried to his office. There he wrote out a plea for executive clemency, attached the twelve thousand names, many of them signed by the hands that had fastened the rope around Nicholas' neck, and mailed it to Governor John Bigler. The governor, being a good politician, was greatly impressed by the names of twelve thousand voters and lost no time in commuting Nicholas' death sentence to ten years in San Quentin penitentiary. Four years later Nicholas was pardoned.

A Sonora man who missed a horse from his corral caught up with the horse thief in Calaveras and found him just sitting down to dinner in the Empire hotel.

"Well, my friend," said the Sonoran, "did my horse suit you?"

"It's not a bad animal," replied the horse thief, a pleasant, good looking young chap.

"But you are not a good judge of horse flesh or you would have stolen the one I'm riding. It's a better horse or I would never have overtaken you."

His ride of thirty miles had given the Sonoran a good appetite and he took a chair at the table and ate dinner with the man who had robbed him.

"You can have your horse back," said the thief after they had passed a chatty half hour over their meat and potatoes.

"Kind of you. Thanks."

"That'll square everything, won't it?"

"There's a minor detail still to be taken care of but that won't take long."

The news of the affair had spread through the camp and a crowd, headed by the sheriff, waited in front of the hotel and took the young man in tow as he stepped out. He looked astonished.

"What are you going to do with me?"

"Hang you."

"But I've already fixed things up with this gentleman."

Having made amends, he seemed to think it was not exactly polite to hang him.

"Here's the rope and there's the tree over yonder."

"Well, if I've got to go, I wish you'd shoot me. I'd rather be shot than hung."

"That'll be O.K. with us. We aim to please."

At the edge of town, a six-shooter squad was selected and the young man took his stand before it. A physician interested in phrenology stepped up to him.

"I'd like to buy your head," he said. "How much will you take for it?"

"What do you want with my head?"

"The conformation of your skull interests me."

"Nobody ever wanted to buy my head before and I hardly know what to ask you for it. Would twenty dollars be too much?"

"O yes, much too high," replied the doctor as if he were accustomed to buying heads every day and kept posted on the latest market quotations. "I'll give you ten."

"All right, I guess I might as well take it. My head won't be worth anything to me in about a minute and a half."

He put the ten dollar gold piece with a lock of his hair in his tobacco pouch and handed the pouch to the sheriff.

"Send this to my old mother in Missouri," he said and gave the address. "But," he added, "don't tell her how I went out. It would break her heart."

The sheriff later wrote to the old lady that her son had died of an unfortunate accident as the result of a horse race.

"Shoot me here," said the condemned man putting his hand over his heart as the firing squad leveled its guns.

"The doctor paid his good money for my head and I want to deliver the goods undamaged."

Then a half dozen six-shooters spoke and he fell dead. The physician drew a scalpel from his surgical case and was preparing to decapitate the corpse when the sheriff stopped him.

"The body goes with the head," said the sheriff. "Your ten dollars takes the whole horse thief."

"But I bought only the head," replied the doctor testily. "The body wasn't included in the deal. Moreover, I don't want it."

"You'll have to take it and you'll have to stand the funeral expenses."

"What kind of a fool do you take me for? I propose to have exactly what I paid for, no more and no less."

With fine professional skill, the doctor cut off the head and dropped it into a gunnysack. Then he dragged the body to an old prospect hole and dumped it in.

"The funeral's over," he said, glaring at the sheriff.

An honest, hard working Mexican was jogging along a mountain trail when he heard a great hullabaloo behind him. Looking back, he saw a dozen horsemen galloping toward him, yelling and firing revolvers. Terrified by this startling spectacle, the poor peon tumbled off his pony and dodged into the brush. He was quickly overhauled. The infuriated crowd wasted no time in explanations but looped a lariat about the neck of the astonished Mexican and strung him up to a tree. Taking a good look at the face of the victim dangling in the noose, one of the lynchers seemed pained by a vague doubt.

"I've got a notion we've hung the wrong feller," he said.

The others took a squint and were inclined to think so too. Before life was extinct, the Mexican was lowered to the ground. The leader of the party bent over him.

"Excuse us, pard," he said. "We mistook you for somebody else."

A wandering miner found gold on the site of Columbia in 1850 and, going to work with pick and shovel, dug a hole on his claim. Within a year that hole in the ground had become a city of fifteen thousand people. A woman named Martha kept a house in Columbia with a bar and a stable of girls. John Barclay dealt faro in one of the town's one hundred and forty-three gambling houses capitalized at a million dollars. Martha and some of her girls used to breeze into the faro bank after midnight and try their luck at Barclay's table. Barclay was taken with Martha's dashing style of play and Martha admired the expert way the handsome young gambler slid the cards out of the box and paid off the bets. In the end Martha won Barclay over the faro layout and they were married. For Barclay, it was like betting the queen to win but, as it turned out, it was the unluckiest play he ever made.

John Smith, a miner in from the diggings, was drunk and loaded for bear. Blowing into Martha's place and blundering about in roystering fashion, he accidentally broke a pitcher. Martha had a tongue with a tang to it and, pitching into the tipsy fellow, she berated him viciously. With loud profanity, Smith made for her. He had her by the throat and was bending her back over a table when Barclay, hearing the uproar, came rushing in and shot him dead. Barclay was arrested and placed in jail.

It was Sunday. Columbia was filled with miners who had come in from the gulches to paint the town on their customary weekly spree. They labored and sweated for their gold with pick and shovel—these hard, rough fellows—and were trimmed out of their dust while drunk quite regularly by slick gamblers. No love was lost between miners and gamblers and when the news spread that a gambler had murdered a miner over a woman of the town, an infuriated mob of a thousand men swarmed around the jail and battered down the door with axes and crow bars. Barclay was taken from his cell and marched to a spot at the edge of town where a water flume built on high trestles crossed the Gold Hill road.

A miners' court was organized. Jack Heckendorn, editor of the Columbia Clipper, was chosen presiding judge. A jury of twelve was selected. James Coffroth was appointed prosecutor and John Oxley counsel for the defense. The crowd formed a ring about an open space where the tribunal went into session with Barclay sitting on the grass. Barclay asked that his wife be called as a witness. The crowd shouted its disapproval;—it would listen to no prostitute. Coffroth addressed the jury. The young lawyer, who had urged respect for law in the Nicholas case, spoke now in fiery defense of lawlessness, his friendship for the murdered man adding fervor to his eloquence. Oxley, whose honest sympathy was with Barclay, made an impassioned appeal. He called the crime justifiable homicide. "Where is the man among you," he thundered, "who seeing the clutches of a drunken brute at his wife's throat would not have done the same thing?" The jury balloted. The verdict was death.

Night had fallen. A great bonfire was built. The flames illuminated the crowd and threw the spidery trestle of the flume into clear relief against the sky. Sheriff James Stewart galloped up and demanded the prisoner. The crowd's answer was to tie a rope about Barclay's neck and hustle him beneath the flume. A dozen miners, carrying the end of the rope with them, went shinning to the top of the trestle fifty feet above the heads of the crowd. Barclay, his hands unbound, stood pale and silent beneath them. They drew the rope taut. The sheriff fought to reach him. A blow from a pistol butt stretched the officer unconscious.

Up with him! The roar was like thunder. The men above gave a mighty pull. A slender figure shot high into the air. The crowd, suddenly silent, watched the doomed man struggle hopelessly for his life. He grasped the strangling rope with both hands and clung to it desperately. The men on the flume jerked him up and dropped him down abruptly again and again but they could not break his hold. "Let go, you fool, let go!" they shouted. Barclay was growing weak—he was dying. One hand fell to his side. Then the other. His writhing ceased and he hung limp and still in the red light of the bonfire. He had been married three weeks. This was the end of honeymoon trail.

Alcaldes went out and justices of the peace came in in 1850 when California was organized as a state and was admitted to the union. The early justices knew nothing of law—some of them could hardly write their own names—but they muddled along the best they knew how and were immensely comical in their serious way. If it had not been for the justices, many a camp and cabin would have had nothing to laugh at on a rainy day.

Justice Richard C. Barry of Sonora had been a captain of Texas Rangers in the Mexican war. He was a red-faced, choleric, little man, czar-like and resolute, who was more interested in his court fees than in square dealing. What he did not know about law would have filled a library but woe to the lawyer who had the audacity to question his authority. Jesus Ramirez was arraigned before Justice Barry charged with stealing a mule from Sheriff Work and the record of the trial has been preserved.

"The sheriff swears the mule is hisn and I believe so

too," said Justice Barry in a masterly summing up of the case. "It seems clear that Jesus Ramirez is guilty of stealing the aforesaid mule, feloniously and against the law made and provided and the dignity of the people of Sonora, and I sentence him to pay the costs of court, which will be $10, and fine him $100 more as a terror to evil doers."

"Pero no tengo dinero," stammered Jesus Ramirez excitedly.

"What is it the greaser says?" asked the justice out of the corner of his mouth.

"He say he no got no money," replied the court interpreter.

"Then," declared the justice with stern decision, "I will rule that George Work must pay the costs of court and the fine as well. This court can not be expected to work for nothing."

"But if your honor please," protested N. B. Barber, the sheriff's lawyer, "such a ruling is unheard of. There is no precedent in the statutes for such a decision."

"Shet up," barked the justice. "I don't give a damn for your law books. I am the law in this case."

"But, your honor, you can not fine Sheriff Work for being robbed."

"Can't I? I'll show you."

Attorney Barber spread out his hands. "What's the use?" he groaned. "I have no chance to get justice in this court."

"No, and if I have anything to say about it you'll never get justice in this court."

"I object strongly, your honor, to the court's conduct and language."

"Object and be damned," roared the justice. "You are in contempt. I will fine you $50 and commit you to jail for five days. I'll learn you to jaw back at me. Mister Constable, take him to the lock-up."

When a young couple came into court and asked to be married, Justice Barry established what is doubtless a world's record for brevity and speed in wedding ceremonies.

"Do you take this woman for your wife?"

"I do."

"Do you take this man for your husband?"

"Yes."

"Spliced. Five dollars. Git."

Justice Jenkins of Sonora, an Andy Jackson Democrat first, last and all the time, ran up the good old Constitution to the matrimonial masthead in marrying a couple. "Hold up your right hand," he said, glaring fiercely at the bridegroom. "Do you solemnly swear that you are twenty-one years old and that you will support the Constitution of the United States and be a true, faithful and obedient husband to this woman?" "I do," answered the bridegroom meekly. "Then I pronounce you man and wife." Nothing was said to the blushing bride but, as obedience of her husband and not to him, was part of the oath, she doubtless was satisfied.

A young man charged with seduction was arraigned in Justice Jenkins' court. A buxom young woman appeared against him. Justice Jenkins discharged the young man, declaring the evidence proved clearly that he had acted in self-defense.

Uncle Jake Emminger, justice of the peace at Rancheria, was noted for his profound ignorance of law and for a long snow-white beard which ordinarily he kept folded up and tied with a ribbon but which, on Sundays and court days, swept in all its glory below his waist line. A lawyer defending a case before him made a motion for a change of venue. The justice stroked his beard thoughtfully. "Motion overruled and judgment entered for the plaintiff," he declared. "Hold on a minute," said the lawyer. "If my case has to be tried in this court, I demand a jury." "A jury?" exclaimed Uncle Jake in astonishment. "What in hell do you expect to prove by a jury?" When Uncle Jake first assumed the ermine, he became famous overnight by sentencing a Chinaman to jail for life for stealing chickens.

Uncle Zeke was known only as Uncle Zeke in Nevada City until he was elected justice of the peace when his fellow townsmen discovered that his name was Ezekiel Dougherty. A man charged with horse stealing was tried before him. The evidence seemed conclusive. The prosecution rested. The defense attorney called a witness to the stand.

"No use calling any more witnesses," said Uncle Zeke.

"If the court please, I wish to prove the good reputation of the defendant," urged the lawyer.

"Why he's already been proved a horse thief."

"I contend the theft has not been established beyond a reasonable doubt. I would like to have my character witnesses heard."

"I won't hear 'em. A horse thief ain't got no character."

"But, your honor, it is a legal presumption that a defendant is innocent until he is proved guilty."

"And it's a dead moral certainty," said Uncle Zeke, "that I'm not bottomed with cast iron. You can keep on with your argument as long as you're a mind to but I'm going out for a good snort o' whiskey right now."

A boy complained to Justice George Vail of Yreka that a man for whom he had worked all winter refused to pay him his wages of $300 and was about to leave the country. Brought into court the man admitted the debt but protested he had no money.

"Stand that fellow on his head," said Justice Vail to his two constables, "and see if anything drops."

The constables obeyed orders. When the man's head was on the floor and his legs were sticking straight up in the air, a bag containing $2,000 in gold dust fell out of his pocket. The boy's claim was paid and the justice adjudged one ounce each to himself and the two constables as court costs. The amounts were carefully weighed on a pair of scales and the sack was returned to its owner who was allowed to depart.

Lawyer Nash Briggs of Jackson had a gambler for a client. The charge against the gambler was grave and, as the evidence piled up, it seemed certain the least he could expect was a term in prison. As the court room was small and crowded, Briggs asked permission of the justice to step outside with his client for a brief conference. When the two men reached the street, Briggs concentrated his counsel into one word—"Run!" Regarding it as sound legal advice, the gambler took it—on the jump.

Squire Yates of Fiddletown became indignant at the testimony of a witness which he considered outrageously false. The dignity of his position, however, would not permit him to voice his resentment from the bench. "I declare this court adjourned for a minute," he said. "Now it is my privilege, Mr. Witness, to tell you you are a damned liar. That's all I wanted to say. I now declare the court in session again. The hearing may proceed."

Two attorneys arguing a change of venue were unable to agree on the jurisdiction to which the case should be sent. One wanted it transferred to El Dorado county, the other to Amador county. The judge suggested a game of cribbage to settle the question. Having spent twenty minutes in an ante-room, the lawyers came back into court. "May it please your honor," said one, "you may send the case to El Dorado." "By how much?" asked the judge. "Two points," grinned the attorney.

Fred Amos was convicted in Judge King's court of robbing a stage and was sentenced to ten years in prison.

"I'd like to make the court a proposition," said Amos.

"What is it?" asked the judge.

"You've given me ten years. Let's play a game of seven-up—you and me—to see whether it'll be twenty or nothing. Twenty years in San Quentin if I lose. Freedom if I win. Are you game, your honor?"

Justice Jesse Niles of Donkeyville was an oracle of the law and a judge of good whiskey. He was the proprietor of the Diana saloon and in the rear of the drink emporium, back of the billiard table and the faro layout, he presided over his tribunal with grave dignity and a bowie knife strapped around him. When two big mining companies brought a suit before him for adjudication, it was one of the proudest days of his life. The two lawyers representing the litigants treated him with the most punctilious formality and observed all the nicetics of court etiquette. It was "If your honor please" and "If the court will permit" at every turn of affairs and the justice swelled out his chest and looked more than usually solemn and important.

In a moment of happy inspiration, it occurred to the distinguished attorney for the plaintiff that a good drink of liquor might relieve the tedious monotony of the trial and possibly incline the justice slightly to his side of the case. "If your honor please," he said, "I move we adjourn for five minutes," and he had the impudence to wink at Justice Niles and jerk his head in the direction of the bar. Instead of resenting this insolent behavior, however, the justice rose with beaming countenance. "I suppose," he said, "the jury and witnesses are included in the invitation?" "By all means," responded the genial attorney, and everybody in the court room lined up and took a drink. And it may be remarked that Justice Niles not only enjoyed his toddy but enjoyed even more the jingle of the gold pieces dropped into his money drawer.

Not to be outdone by his rival, the lawyer for the defense a little later proposed a second adjournment. Adjournment followed adjournment in such rapid succession throughout the afternoon that by night-fall nobody was sure whether the court proceedings were tiddlewinks or the trial of an important law suit. At last came the close. In a voice so thick few could understand him, the justice summed up the case and expounded the points of law for the benefit of the jury. He managed to flounder through this ordeal in some crazy fashion and was vaguely surprised that he had done no worse. Then abruptly out of a clear sky upon that peaceful scene came the deluge.

"In what law book, your honor," piped up a fool juror, "do you find the law you have mentioned?"

Justice Niles glared at the juror with baleful eyes.

"You want my authority?"

"Why, yes, your honor."

"I would have you know," thundered the justice, "that when I tell you a thing is law, it's law."

Up rose Justice Niles in purple wrath. Out flashed his bowie knife. He jumped at that juror like a wild cat. The juror broke for the door. The other jurors leaped out the windows. Lawyers, witnesses, court room hangers-on, scattered in terror. Even the bartender took to his heels. Breathing threatenings and slaughter, brandishing aloft his huge blade, Justice Niles was left swaying unsteadily in the center of the barroom floor soused to the ears in lonely victory. History leaves him in his statuesque triumph. What the result of the trial was remains a mystery to this day.

George Snow, a young man from Maine, had amassed a comfortable fortune as a miner in Shaw's Flat. Three Mexicans and a Chileno living in a cabin in Dragoon Gulch two miles from the town, plotted to kill and rob him. Cold blooded and methodical these fellows were and, having decided upon this job of murder, they worked out their plan with great cunning. First they dug a grave in one corner of the dirt floor of their cabin. When it had been covered with a raw hide and blankets, the grave had the appearance of a bed. Then they bought a long tom from Snow, promising to pay him for it if he would call at their cabin next morning.

Suspecting nothing, Snow rode out to Dragoon Gulch alone and unarmed. Upon entering the cabin he found one of the Mexicans weighing gold dust on a scales on a table. While Snow stood watching him, perhaps bent upon seeing that he received the correct weight, the other three conspirators, who had been lounging about the room, fell upon him with dirks and stabbed him. Shouting at the top of his voice, Snow staggered out the door and fell. Some miners at work not far away ran to his aid. The assassins, having pulled a money belt containing several hundred dollars from about Snow's waist, fled into the hills.

Patricio Janori, the Chileno, and Antonio Cruz, one of the three Mexicans, were caught in Sonora and returned to Shaw's Flat. A miners' court assembled. Two juries were selected and the prisoners were tried simultaneously, convicted and sentenced to die. Janori, tall, powerful, with a swarthy, villainous face, would say nothing. Antonio, young and slight, confessed. He it was who had been weighing the gold dust. He had not stabbed Snow, he said, but had helped dig the grave. He declared the two Mexicans who got away—and who were never captured—did the killing. They had murdered and robbed three other Americans, he said, and planned to kill others.

A thousand miners marched with Janori and Antonio to Dragoon Gulch. When the rope was placed around his neck, Antonio began to cry. "I don't want to die," he whimpered. Janori scowled at him in disgust. "Die like a man," he said in Spanish. Janori went out like a man. Tears were rolling down Antonio's cheeks as he was swung aloft. They were hanged on separate pine trees that stood close together and were buried, one on top of the other, in the grave inside the cabin they had dug for their victim. Cabin and grave have disappeared. The twin hang trees still stand.

Tom Gilman, a young buck as black as the ace of spades, had been born in slavery. He accompanied his master from Tennessee to California in the gold rush and mined for him at Shaw's Flat. As soon as Tom set foot on the free-state soil of California, he was automatically free. But that was something he did not know and, if his master knew it, he kept it to himself. Tom was a strong young fellow and a good workman. If he ever made enough money in the mines, he could have his freedom, his master told him, for a thousand dollars, a price Tom would have brought on any slave block in the South.

Filled with new hope and courage, Tom worked hard from morning to night day after day and every time he swung his pick he thought of freedom and the new happiness ahead of him. Most of the gold he mined went to his master but he was permitted to keep a small amount for himself which he stored in a tin can. Every day he put a little gold dust in the can. Every day he watched his small hoard rise slowly higher and higher.

Then strangely it stopped rising. It even fell a little. What was the matter with that can? Tom puzzled over the mystery. But it got so the more gold dust he put in the can, the less it contained. But with a stout heart Tom kept hard at work and kept on putting a little more gold dust in the can every day, and at the end of a year he had his reward. The can was full at last. Tom paid his master a thousand dollars in gold dust and his master gave him a signed bill of sale that formally closed the transaction.

"Now, Tom, you are free," said his master. "As long as you have this bill of sale to show, you'll not be in danger of being picked up as a runaway slave and returned to me. But if you lose the bill of sale, you will have no proof that you are free and must become a slave again."

"I'll sho' hold tight to it, massa," Tom replied. "Don't you nevah worry about me losin' my freedom paper."

The big moment of Tom's life had arrived. He grinned from ear to ear and was ready to dance for joy. He waved his "freedom paper" about his head. Free! Free!

The master missed his slave. He had to pay for all the labor done for him now and the hire of workmen ate into his profits. With provisions and all kinds of necessities at sky-high prices, his chances for a quick fortune began to dwindle. Then one day when Tom returned to the cabin from his work in the diggings, his "freedom paper" was gone. He hunted for it high and low. He turned the house upside down. But he could not find it. Tears rushed to his eyes. This was tragedy. His "freedom paper" lost, his freedom was lost with it. He recalled the words of his master,—"If you lose the bill of sale, you will have no proof that you are free and must become a slave again." Tom accepted what to him seemed the inevitable and once more resumed his place as his master's chattel.

His master, of course, could have smoothed the matter out very easily by writing another bill of sale. But it seems he was not that kind of master. He was sure now of Tom's labor for another year and sure of another thousand dollars as the purchase price of Tom's freedom. For another year Tom worked in the mines and again filled the tin can with gold dust and again bought his freedom. But this time he carried his "freedom paper" on his person and his mind was made up that any man who tried to take the precious document from him would first have to take his life. So Tom's slavery days ended forever. A little later his master, grown comfortably rich, went back to his plantation in Tennessee.

As a free man, Tom mined for himself and all the gold he found was his own. As he dug one day under the twin pine trees on which Janori and Antonio had been hanged, he picked up a $2,500 nugget. But he picked up a grave problem at the same time. If the news ran through the camp that a nigger had such a bonanza lump of gold, it would probably be stolen from him. If he sold it, he doubtless would be cheated out of the greater part of its value in the first place and robbed of whatever money he received for it in the second. So obsessed by fears born of his life of bondage, he broke his nugget into small pieces. He could sell these fragments or with them buy provisions and what things he needed to wear without exciting suspicion. Disposed of in this way, his nugget kept him in comfort for a long time; and often when he bought his groceries at Bullerdick's store and tavern known as the Mississippi House, he chuckled to himself to think how he had tricked everybody into believing he was just a poor nigger when in fact he had gold to shoot at the birds. It was not until every particle of this nugget was gone that Tom felt safe in telling of his stroke of fortune and his cunning deception. But it became his favorite story after a while. He thought it a great joke on the white folks and he roared with laughter every time he told it.

Tom was a typical darky of the old South, happy-go-lucky, rollicking, always laughing. He could pick the banjo, sing old plantation songs and do a buck-and-wing in fine style. He was, too, one of the kindliest souls that ever lived. It seemed to be a real pleasure to him to do things for people. He staked many a miner who was down and out. Any one in trouble knew Tom would help him. Nobody went hungry as long as he had a dollar. If a neighbor was sick, Tom found time to do his cooking. Among many he nursed through spells of illness was Caleb Dorsey who became one of the best known lawyers in that part of the state and who remained Tom's friend for life. Tom was the only negro in the camp. Everybody knew him and everybody had a genuine affection for him. He became in time a sort of institution. Shaw's Flat would hardly have been Shaw's Flat without Tom.

The years went by and the flush days passed and Tom grew old. He had laid by his money and he built a log cabin just outside the town on the Sonora road and there he lived comfortably for the remainder of his days. He had arrived when Shaw's Flat was young. He saw it grow old and die. The gold gave out, the miners moved away, and about all that was left of Shaw's Flat was the Mississippi House, the red brick school house on the hill and Uncle Tom's Cabin. With his old kindly spirit, Uncle Tom kept a bucket of water from his well always on his front porch for the benefit of travelers. Uncle Tom's bucket of water with the gourd dipper hanging on a nail beside it was known all over that country and, first and last, thousands of wayfarers along the trail stopped at his cabin and refreshed themselves with a cold drink. Nothing made the old fellow happier than to hear some traveler say, "Well, thank you, Uncle Tom. That was a mighty fine drink of water." His bucket of water was Uncle Tom's last benevolence.

Shaw's Flat to-day is only a level stretch of grass-grown land. The red brick school house is still on the hill but it is a country district school now. On a cross beam between two posts beside it hangs a bell that summons the children to their classes but once called together the mob that tried Janori and Antonio and then hanged them. The Mississippi House, a great rambling old structure, is just as it was in early days. It is a store and wayside tavern and its owner, John Ratto, a genial old Italian, who never has been married, has lived in it all alone for nearly thirty years. In its front room is an old-fashioned piano that came around The Horn before the Civil war. In a frame on the wall among some old-fashioned pictures is a page from a newspaper that tells the story of Uncle Tom and Uncle Tom's Cabin and the Old Oaken Bucket. A half mile from the Mississippi House on the Sonora road, an old stone chimney rises above some heaps of rubbish. That's all that's left of Uncle Tom's cabin. The ancient chimney, gray with lichens, calls up a picture of the white-wooled old darky sitting on his porch, smiling a welcome to thirsty travelers, and one seems to hear Uncle Tom's kindly voice coming across the years:

"Drink o' watah, sah? He'p yo'self, sah. Heah's a bucket o' the bes' watah you evah did drink. Fraish and cold fum the well, sah. Drink a gou'dful. It'll do you good. You sho' is welcome to all you want, sah."

CHAPTER VI.

A SENSE OF THEATER.

WHEN six young Mexicans, three men and three women, rode into Mokelumne Hill one day, the town took time to stare at them. Birds of such gaudy plumage had rarely been seen in the rowdy, boisterous gold camp. The women were resplendent in silks and jewels and their companions would hardly have looked out of place in a fashionable parade on the *alameda* in the Mexican capital. Their saddles and bridles were heavily ornamented with silver, and their horses, as clean limbed as antelopes, their satin coats glistening in the sun, pranced and curveted as if to dance music. There was a touch of admiration in the glances that followed them as they made their way slowly along the main street and the crowds wondered who these spectacular strangers might be. They turned into the quarter of Chililito where the Chilenos, Peruvians and Mexicans had their homes and were soon comfortably established in a house that had been provided for them in advance.

Their arrival set the tongues of the gossips in Chililito wagging excitedly. The three showy young beauties were doubtless none too strait-laced and the neighbors expected to be scandalized by their flirtatious adventures. But to the surprise of everyone they lived unobtrusively and the most virtuous housewives could not have been more sedately conventional. Though they piqued curiosity, they had nothing to say about themselves or the men they called their husbands. As the days went by, two of the men were out of town a great deal. The third, a handsome young fellow, remained in Mokelumne Hill.

Mokelumne Hill in these flush and turbulent times had ten thousand people. Situated in a rugged and timbered region on a bench of land two miles or more from the Mokelumne river, brawling in its deep cañon, it was one of the richest camps in the mountains and one of the toughest. Men from many nations, men from everywhere, men from nowhere, elbowed one another on its crowded streets. On the main thoroughfare, almost every other building was a saloon, dance hall or gambling house and life was a riotous hodge-podge of gold, monte and whiskey. Every day pack-trains loaded with ore were starting out for the San Joaquin valley settlements and caravans of heavy wagons loaded with merchandise were lumbering in in an endless procession. The adjacent country swarmed with miners and prospectors and Stockton Hill, French Hill and Nigger Hill, towering almost over the town, were thickly scarred with shafts and tunnels. So Mokelumne Hill was too absorbed with its own affairs to pay much attention to the handsome young Mexican.

When dusk stole over the town and the candles and kerosene lamps were lighted in the saloons, he mingled with the throngs at the bars and gaming tables and discussed with polite animation the latest gold strike, some overnight shooting affray or the most recent Chinese massacre perpetrated by that bloodthirsty villain, Joaquin Murrieta, with whose daring exploits the whole country was ringing. He made many friends. The miners and gamblers thought him a very intelligent and agreeable young fellow.

One evening when the El Dorado saloon was filled with a noisy crowd—packers, teamsters, riffraff adventurers, miners in from the diggings—the young Mexican sat quietly at a monte table intent upon the game.

Weapons were everywhere in sight; six-shooters dangled from belts, the handles of bowie knives protruded from boot-legs. Beneath the bar reposed the white-aproned bartender's double barreled shotgun ready for instant use; derringers lay in drawers within convenient reach of the dealers at the monte and faro tables. Two heavily armed men, half-seas over, talked in loud voices at the bar.

"I'm gittin' good and tired o' all this crazy guff about this here Joaquin Murrieta. Terrible feller, eh? He's a yellow cur—that's what he is. Any good man could take him. Stick a gun in his belly and the cowardly whelp would mighty quick throw up his hands."

"I'd like to git within shootin' distance of him jest once—jest once, that's all. I'd shoot him like I would a rattlesnake. The first time I git my eyes on him, I'll bet five hundred dollars, I kill him."

A sudden commotion behind them made the two swash-bucklers turn their heads. All eyes were riveted on the young Mexican. He had vaulted to the top of the monte table. He stood on the layout among the scattered cards and overturned piles of gold coin, head tilted defiantly, eyes blazing, his silk-lined cloth cloak thrown back from his shoulders and two leveled pistols in his hands.

"You'll bet five hundred dollars you kill him the first time you see him? I'll take the bet. I am Joaquin Murrieta."

The saloon that had been filled with babel and uproar became instantly as silent as a tomb. The two loud-mouthed boasters at the bar, each with a brace of heavy revolvers hanging in scabbards at his belt, trembled in their boots. The crowd was as motionless as if petrified. For a moment, Murrieta remained standing high above the heads of the throng, a target no marksman could miss. But not a weapon was drawn, not a motion was made to harm him. With a sneering smile, he sprang to the floor and, shouldering coolly through the crowd, stepped out into the darkness. A little later, a horseman went galloping at top speed through the main street out of town on the trail to Bear Mountain. Gradually the clatter of his horse's hoofs faded out in the distance.

Mokelumne Hill to-day is a village of three hundred inhabitants. A few dilapidated old stores stand in the shade of spreading elms on the main street that is an unpaved country road, and the town is agog with excitement when the daily motor stages pull in with the mail from Jackson and San Andreas. On a corner of the main street in front of the ancient hostelry known as Peek Inn, that has been owned by the Peek family for three generations, is a hollow in the ground, weed-grown and cluttered with piles of building stones. That is the site, as the graybeards of the village will tell you, of the El Dorado saloon. At the edge of the depression stands an oak in the trunk of which one of the iron shutters of the old barroom somehow became embedded and which has been lifted, as the tree grew, three feet off the ground. It was a long time ago that the El Dorado fell into ruins. The oak tree is three feet thick at the base and forty feet high.

When Murrieta's outlaws invaded Santa Clara valley and spread terror through all the prosperous region south of San Francisco bay, Deputy Sheriff Robert Clark of San Jose with a strong posse took the trail against them. From the Santa Cruz mountains to the Diablos and from Pajaro river to Rattlesnake Butte, the bandits pillaged ranches, ran off herds of horses and robbed travelers on the highways. But Clark hung hard on their traces, allowing them no rest, upsetting their plans, and giving them a taste of his mettle in a running fight now and then. With dare-devil boldness, Murrieta had set up his headquarters in San Jose, county seat and stronghold of law. Here, his identity unsuspected, he lived quietly and directed the operations of his band. When he stood in court one day, closely wrapped in his serape, and heard Clark on the witness stand tell the story that sent two of the marauders to prison, Murrieta made up his mind that Clark must die. But no commonplace assassination would serve the outlaw's purpose. Clark must die in a way that would strike dread among all officers of the law and warn them that the terrible brigand chief kept them under his eye, dogged their footsteps like the shadow of death, and might at the most unexpected moment materialize mysteriously out of thin air and take murderous vengeance on them. So with the adroitness of an artist in melodrama, Murrieta laid his cunning plot.

Lights streamed from the windows of the fandango house on the plaza in San Jose. Fiddles and guitars were playing a lively tune and the floor was pulsating rhythmically beneath the feet of the dancers. Deputy Sheriff Clark entered. He had been misled by whispered information from a Murrieta spy that a thief for whom he was hunting would be at the dance that evening. His guns strapped around him, his sharp eyes searching the crowd, the deputy slowly circled the hall. A sudden commotion arose in a far corner. A woman screamed. The music ceased abruptly. The dancers froze in their tracks. Pushing through the throng, Clark found a girl, apparently in terror, huddled against the wall while standing in front of her, a good-looking, well-dressed Mexican youth, glowering savagely, was brandishing a dagger. Seizing the fellow by the wrist, Clark disarmed him. "You are under arrest," he said. The Mexican cooled off with remarkable suddenness after such a display of violent rage. He submitted quite tamely and was led away for a hearing before a justice of the peace.

Clark suggested leniency to the court. The Mexican had had a little tiff with his woman and in a fit of temper had drawn a knife but nobody had been hurt. He looked like a nice young fellow. No use being too hard on him. Little fracases of that sort were happening every night. So the justice let the prisoner off with a fine of twelve dollars.

"I am sorry I have not that amount with me," said the Mexican. "But if this officer will be good enough to come with me to my home only a short distance from here, I will pay him the money."

That was all right and Clark and the prisoner set off together. Clark had seen this Mexican often about town but had no idea who he was. A clerk in some small shop perhaps. But as he seemed an inoffensive, mannerly young chap, what difference did it make who he was? As they walked along conversing pleasantly, they soon left the plaza and the business houses behind, and, making their way through dark, narrow streets lined with adobe huts, came to the edge of town. The road to Santa Clara Mission stretched before them in the moonlight.

"How much farther is it?"

"Only a little way, *caballero*. That's my house yonder where you see that light."

They came to a point where the road lay dark in the heavy shadow of willow thickets. The Mexican halted.

"One moment, señor," he said politely.

Clark stopped and turned a mildly inquisitive look toward him.

"I have a little surprise for you."

"Yes?" Clark smiled, half expecting some harmless pleasantry.

"I am Joaquin Murrieta," said the Mexican in a cool, level voice, "and I have brought you here to kill you."

That was no smiling matter. It was almost unbelievable that this courteous young Mexican was the murderous bandit famous for his atrocities from one end of California to the other. But Clark wasted no time in astonishment. Death was staring him in the eyes. Lightning-quick action alone could save him. With the fighting spirit of a brave man, he reached instantly for his gun. But before he could snatch it from its holster, Murrieta had plunged a dagger through his heart.

A two-masted schooner slipped her moorings at the Stockton wharf late one afternoon and stood away along a winding tule slough for San Francisco. It carried two sailors as a crew and, as passengers, two miners from San Andreas who had struck it rich in the diggings and were bound for their eastern homes to rejoin wives and children. On both sides of the slough a few miles out from Stockton, desolate, fever-haunted mud flats overgrown with tules as tall as bullrushes extended as far as the eye could see; and with canvas bellying before a light breeze, hull and sails doubled in the sluggish water as in a mirror, the schooner picked its way slowly through the open channel that twisted in a hundred loops and turns through the green marshes like a silver snake.

For hours four swarthy, heavily armed men in a row boat had lurked in ambush among the sedges awaiting the coming of the vessel like cougars watching a trail. As it drew abreast, the row boat darted from its hiding place and drawing alongside with vigorous strokes of the oars, made fast to the shrouds. Over the rail the four desperadoes swarmed like buccaneers boarding a treasure galleon on the Spanish Main and, bounding upon the deck, opened a furious fusillade from their pistols on the astonished crew. The sailor at the tiller caught up a double-barreled shotgun and, as the foremost pirate bore down upon him, sent him sprawling lifeless with a blast of buckshot. A moment later a bullet caught the valiant helmsman between the eyes and he crumpled down in a limp heap across the steering gear. Battling like mad amidships, the other jack tar, swinging an iron belaying pin, crushed the skull of a second robber but was dead himself almost before his victim crashed headlong in the scuppers. Popping out of the little deck-house, the two miners, with revolvers blazing wildly, went down under a squall of lead. Six men had died in five minutes of fighting. Joaquin Murrieta and Three Fingered Jack remained triumphant among the corpses like pirate heroes at Porto Bello or Maracaibo.

Ransacking their prize from stem to stern, the victors dragged from the hold two buckskin sacks bulging with $20,000 in gold dust the two miners had brought from the placers. Then lowering their spoils overside into the small boat, they set fire to the schooner. Flames quickly enveloped the craft, boiling along the bulwarks, coiling up the masts like resplendent serpents, bringing down booms and spars and cross-trees in flaming ruin. Pulling to a distance, Murrieta and Three Fingered Jack rested on their oars while smoke in black clouds rolled off over the marshes and watched the little vessel burn to the water's edge and the charred wreck with its cargo of dead men sink to the bottom. The sun had set; gray twilight had fallen; a streak of lurid red glowed above the horizon. The tule swamps lay once more in dreary loneliness as still and silent as a painted picture.

Stockton at this period had a population of twenty thousand and was the metropolis of the San Joaquin valley as Sacramento, less than a hundred miles north, was the metropolis of the Sacramento valley. Born of the gold rush, both towns were nearly of the same age. Stockton was a village of a few houses when Sacramento was a huddle of huts around Sutter's Fort. Sacramento in boom days was the depot of supplies for the northern mines and Stockton, the outfitting point for the southern mines. As a business center, Stockton was on the top wave of prosperity. Its merchants were rich; its stores were immense establishments stocked with all manner of merchandise; ships from the Bay crowded its wharves; a vast floating population swarmed through it on the way to the mines; and the camp fires of gold seekers were so close together on the east-bound trails that, it was said, a man could travel by their light from Stockton into the hills as easily on the darkest night as in broad daylight.

Stockton and all the region about it were deeply stirred when news of the piratical atrocity on the tule slough was noised abroad. Sheriff's posses and crowds of armed citizens were soon scouring the country. A reward of $5,000 was offered for Murrieta dead or alive. All idea of dealing with the outlaw by legal processes was abandoned. His last merciless crime had placed him outside the pale of mercy. He must be shot like a wild beast wherever found or hanged to the nearest tree.

While the excitement was at its height, a crowd gathered one Sunday morning around the flag pole in the public square in Stockton on which a placard announcing the reward had been posted and was engaged in a lively discussion of the chances of Murrieta's being captured or killed.

"You can bet a lot o' men'll go after that reward. Five thousand dollars is not to be sneezed at."

"More power to them. But they'll never take that fellow alive."

"Dead then and what's the difference? He ought to be shot down like a dog."

The crowd stared as a handsome young Mexican, superbly mounted, came riding into the square, a feather stuck in his hat, his serape tossed back over one shoulder revealing a glimpse of gold-braided jacket and scarlet sash. A gallant figure sitting his horse jauntily and glancing about him with cool unconcern. The placard caught his eye. He reined to a stop at the flag pole and, bending from his saddle, gazed intently at it:

$5,000—REWARD—$5,000

Offered By The Citizens of Stockton

To Anyone Who

Delivers To The Authorities

JOAQUIN MURRIETA

Dead Or Alive.

Dismounting, the Mexican stepped closer to the flag pole and read the placard again with an air of critical interest. Suddenly as if a happy idea had occurred to him, he drew a pencil from his pocket and scribbled something at the bottom. Then swinging into the saddle, he rode off leisurely across the square.

This curious performance piqued the onlookers and they crowded about the flag pole to see what the Mexican had written. They gasped as they read this message inscribed in a bold, free hand:

"I will add $10,000 to this reward.—Joaquin Murrieta."

For a moment the citizens stood stunned. Then they went stark mad. What astounding audacity! The insolence of the scoundrel! They roared with rage, they waved their arms wildly, they shook their fists. "Stop that man!" "That's Murrieta!" "Shoot him off his horse!" "Kill him!" The storm gathering behind him seemed in no wise to disturb the retreating horseman. He rode as jauntily as ever and neither looked back nor increased his speed. As he headed for a side street, he rose in his stirrups and, turning in his saddle, waved his hat about his head. His shout of defiance rang across the square,—"*Carajo, gringos!*"

Twenty-five American miners were camped in a box-cañon on the headwaters of the south fork of the Mokelumne river near the boundary between Calaveras and El Dorado counties. The cañon was enclosed on three sides by steep hills and the only entrance to it was by a narrow trail along a ledge high up on one of the cañon's walls. While the miners were taking breakfast, a lone horseman rode down this trail and drew up at their camp. He spoke English so well and was of such fair complexion the miners were not sure whether he was an American or a Mexican. With gold camp hospitality, they invited him to dismount and have a cup of coffee and a bite of bread and sow belly with them. But he declined and, lounging easily in his saddle with one leg hooked over the pommel, he rolled himself a cigarette and fell into comradely talk.

"What luck, strangers?"

"Can't complain. We've took out right smart dust in these diggin's."

"Struck it rich, eh?"

"Well, you might say we've done pretty good."

"Better watch out or Murrieta'll get you."

"Not much. We're not bad shots ourselves. If that cut-throat tackles us, we'll fill him full o' lead."

While they talked and laughed, Jim Boyce, one of the party, came trudging up from the creek carrying a pail of water. He looked sharply at the visitor.

"What's that devil doin' here?" he roared. "Fill your hands, pards. Start shootin'. That's Murrieta."

"Hello, Boyce," called the bandit cheerfully. "Haven't seen you since Saw Mill Flat days. How they coming?"

Boyce's answer was a shot from his six-shooter. Guns began to speak here and there among the crowd. Putting spurs to his horse, Murrieta galloped off with lead singing about his ears.

Across the stream he dashed, and up a rocky incline, and out on to the narrow ledge that stretched like a string across the face of the precipice. The ledge was not more than ten feet at its widest and narrowed in places to four or five feet. Six inches to one side, a towering granite wall; six inches to the other, a drop of a hundred feet. One misstep of his horse and he would plunge headlong to the mad torrent beating itself into white froth directly beneath him. On he sped until he was opposite the camp across the cañon and broadside on to the fire of his enemies at a distance of thirty yards. Drawing a long knife, he waved it in glittering circles about his head.

"Kill me, if you can," he shouted derisively as the bullets rained about him.

The miners were pegging away at him steadily. Their bullets whined across the cañon and thudded against the wall, before, behind, above, below him—bullets buzzing like bees about him. Death was missing him by inches—but missing him. The miners were growing disgusted at their poor marksmanship. "Dang my ole hide, can't none of us hit him? Bet a couple of ounces of gold dust, he don't never git acrost that cliff alive. Ho, thar goes his bonnet. Somebody was shore cuttin' close to him that time. Hang it all, thar must be somethin' the matter with our guns. T'aint our weapon's, it's us. We couldn't hit a bull in a clover pasture. Begins to look like the son of a gun might git away. That fellow's a devil. It'd take a silver bullet to kill him."

Like a devil, in truth, he seemed with his long black hair streaming on the wind as he flashed along with dizzy speed high against the mountain wall—a winged devil conjured from some witch's cauldron and protected by devil's magic. With a display of superb horsemanship that few of the world's best riders could equal, he ran that amazing gauntlet of a hundred yards unscathed with death nipping at his heels every inch of the way. At last he reached the end of the ledge and disappeared among the pine trees.

Boyce raged over Murrieta's escape. Just when he had him dead to rights, the slippery rogue had wriggled through his fingers. A heavy price on his head, too. Rewards for his capture, dead or alive, posted up along every trail in the country. The outlaw would have been worth bagging. Boyce was keen for immediate pursuit. Why not? The diggings in the cañon were about played out. The miners had fattened their pokes and were ready to slope back to civilization and good liquor at Mokelumne Hill. Then there was that little matter of disgraceful marksmanship that called for vindication. An exciting man hunt would be more fun than a bear hunt to top off their stay in the backwoods. So twenty-five men were soon in the saddle and off over the hills on the trail of the outlaw.

Three miles away they ran on Murrieta's abandoned camp. The outlaw was too wise a fox to be caught napping. Evidently he had expected Boyce to pursue him and had lost no time in hunting cover. But fourteen of his men were with him now. Their trail was plain. It headed east toward the high country.

For a week Boyce and his companions made a picnic of the hunt. There were no roads in this country—no paths even, except those beaten by elk and deer on their journeys to drink at some forest pool. But the trail of fifteen men on horseback was easy to follow and every night the miners camped where the outlaws had camped the night before. With Murrieta only a day's march ahead of him, Boyce speeded up the pursuit. But perhaps Boyce would not have been in such a hurry if he had known the men Murrieta had with him. Three Fingered Jack, Valenzuela, Claudio, Vulvia, Gonzalez, Savolio, Fuentes, Sanchez, Florencio Cruz—these famous fellows were riding at their chieftain's back. The miners were chasing the most desperate cut-throats in California as if it were a lark.

Murrieta was not going it blind and trusting to luck. That was not his way. He was a smart campaigner and his plans were definite. His scouts kept him informed of the movements of his enemies and it was part of his strategy to draw them on into the deeper wilderness. Suddenly he doubled on his tracks. Keeping to rocky ground and dry creek beds where his horses left no hoof prints, he worked in behind Boyce. By this adroit trick, a situation that was growing critical was reversed with startling rapidity. The hunters became the hunted. The broad trail that Boyce's party had been able to follow at a hand gallop went out abruptly like an extinguished candle. The miners circled and quartered like baffled fox hounds but they could not pick it up again. Not a clew was left behind to indicate even vaguely the direction the outlaws had taken. Apparently they had vanished without trace into thin air.

Boyce's last camp was in sight of the main range of the Sierras. One more day of chasing Murrieta and the miners would have butted their heads smack against those mighty, snow-wrapped mountains. The camp was in a glade deep in a forest. Oak thickets hemmed it in. The vaulted boughs of gigantic sugar and yellow pines steeped it in cathedral stillness. The night was cold; the wind off the snow fields had a tang of frost. Building a roaring fire of pine logs, the miners stretched out on their blankets and were soon warm and comfortable in its mellow glow. The radiance of the firelight made the surrounding darkness deeper. The camp seemed ringed by a solid wall of blackness.

No sense of danger disturbed these men. They could not know that death was closing in upon them. They could not see the murderous eyes glaring at them out of the darkness. A twig cracked. What was that? A bear? Some wild animal on the prowl? A startled fellow sat up tautly. A sudden crackle of guns split the silence. The circle of darkness was dotted with points of fire. The miners sprang to their feet in panic, cocked six-shooters in their hands. But there was nothing to shoot at. All they could see was the serried pines, the chaparral thickets, the deadly spouts of flame. Helpless under the fire of an invisible foe, they fell lifeless in their tracks by two and threes—by the dozen—as their death screams went up to the stars. Those left alive made a mad rush to escape from that fatal firelight. But they died in headlong plunges against the wall of darkness that had become a wall of death. The silence of the forest settled down once more. In the tiny spot of red radiance in the vast blackness of the night, twenty-four men lay dead.

Murrieta, Three Fingered Jack, Valenzuela, Savolio and the rest stalked like grim specters out of the gloom. Scrutinizing the limp forms that lay in ghastly huddles in the firelight's lurid glare, Murrieta peered into the face of this one, touched that one with the toe of his boot, to see if life remained in them. Here was one groaning in agony. Three Fingered Jack quickly remedied that. There was another still breathing feebly. Savolio saw to it that he breathed no more. A perfect job was soon given its completing details. Thirty thousand dollars in gold dust was the spoils of the tragedy.

But a disturbing sound came on the wind to Murrieta's ears. It was the muffled drumming of a horse's hoofs in the distance. Jim Boyce, the sole survivor, was on that horse's back riding for his life. He lived to make a modest fortune in the mines and tell the tale of the massacre in a comfortable home in New England.

CHAPTER VII.

THE PACK IN FULL CRY.

A SERIES of mysterious murders of a peculiarly atrocious kind spread terror through the regions around Bidwell's Bar and Marysville. Eleven men were killed on Feather river and Honcut creek near Bidwell's Bar and, within a period of two weeks, the bodies of seventeen murdered men were found in the brush and along the trails in the vicinity of Marysville. All the victims had been lassoed and robbed. This wholesale butchery—a veritable massacre—was traced to Joaquin Murrieta and his band and in the end their guilt was indubitably established.

Two miners were walking along Feather river to Bidwell's Bar after a day's work on their claims in the hills when they saw far ahead of them four horsemen dragging something along the trail at the end of a lariat.

"What is that them fellers are draggin'?" asked one.

"Can't make it out," replied the other.

"It might be a catamount or a coyote."

"Looks too big fer a catamount or a coyote."

"Mebbe it's a mountain lion."

"Mebbe."

"Any feller fool enough to rope a mountain lion can do so if he is so minded. But as fer me, I want a good rifle when I tackle one o' them varmints. Lions is dangerous critters. It won't do to take no chances with 'em."

"I've heard tell of a lot of old timers around here ropin' 'em."

"But you won't never hear o' me ropin' none. I got too much sense."

"Or not enough guts."

"Dang my cats," said the first miner growing a little excited. "That thing at the end o' that lariat ain't no catamount nor coyote nor mountain lion neither. It looks to me like—well, dang my cats."

"Looks to you like what?"

"Take a good hard look yourself. See if it appears to you the same as to me?"

"By gosh, it looks a little like a man."

"You said it, pardner."

"But it can't be a man."

"No, it can't be a man."

"But it shore does look like a man."

"By thunder, it is a man. Yes sir, it's a man as shore as you are a foot high."

"Well, I'll be damned."

Afraid to venture any farther along that dangerous trail, the two miners struck across the hills to Bidwell's Bar where they gave the alarm. Citizens rode out and found in the brush on the banks of Feather river the bodies of Charles Miller and an unidentified man. Both had been lassoed and robbed.

A few days later the dead bodies of George Mather, John B. Gaidner and C. Jinkerson were found on Honcut creek. All three, it was evident, had been lassoed. It was believed Gaidner and Jinkerson had seen Mather being dragged along the trail and had lost their lives in a heroic attempt to rescue him. Six other dead men who had been roped and robbed were discovered in the brush within the next few weeks.

The excitement aroused by the murders was still unabated when the killings around Marysville began. Seventeen men lassoed and slain within two weeks was at the rate of more than one a day. All the bodies were found but no one had even a distant glimpse of the elusive bandits of the flying loop who flitted through the hills like shadows leaving death behind them. Fear of these phantom riders gripped the countryside. Travel ceased. Trails were deserted. Marysville's trade with the mines fell off.

Marysville at the eastern edge of the Sacramento valley at the confluence of the Feather and Yuba river, was a town of eight thousand inhabitants. It was the county seat of Yuba county and an important depot of supplies for the northern mines. From the time it was founded in the very first days of the gold rush, it had prided itself upon its enforcement of law. Its first *alcalde* had been Stephen J. Field, afterwards chief justice of the U. S. Supreme court, who was elected to the office on the strength of his being an old timer in Marysville. He had lived in the town two weeks whereas the rival candidate was a mere tenderfoot who had lived there only one. Shamed by the startling situation at its very doors, Marysville, bulwark of law, bestirred itself to end the operations of the murderous bandits.

The Marysville vigilance committee composed of some of the town's foremost citizens raided a Mexican settlement, known as Sonorian Camp, three miles away. Among the prisoners taken was a notorious Mexican thief. The committee was convinced the prisoner could throw much light upon the seventeen murders but he stoutly maintained he knew nothing about them. In common with the men of those days, the vigilantes had an abiding faith in a rope as a means of refreshing the memory and loosening the tongue and they strung the thief up to a tree. Stringing him up once and then again did no good—he was a stubborn brute,—but when, with the unwavering confidence of a doctor in the efficacy of his pills, they strung him up a third time, he unburdened his soul of many secrets. He disclaimed all personal guilt but he declared the mysterious crimes were the work of Murrieta and his band who had established themselves in Sonorian Camp. His revelations, it may be remarked in passing, important as they were to the committee, proved fatal to the Mexican. He was found next day with his throat cut and probably went out into the big dark with a grave doubt in his mind whether it might not have been just as well to let the vigilantes choke him to death as to die at the hands of Murrieta avengers.

Sheriff R. B. Buchanan of Yuba county and a posse closed in on Sonorian Camp one moonlight night a little later. With Deputy Ike Bowen at his side, the sheriff came upon a tent at the edge of town with a camp fire burning in front of it beside which stood a Mexican wrapped in his serape. A dog barked. The Mexican vanished. By tactful maneuvering the sheriff managed to silence the dog with a bowie knife and then on hands and knees, he and Bowen crawled silently toward the tent. But the dog had given an effective alarm and as Buchanan and Bowen were wriggling through a fence, three Mexicans opened fire on them from behind a strip of chaparral. A lively exchange of shots followed and when Buchanan fell founded, the Mexicans disappeared. Bowen and the other possemen took the sheriff back to Marysville. The bullet that brought him down had passed through his body and for weeks he lingered between life and death but eventually recovered. He had no idea who had shot him until Murrieta sent him word that he himself was the man. The Mexican standing by the campfire wrapped in a serape was the famous outlaw.

When the Marysville district grew too hot for him, Murrieta moved south and made his headquarters three miles from San Andreas at Yaqui Camp, a Mexican mining village. Several minor adventures, some touched with humor, marked his return to his old stamping grounds.

On the trail between Jackson and Volcano, Murrieta and Three Fingered Jack met the postman who regularly carried the mail between those towns and who rode a fine horse. Three Fingered Jack, who plumed himself on being a judge of horse-flesh, had no sooner clapped eyes on the animal than he determined to have it and drew his six-shooter. The mail carrier fled at top speed with the robber in pursuit. But Jack was not able to get within fifty yards of the fugitive and, pulling up his mount in huge disgust, he emptied his gun at the mail carrier and trotted back to Joaquin.

"When I stole this animal of mine," said Three Fingers, "I thought I had the fastest horse in California. I seem to have been mistaken."

While Joaquin was laughing at Jack's discomfiture, a man named Horsely hove in sight.

"This fellow seems to have a pretty fair nag himself," said Three Fingered Jack. "I'll just take it away from him and make up for my bad luck."

Horsely turned tail and streaked it back for Volcano. Jack pounded after him, determined this time to vindicate his horse's reputation. Up hill and down they went for five miles, Horsely unable to pull away from Jack and Jack unable to gain on Horsely. Jack belabored his steed with his quirt and dug his spurs into its flanks up to the rowel-heads but the distance between the two men remained the same. The race ended at Volcano. With deep humiliation and chagrin, Jack saw his intended victim turn in his saddle and wave his hat triumphantly as he rode into town.

"Where's the other fellow's horse?" sniffed Joaquin when Jack rejoined him. "You look like a coyote that had missed a jack-rabbit by one jump."

"It was what you might call a dead heat," explained Jack apologetically. "My horse is as good as his. He had too much the start of me or I should have caught him."

Three miners bound for the San Joaquin valley settlements with their packs heavy with gold dust were trudging along the trail near Murphy's Diggings. Murrieta and Three Fingered Jack, riding that way, might have passed them by without molesting them if the miners had not suddenly scattered in flight.

"There is nothing frightful in our appearance," said Joaquin. "Those fellows must have money."

With this philosophical reflection, he and his fellow desperado spurred in pursuit and having killed and plundered the fugitives, dragged their bodies with their lariats a short distance and threw them into an abandoned prospect hole.

Four miners of Angel's Camp awoke at midnight to find their cabin filled with armed ruffians. Three Fingered Jack demanded their money. They handed over $200. Infuriated at such paltry loot, the robber flourished his tremendous bowie and declared he would dig out their hearts if they did not produce more. But they protested it was all they had. "Then," roared Three Fingered Jack, "I will kill you for having so little." When a massacre seemed imminent, Murrieta interfered and saved the miners' lives.

Soon after he had established himself at Yaqui Camp, Murrieta embarked upon a widespread campaign of pillage and murder that was one of the bloodiest and one of the most disastrous in his career. His operations extended over all the country about San Andreas, Mokelumne Hill, Jackson, Campo Seco, Lancha Plana, Murphy's Diggings and Angel's Camp. Cold blooded atrocities became every day occurrences. Men were robbed on the highways. Chinamen were slaughtered and their camps sacked and burned. Miners heading for distant homes with sacks filled with gold dust accumulated by toil in the diggings, were lucky to get out of the hills with their lives. The law was a dead letter. Citizens were helpless and dared not defend themselves. The marauders came and went as free as the winds with reckless bravado but they left no clews behind. Their trails were red with blood but from the scenes of their crimes they vanished like phantoms.

With Murrieta's crimes piling up with tragic rapidity, the citizens at last awoke from their nightmare and launched a movement to exterminate the outlaws. Mass meetings were held in San Andreas, Mokelumne Hill, Jackson, Murphy's Diggings and Angel's Camp and concerted action decided upon. Deputy Sheriff Charles H. Ellis of San Andreas took the field with a posse of thirty men. Under-Sheriff Charles A. Clark of Mokelumne Hill went out on the hunt with a force as large. A company of citizens was organized and armed at Jackson. Murphy's Diggings and Angel's Camp raised posses. All trails were patroled by armed citizens and guards were posted at every ferry, ford and bridge on the Calaveras, Stanislaus and Mokelumne rivers. It was war. The whole country was up in arms and Murrieta faced the most desperate crisis of his life.

Out alone on a hunt for some thieves who had stolen a horse overnight in San Andreas, Deputy Sheriff Ellis saw two mounted Mexicans on top of a hill beside the road and called to them to come down and have a talk with him.

"If you want to see us more than we do you, come up here," one flung back.

When Ellis had dismounted and started up the hill, he heard a rustle in the underbrush. Suspecting an ambush, he looked behind him and shouted, "Come on, boys," as if he had a company of men waiting out of sight. His stratagem doubtless saved his life. Five mounted Mexicans dashed out of the chaparral and, with the other two, quickly disappeared.

Ellis rode on to Yaqui Camp unaware that Murrieta was making his headquarters there and that every Mexican in the place was his friend or secret partisan. There he expected to drum up a few men to take the trail of the outlaws. While sitting on his horse in front of a saloon, he saw a Mexican with a serape drawn about his face regarding him intently. As their eyes met, the Mexican, dropping his hand in casual wise to the butt of his pistol, moved away. Though Ellis was in ignorance of the fact, he had been for the first time in his life face to face with Joaquin Murrieta. Ellis wondered afterward how he happened to escape with his life from this outlaw stronghold.

Ellis' efforts to raise a posse left Yaqui Camp cold. Only one responded to his call for aid. That was Atanacio Moreno. But it was something that Atanacio Moreno was one of the town's leading citizens. He was an impressive looking man, tall and rather stout, a smooth and voluble talker and of manners suave and ingratiating. This obliging person came forward with an offer to guide the deputy sheriff to the exact spot at which Murrieta could be found. The offer surprised Ellis but he could not doubt the good faith of so distinguished a citizen. It would have surprised him even more if he had known that Murrieta himself was standing only a few feet away whiffing coolly at a cigarette when the offer was made. Atanacio Moreno was a merchant and quite prosperous. Also he was Murrieta's spy and secret agent and at times took personal part in the murderous crimes of the outlaws. There seem to have been many things in Yaqui Camp with which Ellis was unacquainted.

"Murrieta and his men trade at my store," said Atanacio Moreno. "I am on friendly terms with all of them. In leading you to their hiding place, I will merely be doing my duty as a good citizen. I want to see law and order established in this country. They are a bad lot and the sooner they are wiped out the better."

So accompanied by this public spirited citizen, Ellis returned to San Andreas where he summoned a posse together and set out after the bandits.

"Where do you think Murrieta is hiding?" Ellis asked.

"Ah, señor," replied Moreno, "I do not think—I know. We will find him in Bear Mountain. There we will take him unawares and you and your men will win much glory by ridding the country of this monster of crime."

Moreno was an enthusiastic guide and he communicated some of his own buoyant confidence to Ellis and his posse. Sustained by an abiding trust in Moreno, they traveled all day and far into the night. They climbed mountains, they forded rivers, they picked their way through pathless woods and threaded wild ravines. After leading them forty miles or more from Yaqui Camp, Moreno halted against a stone wall at the head of a cañon. He seemed disappointed.

"This is Murrieta's hiding place," he said.

"But where is Murrieta?" demanded Ellis boiling with wrath.

Moreno gave a shrug. "That I cannot tell."

"But I thought you knew we should find him here."

"He has been here. Without a doubt, he has been here. But he has vanished. I will tell you what has happened, Señor Ellis. Murrieta in some mysterious way has had word you have taken his trail. He knows what a brave, relentless enemy you are. With you in the field against him, he was well aware he would be killed if he remained in this country. He has taken flight. By this time he is miles away. Pursuit is now hopeless."

But Ellis and his men did not take the matter so lightly. They realized Moreno had made fools of them but they were not certain whether he was an honest ass wise in his own conceit or a treacherous scoundrel who had deliberately tricked them. As it was, Moreno had need of all his eloquence and adroitness to argue them out of stringing him up to a tree but, in the end, they gave him the benefit of the doubt and let him off with his life. Upon his return to Yaqui Camp, Moreno hurriedly packed his effects and left for parts unknown, and was never seen in that region again. He figured later in Los Angeles as the hero of a sensational adventure—an adventure that landed the hero in San Quentin penitentiary.

The organized war against Murrieta opened at Chaparral Hill. With a posse of five—Jeff Gatewood, John Hall, Sam Davis, Peter Woodbeck and one other—Deputy Sheriff Ellis struck the trail of the outlaws on Murray's creek. Seeing from the tracks there were nine in the band, Ellis sent Woodbeck back to San Andreas with instructions to Alcalde Talliaferro to rush reinforcements to him. The alcalde was unable to carry out the order but, confident that the reinforcements would soon arrive, Ellis pushed on. As he and his men climbed the pass leading over Chaparral Hill nine Mexicans in command of Murrieta himself rose from the brush and opened fire upon them.

The possemen sprang from their horses and concealed themselves behind rocks and trees. A bullet bored a hole through Ellis' hat. Another burned a streak across his vest. Gatewood's horse was shot. Davis wounded one of the Mexicans. Ellis shot another who disappeared over the hill. Thrown into panic by the fusillade, Ellis' horse ran away. The animal soon came trotting back to join the other horses but was pursued by a mounted brigand who, when a bullet from the deputy sheriff's revolver struck him in the breast, fell over on his horse's neck, evidently dangerously injured. To cover this fellow's retreat the other outlaws with Murrieta at their head, mounted their horses and, dashing down the hill in single file between the wounded man and the possemen, discharged their revolvers at Ellis' squad at close range but without effect.

While the scrimmage was at its hottest, a Mexican on a white horse rode to the top of a rocky eminence and emptied his six-shooter at Ellis at a distance of thirty yards. Drawing a careful bead, Ellis knocked the sharpshooter out of his saddle with a bullet. But the Mexican quickly remounted and galloped over the hill. As the outlaws, again on foot, worked through the brush to close quarters, Ellis and his men slowly retreated, dodging among the boulders, and reached shelter in the dry bed of Willow creek at the bottom of the hill. There they jumped on their horses and galloped away for San Andreas with the bandits firing at them as long as they were in range. Though Murrieta won this hard fought little battle, four of his men had been wounded while Ellis' party came off without a scratch.

Next day, Murrieta with five men appeared at the Phoenix quartz mill a few miles from Yaqui Camp. There he found Peter Woodbeck and the caretaker of the property. Woodbeck had just mounted his horse. "You got away yesterday," said Joaquin throwing his six-shooter down on him. "But you die to-day." Woodbeck drew his gun and both men fired at the same time. While they fought, Three Fingered Jack threw himself from his horse and attacked Woodbeck's companion with a bowie knife. Having fired the single shot in his derringer, the caretaker, with Three Fingered Jack after him, ran inside the mill where for a time he defended himself with an iron bar. But after a desperate struggle, the huge blade of his ferocious antagonist flashed across his throat and Three Fingered Jack emerged from the mill dragging his victim by the hair. Just at this moment Woodbeck, who had emptied his revolver, put spurs to his horse and fled. He was almost out of range when, with the last ball left in his six-shooter, Murrieta dropped his horse dead in its tracks. While Woodbeck lay stunned from his headlong fall, Three Fingered Jack rode up and slashed his head half off his shoulders.

Deputy Sheriff Ellis arrived at the Phoenix mill with a posse before the bodies of the murdered men were cold. The trail of the outlaws was plain. Ellis followed it across Bear Mountain, back and forth across the Calaveras river to Lancha Plana, to Angel's Camp and back to within a mile of San Andreas where it was lost. Jesus Ojoa, a friendly Mexican, reported he had seen Murrieta and his band at Greaserville. At that point Ellis picked up the trail again. It led to a cabin on the Calaveras about which Ellis found the tracks of several horses. In the hut lived an evil-looking Mexican who treated the possemen with great haughtiness and ill-concealed contempt. He had no explanation to offer for the hoof prints at his door and, with a lariat looped about his neck, he was sent up into a tree "to see," as an old chronicler quaintly puts it, "if he could obtain the desired information." After he had been swung up twice, he remembered that Murrieta and two of his men had stopped at his cabin the night before on their way, as they had told him, to Campo Seco. "But," said the old Mexican, "Murrieta's last word to me was that he would surely return and would never rest until he had had the heart's blood of Deputy Sheriff Ellis and that traitor, Jesus Ojoa."

Ellis kept on to Capulope where he learned Murrieta recently had passed the night. Alex Bidenger, a Capulope storekeeper, had heard of the outlaw's visit and next morning had dispatched a note by a Digger Indian to Justice Beatty at Campo Seco. The note read:

"I hereby gave Notice thar is a Thief and robber in this capulope by The name of wakeen he slep here Last nite and he Is xpected to Sleap here tonite thar is not men Enough here in capulope to Take him he has tied horses Back in the hills And six men."

Upon receipt of this startling message, Justice Beatty sent word to the keeper of the ferry at Winter's Bar on the Stanislaus to let no one cross during the night and hurried off a constable with a posse to rescue the six men the terrible brigand had tied back in the hills. When the constable arrived at Capulope, Bidenger explained somewhat heatedly that his note had been intended to inform Justice Beatty that Joaquin's party numbered six men.

"It seems a pity," remarked Bidenger stroking his white beard solemnly, "a man of the squire's book larnin' can't read no better."

As Justice Beatty had anticipated, Murrieta and his band struck the Stanislaus at Winter's Bar the night after leaving Capulope and asked the ferryman to put them across.

"No, sir-ee," replied the ferryman with decision. "I've got orders. Nobody crosses this river to-night. Not even if he was the governor o' the state, by gosh. I believe in obeyin' orders—I do. I'm sorter o' old-fashioned that a-way."

Joaquin threw a cocked revolver in his face. "You'll take my orders," he said. And the ferryman did.

At Lancha Plana, Murrieta and his band were ferried

over the Stanislaus river, as Ellis ascertained, and were attacked on the opposite bank by a party of Americans. Under a galling fire, the outlaws fled with such precipitation they abandoned several fine loose horses they had recently stolen.

While Ellis was at Lancha Plana, one of his scouts brought him information that a badly wounded Mexican was in hiding at Cherokee Flat and was being nursed by one of his countrymen. The deputy sheriff hurried to Cherokee Flat. As the posse rode into the village, the Mexican who was tending the wounded man broke for the chaparral. He died under a six-shooter volley before he reached cover. The wounded Mexican was found lying on a cot in a cabin. He had been, he confessed, the man on the white horse who had shot at Ellis from a rocky eminence at Chaparral Hill and had been tumbled out of his saddle by Ellis' return fire. He was dangerously hurt, he said, and expected to die. The possemen quickly made sure he should not be disappointed. They carried him with great gentleness to a shady spot under a live oak and as he lay comfortably on his back at full length on the grass, they slipped a rope about his neck and hanged him.

A Mexican carrying across his shoulder a sack of provisions he had just purchased at a grocery was leaving Carson's Creek on foot when Ellis and his men rode into town. Taken into custody, the Mexican pretended to be a *bobo*—a fool—and jabbered incoherent nonsense in answer to all questions. It had not been known that a rope was a panacea for imbecility but Ellis risked the experiment and found that it quickly restored the poor fellow to reason. Having been swung up to the limb of a live oak, the Mexican admitted he had been on his way to deliver provisions to Murrieta, who, he said, was hiding with Three Fingered Jack, Valenzuela, Claudio and

Reyes Feliz, in one of the band's old haunts on Bear Mountain. Ellis left the Mexican for the night under guard of two of his men. "See that he does not escape," the deputy sheriff warned them. "I expect you to give a good account of your prisoner." At midnight Ellis was awakened in his camp by the two guards. They had come, they said, to give a good account of their prisoner and they related it in entertaining detail. The Mexican was found swinging to a tree beside the road next morning.

On information that Murrieta had holed up in Camp Opera, Under-Sheriff Clark and a posse closed in on the place at dawn. Opera was a tiny village of fifty people, mostly Mexicans, and twenty houses, twelve of them saloons; and was chiefly famous for its cemetery known as the Graveyard of Drunks, every one buried in it having died of alcoholism or delirium tremens. Into a big tent across which was painted "Grand Palace Hotel," Clark herded all the inhabitants and grilled them with questions. An old woman, shaking with fear, told him a Mexican had ridden in the day before and inquired of some women washing clothes at the creek if they had seen Murrieta in the camp lately and had paid one fifty cents to wash out a handkerchief deeply stained with blood. When Clark asked her if she knew where the Mexican was, she pointed out a man in the tent. "There he is," she said. He proved to be Juan Sanchez and when a rope was looped around his neck, he admitted he was one of Murrieta's bandits and had been in the battle at Chaparral Hill and at the Phoenix quartz mill when Woodbeck and his companion were murdered. He met death with a shrug and a smile. He took a deep inhalation from a cigarette just before he was swung off and the smoke trickled from his lips and nostrils while he dangled in the air.

While the chase was on, the citizens of Angel's Camp

arrested a Mexican who had aroused their suspicions. A young Mexican gambler who had witnessed the arrest ran to a horse hitched at a rack and was preparing, it was supposed, to carry the news to Murrieta. As the young fellow stood with one foot in the stirrup, a miner jabbed a six-shooter in his ribs. "Better stay whar you be, pard," said the miner. "It looks a little like rain and you might git wet." The Mexican under arrest was identified as Miguel Salazar. He was, he confessed, a veteran outlaw and had been with Murrieta at Chaparral Hill. When the noose had been adjusted around his neck, he asked for a drink of whiskey. A grim-faced, red-shirted old timer getting ready to pull on the other end of the rope, handed him a flask. Salazar took a long swig and returned the bottle to its owner. "That's good liquor," he said smacking his lips. The tree on which he was hanged still stands in Angel's Camp.

At Los Muertos, Ellis arrested a Mexican who had been curiously wounded. A pistol ball had pierced his body in such a way as to leave four holes due to some peculiarly twisted attitude he had assumed when struck. The prisoner was taken to San Andreas where he was tried before a lynch court and sentenced to death. Finding he must die, he admitted he was the brigand who had been shot while chasing Ellis' horse at Chaparral Hill. He gave his name as Ramon Blanco and said he had been for a long time one of Murrieta's secret agents. The bandit organization, he declared, "went all the way through to Shasta," by which he meant it was state wide.

"No member is considered of much account who has not killed at least half a dozen men," he said. "Each ranks in importance according to the number he has slain. Secret agents of the band are located in every town in the mining country. They are bound by a solemn oath to obey their leaders and disobedience is punished by death. Each agent is assigned to a particular district. He is required to observe passing events that may affect the band's welfare. He must be ready to turn out immediately on receiving an order from his superiors. He must provide food and shelter for members of the brotherhood and aid and protect them in time of danger even at the risk of his life. He must locate horses to be stolen, direct the operation of the horse thieves of the gang and when a raid is under way, see to it that relays of fresh horses are stationed at designated points along the route selected for escape."

The completeness of Murrieta's organization and the absolute power wielded by the young chieftain were never more impressively set forth than by this Mexican waiting for the rope to be tied around his neck. A few minutes after he had ended his amazing recital, he was dead.

San Andreas in the valley of the Calaveras river, once a California Pactolus rolling over sands of gold, was the county seat of Calaveras county and a legal and business center. Lawyers flourished. Many cases that in their time made a stir in the mining country were tried in the court house and several men were hanged there by legal process, which, for a town of gold rush days, was a rare distinction. The region about it was alive with miners. Many Chinese camps were near by. Merchants were prosperous. Saloons and gambling houses never closed. Everybody had money to burn and burned it. San Andreas was a live camp.

To-day in its old age it suggests a gray bearded grandfather sitting in an ingle corner with his pipe and memories. Farms and orchards and vineyards are about it. If you did not know the region had been the scene of the wildest gold rush in the history of the world, you might think it a peaceful New England countryside. Here and there about the town are ancient weather-beaten buildings that date back to the old days. On Main Street is an old one-story stone house with rusty iron doors and rusty iron window blinds. This, as a half-obliterated sign informs you, was once the American hotel known from Hangtown to Mariposa and considered quite palatial. Now it gathers cobwebs in empty squalor. Opposite it is the modern Hotel Treat. The past and present stand face to face across the narrow street. Once San Andreas had eight thousand people. Now it has seven hundred. In flush times there were eight hundred Chinamen in town. Now there is one—a poor lonely Chink who is like a fossil footprint left over from a forgotten age. He keeps a restaurant.

San Andreas has only two relics to show of Murrieta who operated through all the country about the town. They are two silk sashes once worn by the outlaw. Both are of the same kind—eight or ten inches wide, three yards long with tassels at the ends, and of the color of port wine held up to sunlight. The Chamber of Commerce has one in its collection of documents and curiosities of early times. The other is owned by Mrs. Ira Hill Reed, widow of a lawyer who was once district attorney and county judge at San Andreas.

"The sash," said Mrs. Reed, "was given to my husband by a Mexican whom he defended in 1875. It is stained with blood in several places and the Mexican said he himself had taken it from the dead body of Murrieta after the fight with Harry Love's Rangers near the Arroya Cantova. Who the Mexican was I do not know. He probably had been a member of Murrieta's band and may have taken part in his leader's last battle. The dark stains on the sash, he declared, were made by the blood trickling from the wounds that killed the famous outlaw."

A few days after Ramon Blanco was hanged Murrieta gave San Andreas a spectacular surprise. Enraged by the loss of so many of his men and impelled by his inordinate fondness for lurid melodrama, he rode alone at a hand-gallop through the main street of the town from one end to the other and shot and killed three Americans whom he did not know and who did not know him. Hundreds of people saw the lone horseman as he rode in from the direction of Angel's Camp. No one at first paid any attention to him. But the first crack of his revolver focused all eyes upon him. The cry of "Murrieta!" ran along the street. Nothing in his appearance indicated any murderous purpose. His face was not ferocious; his eyes did not blaze. He rode leisurely and fired with an air of languid indifference as if he might be practicing marksmanship while enjoying an easy gallop to stimulate a delicate appetite. He fired only three times and his victims fell at least a hundred yards apart. No shot was fired at him, no effort was made to capture him, and when he rode out of town still at a slow gallop on the trail to Mokelumne Hill, no move was made to pursue him. The town seemed paralyzed by the daredevil audacity of the performance.

The Alta California of contemporary date printed a brief item about this ride which read: "On Thursday Joaquin rode through San Andreas at a gallop and shot three Americans as he passed through the street. Joaquin is a young man and must be one of the best shots with a revolver in this or any other country as all three men were shot through the neck."

Who the three men were who died beneath the brigand's gun is not known. One might fancy death at the hands of so celebrated an outlaw would have been in the nature of an accolade and insured them at least a modicum of fame. But even their names have been forgotten.

Fording the Calaveras river near Jesus Maria at blue dawn, Murrieta and six of his followers were fired upon from ambush by a small party of San Andreas men. Wheeling their horses, the bandits dashed back across the stream and disappeared in the brush. All but one. Claudio's horse had been shot under him and that young robber was captured. When the Americans arrived at Yaqui Camp with their prisoner, a live oak standing beside the trail with spreading foliage and stout lower limbs met their eyes. It struck them as a very nice tree. Standing beneath it with the loop of a lariat about his neck, Claudio was asked if he had anything to say. The shadow of a sneer swept across his handsome face.

"I was taken with Joaquin," he said. "That is enough. You will hang me no matter what I might say."

Suddenly out of the distance came a faint rumble like a low growl of thunder. Far across the level plain bathed in the brightness of the newly risen sun, six horsemen came riding like devils with clouds of red dust boiling up from the heels of their flying horses.

"Joaquin!"

This after all was no time to hang anybody. The Americans scrambled for their horses and leaping into their saddles galloped off in mad flight on the road to San Andreas. As the outlaws swept past the live oak, their guns spouting fire, Claudio with the rope around his neck waved at them with a joyous grin. On through the town, over the hills, among the chaparral thickets of the winding trail, revolvers of pursuers cracking at every jump, bullets from the pursued whistling back, the wild race kept up until the Americans found refuge in San Andreas.

Murrieta rode back to Yaqui Camp flaming with rage. Having failed to empty any saddles in the chase, he was determined to revenge himself with some American blood no matter whose. The stirring events of the morning had brought many people into the street. Seeing an American in the crowd, Three Fingered Jack shot him dead. Valenzuela brought down another. A third took to his heels and Murrieta spurred his horse after him. Darting out of town, the fugitive headed for the hills across ground covered with ditches and gravel ridges left from sluice mining. While Murrieta's horse floundered among these obstructions, the runner lightly hurdled them and kept well in advance of his pursuer. Murrieta emptied two revolvers at him. He made desperate casts with his lasso. Still the agile sprinter went bounding ahead. As a last resort, the bandit hurled his long, two-edged knife at him. The flashing blade slit the American's ear as he dodged behind a giant boulder. With the nimbleness of a monkey he shinned up the face of a sheer cliff to safety.

San Andreas buzzed with excitement when the news was bruited about that Murrieta was within three miles of town. Deputy Sheriff Ellis with a hundred armed citizens rushed to Yaqui Camp. But when they arrived, the outlaws were miles away in the hills. But the wantonly murderous work of the bandits called for retaliation. Murrieta's spies and secret partisans were hunted out mercilessly and sent packing to distant parts of the country. Pedro Lopez, who for a long time had ridden with Murrieta and had taken part in many of his desperate crimes, had recently forsaken banditry and settled down in Yaqui Camp as the proprietor of a saloon. Betrayed by Mexican informers, he was seized by the mob and tried before a lynch court. Sentenced to die, he begged for his life. But seeing his prayers were in vain, his brow darkened and he faced his judges with proud defiance.

"If you search my trunk," he sneered, "you will find

a knife from whose blade no handkerchief has yet wiped the American blood."

The close of the day found the Americans in a mood of bitter resentment against all Mexicans. While Lopez twisted in the breeze on the same live oak from beneath which Claudio had been rescued, the mob, scattering among the houses, began to ply the torch and soon the flames were roaring over the town. When the crowd rode back to San Andreas late that night, Yaqui Camp had been wiped off the map and its site was a black and smoking desolation.

But the mob's work at Yaqui Camp was only the beginning. Murrieta's outrageous crimes had inflamed the whole region against his countrymen. The entire Mexican population of San Andreas was driven out of town by the enraged citizens. The quarter in which they had dwelt was given to the flames and Mexican men, women and children, fleeing in fear of their lives, swarmed along the trails while the smoke of their burning homes rolled in billows over the hills.

CHAPTER VIII.

THE BREAK OF THE LUCK.

HORNITOS was taking its siesta. The afternoon sun filled the main street with lazy warmth. Few pedestrians were abroad. The shops were empty. Gamblers off duty lounged about the doors of the saloons. As Deputy Sheriff John Prescott sauntered along he was stopped by a Mexican wrapped in a serape.

"Give me some tobacco," said the Mexican.

Prescott handed him his pouch.

"Be on your guard," muttered the Mexican out of the corner of his mouth as he poured some tobacco into his pipe. "I have some information for you. Murrieta is in town. Four or five are with him."

"Where is he?" asked Prescott with the air of one wholly uninterested.

"In an adobe in the outskirts."

"Meet me at the three pines on the Mariposa road at midnight."

The Mexican laughed loudly as he puffed at his pipe. Anyone seeing him would have thought Prescott had told him a good joke. Prescott strolled off with a jovial smile on his face.

Promptly at midnight by the three pines Prescott and fifteen men met the informer, or stool pigeon as he would be called in the police nomenclature of to-day. Leading the posse through the chaparral the Mexican pointed out an adobe standing dark and silent in the moonlight at the edge of town. "That's the house," he said. Prescott and his men surrounded it. Doors at front and rear crashed in beneath the battering rams of powerful shoulders and Prescott and half a dozen possemen burst inside.

Five shadowy forms huddled in blankets on the floor sprang to their feet. Their revolvers blazed. By the light of burning gunpowder, Prescott recognized a tense figure standing at bay against the opposite wall with a flaming six-shooter in each hand. That was Murrieta. Prescott fired at him with both barrels of a double barreled shotgun. The distance of ten paces gave the charge no chance to scatter and the buckshot bored two great holes in the plastering beyond the outlaw but left him unharmed. A bullet from his revolver struck Prescott in the breast and the deputy pitched headlong. Twice more Murrieta fired and each shot brought down a man. Three of his foes lay stretched out in the darkness as he rushed through the door. Outside he bumped into another. Clubbing the fellow with his gun, he knocked him down. The ring of guards about the house opened fire. Bounding through them Murrieta ran for the brush, his men scrambling pell-mell after him. They faded in the moonlight with bullets whistling about them and darted out of sight among the thickets of chaparral.

Prescott nursed his wound in bed for six weeks. In his hiding place in the hills, Murrieta kept informed of his condition and was deeply disappointed, it was said, when the deputy sheriff finally recovered. A week after the fight, some travelers riding into town in the gathering dusk noticed with curiosity some strange looking object hanging from the limb of a tree. Upon closer view, it turned out to be the body of a Mexican. For the information that had almost cost Murrieta his life, the stool pigeon had been paid in full.

The affair at the Jamison ranch on the Consumnes

river had a certain fame in its day and increased the bitterness between Americans and Mexicans in the mining country. Some cattle were stolen from John Crouch who found the hide of one of the animals in a Mexican camp known as Yeomet at the forks of the Consumnes. Crouch and his friends rounded up five or six of the Mexicans in the village and took them to the Jamison ranch for "trial," as it was called, before a "citizens court," which interpreted meant Crouch and his crowd. Mr. Beebee, a storekeeper and several other citizens of Yeomet, who believed the Mexicans innocent, sent for Sheriff R. B. Buchanan who soon arrived with a posse. The sheriff demanded the prisoners. The crowd refused to give them up. An angry colloquy ensued. Several Mexicans with guns were discovered hanging around the edges of the crowd. They were fired at and chased away. The crowd swarmed about Sheriff Buchanan with rifles and six-shooters and ordered him to leave. One man struck the sheriff's horse with the barrel of his rifle. With his life apparently in danger the sheriff rode off followed by friends of the Mexicans.

Then the crowd formed a court, selected twelve men to serve as a jury and placed the Mexicans on trial. No evidence was produced to show that any of them had been concerned in stealing Crouch's cattle. But as the hide of one of the stolen steers had been found in Yeomet the jury concluded that some Mexicans in the settlement had taken part in the theft and sentenced all the prisoners to thirty lashes on the bare back. One of the Mexicans addressed the jury in defense of himself and others. He was well-dressed, intelligent, young and good looking and spoke excellent English.

"There are some bad Mexicans in the settlement," he said, "but none of us had anything to do with stealing the cattle and it is unjust to hold us responsible for the deeds of criminals as ready to rob their own countrymen as to rob Americans."

One after the other the prisoners, stripped to the waist, were tied to a tree and given thirty lashes on the bare back with a rope. When it came the turn of the good looking young fellow, he bowed to the crowd with a smile and said, "Gentlemen, I am as innocent of this stealing as any of you" and held out his hands to be tied around the tree. Whirling his rope the executioner said, "God damn you, I'll take that smile off your face." John McCauley, one of the jury, protested against the Mexican's receiving any severer punishment than the others. "I'm doing this," said the man with the rope and he laid on the lashes until the blood came.

The identity of this Mexican became a question of interest and controversy. The belief became widespread that he was Joaquin Murrieta and J. D. Mason in his history of Amador county mentions this belief. That this opinion was erroneous now seems established beyond a doubt. But there is reason to believe the Mexican who was whipped was Claudio, sometimes known as Claudio Murrieta and thought by many to be a brother of Joaquin to whom he bore a striking resemblance. The affair at the Jamison ranch occurred in 1852 and at that time Joaquin was at the heyday of his outlaw career. But the date at which Claudio joined Joaquin's banditti is uncertain and it now seems probable the undeserved and merciless lashing he received drove him into outlawry and inflamed him with hatred for Americans comparable in bitterness to that of Joaquin himself. Their mutual hatred of the gringo race became a bond between the two men and there was no member of his band to whom Joaquin was more warmly attached than Claudio. The killing of four Americans by Mexicans at Turnersville a few weeks later was believed to have been in revenge for the Jamison ranch outrage. Tom Olin, William Boose and two brothers named Steward died in this butchery and Tomas Domingo, one of the murderers who was caught and hanged by the citizens, confessed that Murrieta's outlaws were concerned in the atrocity. Both Joaquin and Claudio were supposed to have taken part in it.

The aftermath of the floggings involved the participants in serious difficulties. Sheriff Buchanan returned in a day or two with a posse of three hundred men and scoured the region for the rioters. Runners were sent up and down the Consumnes river warning the members of the party and most of them fled the country, some taking refuge in Indian villages far back in the mountains, and remained away for several months until the storm had blown over. John M. Jamison, owner of the ranch, and his son were arrested and after a vexatious and costly law suit paid nominal fines. The Jamisons were prominent people in El Dorado county and were from St. Louis, Mo., where the father had held "many positions of trust and honor."

A dance had just ended in the fandango house at Quartzburg. The last notes of *"El Mal Criado"* had died on the air from the fiddles and guitars and ladies and gents had chasséd to the bar. There was a sudden commotion at the door. A handsome young *caballero* entered in state, five or six obsequious fellows in his wake. He might have been some grandee of old Mexico with a train of retainers. In his sumptuous regalia—velvet jacket, scarlet sash, black pantaloons seamed with silver discs and split at the knees to show the snowy white calzoneras beneath—he was as gallant a figure as ever inflamed a rival with jealousy or swept a dance hall girl off her feet. Señor Joaquin Murrieta, if you please, was dressed for the ball.

The table in a far corner at which my lord and his retinue took seats was soon cluttered with bottles and glasses and surrounded by dusky beauties. With noisy gaiety the charmers flopped into the laps of these jovial gentlemen, petted them, toasted them in merry bumpers of *aguardiente*. It might have been the coquettish creatures did not know the names of their cavaliers but at least they had a kissing acquaintance with them.

Across the room by the bar among some tipsy Americans, the eyes of a jealous greaser burned green. He knew, as no one else in the house did, that the young dandy was Murrieta the notorious robber. And that was the greaser's gal in the blue and yellow grenadine with the jeweled comb in her hair and the loops of gold in her ears—the lady with her arms wound lovingly about the outlaw's neck. That was getting away with murder. Was he to take it standing still? Name of God—no! He would teach that cheap thief to steal his gal.

"Joaquin!" he yelled at the top of his voice. "There he is. That's Murrieta. Get him. Shoot him."

Now that was a devil of a note. A gentlemanly bandit, it seemed, was not to be permitted to relax for one brief interval among the petticoats or sip his *tequila* in peace. But as the cards fall, so goes the game. Spilling the siren on the floor and drawing his six-shooter, Joaquin rushed for the greaser of the green eyes. He would kill him the first thing if it were the last thing he ever did, and in a swirl of lead the poor devil went down. The Americans started shooting. The other outlaws got into the scrimmage with popping guns. The kerosene lamps swinging from the ceiling were shot out. The battle went on in the dark. Men fell here and there and lay still. The outlaws fought their way out the door, leaped on their horses and escaped to the hills. An evening of polite amusement was spoiled for Joaquin; the jealous

Mexican who had sought to save his lady love from the arms of a rival lost both his gal and his life; and, according to the newspapers of the period, "two or three Americans were killed and others wounded."

From the cluster of cabins that marks the site of the once flourishing gold camp of Los Muertos you can see on a clear day a peak in the Bear Mountain range that is still called Joaquin's Lookout. From the top of it, the lights of Stockton can be seen at night. Below this summit, and overlooking the Stanislaus river, is a cave once used by the outlaws as a refuge and now known as Joaquin's Cave. The cave opens under a shelf of rock that projects far out from the mountain wall and from the mouth a narrow tunnel runs back to a spacious chamber. When the cavern was located a few years ago, the low rock platforms on which the robbers made their beds were still to be seen about this chamber and the outer space under the overhanging rock where they did their cooking was a foot deep in ashes. Many people have dug in the cave for treasure but all they ever found was a skeleton, the remains, it was believed, of one of the outlaws who had ridden with Murrieta on his wild adventures.

"Joaquin Romero, a Yaqui Indian who lived in Los Muertos," said Frank Marshall, "was one of the best friends Murrieta had in that region. They had known each other as boys in Mexico, and when Murrieta and his wife Rosita first arrived in the mining country they lived for a while with Romero and his wife in a cabin in Los Muertos. When in later years, the robbers made the cave in Bear Mountain their headquarters, Romero regularly carried provisions and liquor to them on mule back. When he was an old man, I knew Romero well and he used to tell me a lot of stories about his visits to the outlaws' cave.

"The cave was in a rugged, deeply forested country into which even the hardiest prospectors rarely ventured, and, besides the outlaws themselves, Romero said he was the only man who knew where the cave was. When the sheriff's men were hard on his heels, Murrieta's trail often ended abruptly as if he and his band had gone straight up in the air. The cave was the explanation of their disappearance. They lived there for weeks, Romero said, safe from pursuit and as snug as bugs in a rug. Sometimes they had their women with them and as Romero kept them supplied with food and liquor, they caroused and feasted to their hearts' content. Romero bought all their liquor at Maldives' saloon and Maldives was my godfather. The stone walls of the saloon with iron bars on the windows still stand in Los Muertos.

"Murrieta, so Romero told me, had another cave he used as a hiding place which was known only to himself, Three Fingered Jack, Reyes Feliz and Claudio, who were his closest friends among the robbers. Romero was never permitted to visit this cave which was somewhere on Funk Hill between Copperopolis and Reynold's Ferry near where Black Bart held up his last stage in 1883. Many people have hunted for this cave but so far no one has ever located it.

"Joe Dixie, an Indian who still lives in Angel's Camp, nursed Romero in his last illness and I was present when the old man passed out. 'I'm not afraid to die,' Romero said to me, 'but after all the money I made in the mines, I hate to die without a dollar.' 'You ain't going to die without a dollar,' I told him and I put a silver dollar in his hand. 'God bless you,' he said. Dixie bought a shirt and a pair of drawers with the dollar and buried Romero in them."

It was at the Bear Mountain cave that Murrieta killed Florencio Cruz and the skeleton found there may have been that of this noted lieutenant of the robber band. Florencio secretly resented what he regarded as the favoritism shown by the young chieftain to Three Fingered Jack, Valenzuela and several others and, considering himself unjustly slighted, resolved to serve no longer under Murrieta. Instead of slipping away as he might have done, he foolishly brought the affair to a head. Saddling his horse, he confronted Murrieta as the latter sat among his outlaws at the mouth of the cavern.

"I am going to Stockton on business," he announced.

"What business?" asked Murrieta.

"Personal business."

"The business of my men concerns me."

"This matter concerns only myself."

Murrieta did not miss the insolence of Florencio's tone.

"Your announcement comes as a surprise."

"Possibly." Florencio shrugged.

"You are aware that just now we are being hard pressed. Posses are hunting for us all over the country. At any time we may be cornered and have to fight for our lives. I need all my men. The time you have chosen to leave us is inopportune."

"Opportune enough for me."

"I will not permit you to go. That settles it."

"I am not asking your permission. I am going without it."

"Do you mean to defy me?"

"Think what you please about it."

"This is rebellion."

"Call it that if you like."

"Do you know what rebellion means in my command?"

"It may mean my death."

"Unless you reconsider, that is exactly what it means."

"Or," added Florencio, reaching for his six-shooter, "death to yourself."

With a lightning quick movement, Murrieta whipped his own gun from the scabbard and fired twice. Before he had time to pull the trigger, Florencio fell dead with a bullet between his eyes and another through his heart.

Murrieta's adventure among the Tejon Indians stands out in perspective as the one side-splitting comedy sandwiched among the many tragedies of his career. With Reyes Feliz and Pedro Gonzales, Murrieta stole twenty head of horses from the ranch of a Mexican at Avisimba near Orris Timbers, thirty miles or so from San Jose. They drove the horses south intending to sell them in Los Angeles. On the way they picked up Maria Ana Benites, Carmelita and Mariquita at Rancho San Luis Gonzaga at the east end of Pacheco Pass where their three inamoratas had been sojourning for a while. Traveling across the Tulare plains, they came after a journey of several hundred miles into the Tehachapi mountains and went into camp to rest themselves and their stock in the country of the Tejon Indians. The Tejons were as lazy and good for nothing as Indians ever get to be and were regarded as no more dangerous than the rabbits and ground squirrels they trapped for food.

The rancher of Avisimba, who had followed the trail of the outlaws, hunted up Sapaterra or Zapatero, the chief of the tribe, and offered him half of the stolen horses if he and his braves would recover them. When his runners returned after locating the camp, Sapaterra was inflamed with avarice at their report of the fine apparel, jewels and apparent wealth of the travelers; and at dawn one morning several hundred savages closed in on the slumbering outlaws and took them prisoners. They stripped them of their clothes, took possession of their arms and horses, robbed them of $7,000 in money and gold dust and $3,000 in jewelry and marched them stark naked fifteen miles across the mountains to Sapaterra's village.

But captives were something new in the experience of the fat old sachem who had never taken a war trail. He felt that his victorious coup called for something or other but he was unable to determine what. For a week he pondered whether to shoot them, hang them or offer them up as a burnt sacrifice to the Great Spirit. But he hesitated for fear he might displease the Great White Father and call down his wrath upon the tribe. In his dilemma, he finally dispatched a runner to Los Angeles to get the advice of the *alcalde*, and the *alcalde*, being a kind hearted old Mexican, sent him back word to set them free. Sapaterra did. But first he tied them to trees and switched them; after which he made them a speech in Tejon gibberish which they did not understand but which obviously bristled with solemn warnings and the wisdom of the ancients. Then they were escorted to the border of Sapaterra's domains and turned loose to shift for themselves.

Behold now these six men and women trudging sadly through the woods in the nude simplicity of Adam and Eve before fig leaves had become the *dernier cri* in fashionable attire in the Garden of Eden. For two sleeps they journeyed southward—and the dew was heavy and the mountain air was cold—and as they emerged from the mouth of Tejon Pass, Mountain Jim Wilson, old time pal of Joaquin and Three Fingered Jack, espied them from afar off and stood aghast at the startling vision. Holy Mackerel! What the hell? The after effects of bad whiskey? Pink elephants next? Then one of the apparitions hailed him in a voice that sounded human—called him Mountain Jim, good old Mountain Jim. And before he knew it the veteran horse thief was blushing to his ears as fauns and hamadryads danced joyously about him.

Mountain Jim hustled up clothes for them at San Francisco rancho and soon had them equipped with arms and horses. As by magic, three cowering creatures of the female sex became beautiful women, gay, smiling, coquettish. One moment the famous Joaquin Murrieta was as pitiful and helpless as a stray cur pup. The next he was the dangerous outlaw chief at whose glance men shook in their boots.

"What do you suppose this thing called luck is anyhow?" remarked Mountain Jim to Joaquin over the glasses in a San Gabriel *cantina.* "Needin' the price of food and drink, you play your cards close to your belly and are trimmed out o' your last white chip. Sittin' into a game to pass the time, not givin' a damn whether you win or lose, and in three shakes of a mule's tail, you've got a wall of reds and blues in front of you as high as your chin. You call the turn for a dollar and win. You call it for a hundred and the dealer takes your bet. I start out to be a preacher and wind up as a horse thief. You shoot your way out of tight corners in many a fight with good game Americanos and get took like a sheep by a bunch o' lousy Redskins. You figure it out and take the money. As for me, I pass the pot."

J. A. Carter, a lawyer of Drytown, missed a valuable horse from his barn. Robert Cochran, his law partner, trailed it to within a mile of Oleta, once Fiddletown. There he saw the animal hitched with a number of other horses in front of a wayside tavern kept by John Clark. The Mexican who had ridden it was eating his dinner with several companions inside. Clark, a powerful man, had no idea as to the horse thief's identity and offered to help Cochran arrest him. If he had known it was Joaquin Murrieta he would not have been so bold. The two men entered the dining room and stepped up to Joaquin. Clark laid a heavy hand on his shoulder and said, "You are my prisoner." Joaquin, with his mouth full of beans, looked up at him in surprise. "I think you are mistaken," he replied politely and drawing his six-shooter killed Clark instantly and dropped Cochran to the floor severely wounded. The outlaws then mounted and disappeared, leaving behind Carter's horse which was recovered by the owner.*

During a stay of several months in the mountains about Mount Shasta, Valenzuela's band devoted itself to stealing horses and was assisted in its depredations by the Modocs, a wild tribe that in subsequent years rose against the whites and was all but exterminated in a long war among the lava beds. The ranchers of the valleys whose herds were being seriously raided pursued a bunch of Mexican and Indian marauders on one occasion and, hemming them in between a river and a wall of bluffs, massacred them almost to a man. Plunging on his horse into the foaming river torrent one of the outlaws tried to escape. A dozen men fired at him. He swam on with bullets knocking up spouts of water about him. He had reached the middle of the stream when an old mountaineer who in his backwoods home in Missouri had been accustomed to "bark" squirrels in the tallest hickory tree and bring them to earth without breaking the skin, jumped from his horse and, dropping on one knee, drew a steady bead. At the crack of his musket, the Mexican threw up his hands and toppled sidelong from his saddle. His body was swept away in the swift current while his horse made the opposite shore unhurt and galloped off into the woods.

Only a few gold hunters passed through the mountain wilderness where the outlaws had established themselves

* J. D. Mason's History of Amador County.

but a number of skeletons of these adventurers were found in lonely cañons, sometimes with a bullet hole through the skull, sometimes with Indian arrows among the bones. Once some Redskins, wearing the clothes of four prospectors killed by the outlaws, were believed themselves to be the murderers and shot on sight. Several hundred horses stolen in this region were driven to Arroya Cantova and later sold in Mexico.

On Bear river twenty miles above Marysville an elderly widow was sitting at her front door with her grown son and daughter when Valenzuela with four revolvers and a bowie knife strapped around him and accompanied by three heavily armed Mexicans rode to the house and asked for supper. Suspecting they were robbers but afraid to refuse them, the widow invited them in. Valenzuela was the pink of politeness until he had eaten his supper. Then he robbed the house of several hundred dollars and left the family gagged and bound. The same night, the robbers broke into another house a few miles away and there also gagged and bound the inmates. Ransacking a drawer, Valenzuela found a woman's gold watch and looped its long gold chain about his neck. When she saw him at this, one of the women lying gagged on the floor rolled her eyes wildly and grew purple in the face.

"Take the gag out of that lady's mouth," said Valenzuela. "She wants to say something and looks as if she would choke to death trying."

"O please don't steal my watch," cried the woman in an agonized voice when the gag was removed. "I'm a widow and it was a present from my husband."

"You needn't take it so hard, madam," said Valenzuela. "I'll give it back to you."

The widow was gagged again and the family was not released from its bonds until next day when neighbors happened to call and found men, women and children lying silent and helpless about the floor.

"All I've got to say," said the widow spitting out the rags that had been stuffed into her mouth, "is that the leader of those robbers was a perfect gentleman. I never met a nicer, more polite man."

Bear river hospitality had been famous, but after these two robberies a traveler was unable to obtain a night's lodging for love or money. A young man from the mountains, on his way to the valley, called at every house he passed and found every door barred at his approach. A muffled voice from the dark interior would say, "We ain't got no room fer you here," and direct him to a house a mile away. Arrived there, he would be told through the keyhole that the people across the river would take him in. And the people across the river would direct him to the house just over the hill. Having wandered around nearly all night, the young fellow left his horse hitched on the bank of a slough, paddled to the other side in a canoe and, after a pitched battle with a pack of savage dogs, thumped on the door of a tumble-down shanty in a field overgrown with weeds. A gray-haired old man opened the door. "Why, shore, stranger, come in," he said. "If you're an honest man you're welcome to what I've got, and if you're a robber you won't find nothing to steal because I ain't got nothing."

Murrieta set out on a marauding expedition through the country along the coast after Valenzuela, returning from his northern adventures, rejoined him at Arroya Cantova. His depredations were extensive in the Pajaro and Salinas valleys and he sent the horses he stole through Priest's valley to Arroya Cantova. On the Salinas plains, three Mexicans stopped at a ranch house and asked for lodging for the night. The leader, according to the rancher's description, was young and handsome, wore what seemed to be false whiskers and a mustache and had four heavy revolvers buckled around him. Suspecting he was Murrieta, the rancher asked him if there was any news from the placers regarding the "robber chief of the Stanislaus." The young man put his hand to his heart and bowed with grave politeness. "I am that Joaquin," he said, "and no man takes me or comes within one hundred yards of me as long as I have these good weapons." He talked at first with composure but as he went along he seemed to labor under intense excitement. He told of the outrage upon his wife, the lynching of his brother, the flogging he himself had received, and declared he had been swindled out of $40,000 by Americans.

"I was once a great admirer of Americans," he said. "I thought them the noblest, most honorable and high-minded people in the world. I had met many in my own country and all forms of tyranny seemed as hateful to them as the rule of the Gachupines to the Mexicans. I was sick of the constant wars and insurrections in my native land and I came here thinking to end my days in California as an American citizen.

"I located first near Stockton. But I was constantly annoyed and insulted by my neighbors and was not permitted to live in peace. I then went to the placers and was driven from my mining claim. I went into business and was cheated by everyone in whom I trusted. At every turn I was swindled and robbed by the very men for whom I had had the greatest friendship and admiration. I saw the Americans daily in acts of the most outrageous and lawless injustice or of cunning and mean duplicity hateful to every honorable mind.

"I then said to myself, 'I will revenge my wrongs and take the law into my own hands. The Americans who have injured me I will kill, and those who have not,

I will rob because they are Americans. My trail shall be red with blood and those who seek me shall die or I shall lose my own life in the struggle!' I decided to submit tamely to outrage no longer.

"I have killed many; I have robbed many; and many more will suffer in the same way. I will continue to the end of my life to take vengeance on the race that has wronged me so shamefully." *

The next thing heard of Murrieta was that he was camped with fifteen men near San Luis Obispo. He sent word to the citizens that he proposed to remain in their vicinity only a few days to rest his men and his horses and warned them that should any attempt be made to molest him, he would sack the town. He moved into San Luis Obispo next day and camped in the priest's garden at the old Mission founded by the early padres. San Luis Obispo, now a city of 10,000 inhabitants, was then an adobe village of two or three hundred Spanish Californians, Mexicans and Mission Indians with five or six American families.

"The bandits," says an old account, "were dressed in buckskin clothes, some having coats or jackets of green and all were heavily armed. The leader was symetrically formed with regular features and an open countenance but with a gloomy expression. The Americans were in a state of dread during Murrieta's stay on account of his known enmity to their race. They went abroad but little during the day and at night slept together with arms by them in Pollard's store. The robbers however harmed no one except a gambler whom they despoiled of his ill gotten hoards."

While the outlaws were camped here, Murrieta re-

* This statement was first published in the San Francisco Herald and was known as "Joaquin's Confession." It was investigated by a Stockton paper, and in an interview the rancher said it was printed almost verbatim as it came from Murrieta's lips.

ceived a message from a Spanish *haciendado* along the coast that a strong force of Americans had come up from the south on the hunt for him and had camped the night before at Los Coyotes rancho fifteen miles from San Luis Obispo. The Americans were mostly ranchers from about Santa Maria, Los Olivos and Santa Ynez in Santa Barbara county. They numbered twenty-five and were well mounted and armed and determined to rid the coast lands of the band of horse thieves that had been making such heavy inroads upon their herds.

Joaquin's situation was grave. He was outnumbered, and his enemies with injuries to avenge might be depended upon to fight desperately. Flight seemed the part of wisdom. But he was enough of a general to know that an attack is the best defense, and he decided upon a strategic maneuver. He rode hard by a roundabout trail for Los Coyotes rancho. It was night by the time he arrived at the deserted camp of the Americans but he was able to see that they had left the main road and, taking to the woods, had pressed on toward San Luis Obispo hoping to surprise the outlaws there and overwhelm them in a night attack.

Unable to follow their trail in the dark, Murrieta and his men camped for the night but were up with the dawn and in the saddle. At sunrise they halted within two miles of San Luis Obispo. Scouts were sent forward who soon returned with word that the Americans had bivouacked in the town overnight and had headed south that morning on the trail of the outlaws. The same tactics were evident on both sides and had evolved a rather remarkable situation. The Americans were trailing the outlaws and the outlaws were trailing the Americans. But with the intuition of a leader, Murrieta saw that the enemy was playing into his hands. The early morning radiance now bathing the dingy little village of San Luis Obispo held a glint of the sun of Austerlitz.

Cutting across country to his trail of the day before and well in advance of the American posse, Murrieta placed his men in ambush on both sides of a narrow pass through the hills. All that was left for him now was to wait for his foes to ride into the trap and be slaughtered. He waited for two hours. The Americans came in sight riding leisurely. They reached the gap in the hills. Woods and thickets were silent and peaceful in the sunlight.

"We ought to ketch up with 'em around Santa Maria ef we have good luck."

The words carried on the still air with clear-cut distinctness. The hillsides suddenly sparkled as the guns of the outlaws blazed. Five men lay dead in the road. Five riderless horses went galloping into the distance.

"Git into the brush, boys. Take to cover."

The Americans flung themselves from their saddles and sought shelter behind boulders and trees. The surprise had been deadly but it had passed. From now on it was steady fighting with no advantage on either side. Here and there a head showed above a thicket for an instant. Here and there a six shooter or a rifle flamed from behind a live oak. But the antagonists in this battle were expert marksmen, the American trained as stalkers of deer and antelope, the outlaws as stalkers of men, and for both a fleeting glimpse of a target was usually enough. No volleys roared. No clouds of smoke rose to the sky. A gun cracked now and then. A tenuous blue wisp wriggled off over the chaparral. That was all to be seen and all to be heard except once in a while a yell of agony as some poor devil sank behind a rock and died.

For two hours this strange battle of hidden foemen kept up—a battle of law against lawlessness—with now an interval of silence, now a shot or two like the tapping of a woodpecker on a dead sycamore. At last the firing ceased. Outlaws and posse had had enough. Both worked their way gradually over the hills, the Americans in one direction, the bandits in another. Neither stopped to take count of the casualties, but the Americans on foot, having lost their horses, and the outlaws on horseback fled from the scene swiftly.

A pick-and-shovel squad came out from San Luis Obispo toward sundown. Eleven Americans and nine outlaws, according to the tally, had been killed. Wherever the bodies were found they were buried and the two hills beside the trail remained dotted for years with the mounds of stones that marked their nameless graves.

CHAPTER IX.

AS IN A STORY BOOK.

THE circus elephant that gratefully remembered the old gentleman who as an urchin had given it a peanut—that was Joaquin Murrieta. The "little unremembered acts of kindness" were as big as mountains to him and as beautiful as mountains in the dawn. His gratitude was not merely a complacent recollection. He watched and waited for an opportunity to repay a kindness. But the memory that cherished a courtesy treasured an injury as tenaciously. He held in warm esteem those who had been kind to him—even carelessly kind—but he held in deadly hate those who had been unkind. He repaid kindness with kindness but death alone could repay a wrong. He hated with all the intensity of his being. Only by killing him could it have been possible to kill his hate. His hate was the kind that burns like a steady flame and endures to the grave. Gratitude is admirable. But in passionate and unquenchable hate there is also something admirable—something of the nobility of Greek tragedy.

But Murrieta could be magnanimous. Nor was his code wholly devoid of honor. He never betrayed a confidence and those who had faith in his honesty were never disappointed. His melodramatic soul must have reveled in his antic adventures in disguise. But in his rôle of Haroun Al Raschid, his mood was as often tragic as gay. His masquerade might mean either a droll prank or a murder. His humor at times turned a crime into a comedy and the fantastic escapades that now and then relieved the somber sequence of his career form a diverting chapter of the Murrieta chronicle.

Preserved in the State Library at Sacramento is a manuscript written by James E. Hunt, who came to California as a soldier during the Mexican war, and among the old timer's reminiscences—never published—is an interesting story of Murrieta's gratitude.

"While I was living in the Mount Diablo valley," writes Hunt, "I went one day with Mr. Brand, foreman of Widow Welch's ranch where I was working, over to the Variasse ranch where *vaqueros* had assembled from all over the country to compete in exhibitions of horsemanship and skill at throwing the lasso. The prize for the best rider was a pair of buckaroo silver mounted spurs and a silver mounted bridle; the prize for the best lassoer a saddle and silver mounted bridle. In one of the contests a silver quarter of a dollar was laid flat on the grass and the winner was the man who, in a dash of fifty yards at full speed, could bend from his saddle and pick up the coin. The most expert of the cowboys was Ned Le Grande, half Mexican, half American, who had served as interpreter for Major Robert Allen in the Mexican war. He was the only one among the contestants who succeeded in picking up the quarter. A handsome young Mexican *vaquero,* who had had his try and failed, declared Le Grande had pulled his horse down to a slow gallop and had won the prize on a foul. A quarrel started. The Mexican drew a knife and made for Le Grande. Le Grande hauled out his six-shooter. As he fired, I jerked his arm and his bullet went wild. But my jerk was the only thing that saved the Mexican's life, for Le Grande was a dead shot. While I grappled with Le Grande, the crowd hustled the Mexican away.

"During the gold rush, I moved up into the hills and

opened a saloon at Middle Bar. Murrieta and his robbers were operating in that part of the country just then and almost every day I heard of some miner being lassoed and murdered on the trails. Late one night while I was snoring in my bunk a loud rap came at my door. When I opened the door, in walked seven rough-looking Mexicans. One put a pistol to my head. Another dropped the noose of a lariat over my shoulders and pinioned my arms against my body.

" 'Where is your money?' the leader demanded.

"I pointed to a chest in a corner in which I had $740 stored and told him the key was in the pocket of my pants hanging over the back of a chair. He lit a candle and unlocked the chest. While he was rummaging through it, with the candle held close to his face, I recognized him as the young *vaquero* whose life I had saved in the Mount Diablo valley.

" 'This is a poor way to pay a man for saving your life,' I said in Spanish as he raised up with my two sacks of gold dust and money.

" 'Where did you save my life?' he asked.

"I told him. He looked hard at me.

" 'I remember,' he said.

"He dropped the two sacks back into the chest and closed down the lid. Loosening the hitch in the lariat, he slipped it over my head and freed me. The other Mexicans gasped.

" 'What are you doing?' growled a savage looking fellow with a bowie knife almost as long as a sword hanging in a scabbard at his belt.

" 'This man saved my life once,' the leader answered.

"Then he said to me, 'You have a nice saloon here. Let's all take a drink.' We walked out into the saloon—me barefooted and in my undershirt and drawers—and he threw a twenty dollar gold piece on the bar.

" 'Fill 'em up and take one yourself,' he said and I set out the bottle and glasses. 'If any of you fellows ever pass this way,' he said to his gang, 'leave this man alone. He is my friend.' Then we all clicked glasses and drank.

"I was not sure who he was until one night long afterwards when I was in the El Dorado saloon in Mokelumne Hill, I saw him jump on a monte table and shout, 'I am Joaquin Murrieta.' "

Jack Sutherland, a well to do cattleman, lived on a ranch on Dry Creek near Ione and when he went to Stockton on business one day he left his son, Billy, eighteen years old, in charge of the place. While his father was absent, Billy, as he had been instructed to do, sold a bunch of steers for several thousand dollars in cash. Before putting the money away in a hiding place, Billy counted it on the kitchen table, piling it about in glittering stacks of gold and silver. While he was absorbed in his task, Murrieta and a half dozen of his outlaws stalked into the house. Billy's heart sank into his boots.

"Aren't you afraid to be here alone with all that money?" asked Joaquin.

"I guess there ain't much danger," answered Billy, putting on a bold front.

"What if Joaquin Murrieta paid you an unexpected visit?"

"He wouldn't rob me."

"He wouldn't, eh? That fellow would steal anything not nailed down. You don't know him."

"But my dad knows him. My dad did him a favor once. They're friends. Murrieta never harms his friends."

"What's your name?"

"Billy Sutherland."

"Are you Jack Sutherland's son?"

"That's what I am."

Murrieta rubbed his chin thoughtfully as his eyes lingered on the shining heaps of money on the table.

"All right, Billy," he said. "How about a little supper? We're thinking of spending the night with you."

Billy rustled around and cooked a good meal and when he had replaced the gold and silver with steaming dishes, the bandits sat down and fell to with ravenous appetites. After supper they lounged about smoking and talking and finally stretched out on the floor and went to sleep. All night Billy lay awake with eyes and ears open. The snoring of the brigands was sweet music to him. As long as they snored his treasure was safe.

"How much do I owe you, Billy?" asked Joaquin after breakfast next morning.

"O that's all right," Billy answered, thankful he had not been robbed. "You don't owe me a cent."

Joaquin flipped a twenty dollar gold piece on the table. "You're a good cook, Billy. Put that in your pocket for luck."

With his heart thumping with joy, Billy did his best to look unconcerned as he stood in the door and watched the bandits swing into their saddles.

"Good-bye, Billy," said Joaquin gathering up his bridle reins. "Give your dad my best. And say, Billy, if any of the sheriff's men happen to pass this way and ask for fellows answering our description, it might be just as well for you to forget we've been here."

Billy thought so too.

John W. Green arrived in California with his family in 1846 after crossing the plains from the Missouri river with a covered wagon and a six-yoke team of oxen. He took up land near Stockton and went into the cattle business, and John C. Fremont and Kit Carson, riding down from Sutter's Fort, used to visit at his ranch. Green became well acquainted with Murrieta when the latter was a *vaquero,* and remained his friend throughout his outlaw years. While Green was camped one night in the hills above Knight's Ferry on the Stanislaus, Murrieta rode into his camp alone.

"You sold a herd of cattle in Sonora to-day, Juan," said the bandit. "How much money have you with you?"

"Eight thousand dollars, Joaquin," Green answered with frank honesty.

"Three Fingered Jack," said Murrieta, "knows you sold those cattle and knows the exact amount of money you have. He is not far away and he plans to rob you. He usually obeys me. But now he is licking his chops like a hungry wolf at the prospect of getting his clutches on so much money and I can't do anything with him. I thought I'd warn you. You'd better look out for yourself."

This was alarming news and Green remained for a while in meditative silence. If Three Fingered Jack and his cut-throats swooped down on him, it would be good-bye to his eight thousand dollars. Suddenly he had an inspiration.

"I wonder, Joaquin," he said with naïve confidence in the outlaw, "if it would be too much trouble for you to take the money to Tia Lisa (Mrs. Green) at the ranch. If you'd do that for me, I'd certainly appreciate it."

"Why of course I'll take it," returned Joaquin. "It'll be no trouble at all."

Green counted the money in the light of the campfire and, putting it in a buckskin sack, gave it to Murrieta. A moment later there was a clatter of hoofs on the Stockton road and eight thousand dollars went galloping away in the darkness in the hands of the most notorious robber in California. Then Green rolled up comfortably in his blankets and went to sleep.

"Well for the land's sake, Joaquin, where did you

come from?" exclaimed Tia Lisa as Murrieta swung out of his saddle at the door of the Green ranch house. "You're certainly good for sore eyes. I haven't seen you for a month of Sundays. Come on in the house and rest yourself."

"Here's the money Juan got for his cattle," said Murrieta holding out the buckskin bag. "He was afraid he might be robbed and asked me to bring it to you?"

"Money?"

"Eight thousand dollars."

"Well, I'm sure much obliged to you, Joaquin. It was mighty nice of you to bring it. But you must be thirsty after such a long hot ride. Come out to the kitchen and have a glass of buttermilk."

Tia Lisa saw nothing remarkable in the episode. She was no more surprised than if Joaquin had delivered a sack of potatoes. She knew he lived by robbery but there was never the glimmer of a doubt in her kindly old soul of his honesty with her and her husband. Both would have trusted him with their last dollar.

A cattle buyer named Cocariouris was camped at dusk on the San Joaquin river. Several Mexicans in flashy dress rode up and asked for supper.

"You're just in time," replied Cocariouris cordially. "Get down off your horses and come and help yourselves."

Squatting around the campfire, the hungry Mexicans packed their stomachs with fried ham, gravy and pancakes. A little later they threw down their blankets for the night.

"How is Señor Joaquin this morning?" called Cocariouris in cheery greeting as the leader arose next day.

"You know me then?"

"I recognized you as soon as I set eyes on you."

"Where have you seen me before?"

"I have seen you often in the saloons and gambling houses in Hornitos."

"Why did you not kill me while I slept? It would have been a very easy way to fill your pockets with money. The reward for me dead or alive would be worth having."

"I am a man, not a hyena. If other men's palms itch for blood money no more than mine, you'll live a long time. You asked me for food and I shared what I had with you. If every rascal who deserved to be hanged went supperless to bed, there'd be an empty chair at many a table."

"True," replied Joaquin, "and you will never regret your hospitality. I will see that you lose nothing by it. I know how to requite a courtesy."

The bandit kept his word. Frequently after that, Cocariouris was on the road with large herds of cattle bound for market through a country harried by Murrieta's band. But not a head of his stock was ever stolen.

Joe Lake and Murrieta had been great friends in Saw Mill Flat. They had often had a social glass together; Lake had taken a fling now and then at Joaquin's monte table; and in the adobe under the pine tree on the hill, Lake had passed many a pleasant evening listening to Rosita sing songs to her guitar. From Saw Mill Flat, Lake moved to Jackson and opened a butcher shop. He built up a fine trade and was soon ranked among the town's influential citizens. He made many friends and was highly respected.

While riding along the road between Mokelumne Hill and Jackson, Lake was greatly surprised when Murrieta rode alongside and greeted him. The two had not seen each other since their days in Saw Mill Flat and it was a pleasure to both to meet again. With their horses at a walk, they rode together for a mile or so laughing and talking over old times.

"It's no news to you, Joe, that I'm an outlaw," said Joaquin. "But don't believe everything you hear about me. I'm not the devil they try to make me out. I don't ask the respect of an honest man like you but I'm going to ask you, as one of the best American friends I ever had, not to say anything about meeting me. There's a big price on my head. Officers are on the lookout for me. Many men would like nothing better than to kill or capture me. But in this country where I am unknown, I'm safe for the time being. I don't like to threaten an old friend but if you betray me, Joe, I will surely kill you."

"Don't worry, Joaquin," replied Lake. "Your affairs are none of my business. I'll keep my mouth shut about you. I promise you that and you can rely on my word."

But when Lake arrived in Jackson he had doubts about the wisdom of his promise and finally decided it was his duty to notify his fellow citizens of the presence of such a dangerous character in the vicinity. So he called on the *alcalde* and informed him and the news soon spread about the town.

Late next day Lake was having a drink with some friends at a bar on Jackson's main street when an old man with white hair falling about his shoulders and a white beard sweeping his breast pulled up his horse in front of the saloon.

"I wonder," he said to some loungers on the sidewalk, "if one of you men will step inside and tell Mr. Lake I'd like to see him?"

Lake came out of the saloon looking a little surprised. "You want to see me?"

"Just for a moment," the old man replied politely. "I have a little business to settle with you."

"Business? I don't remember ever having had any business dealings with you."

"Don't you recall the promise you made me?"

"I made you no promise. You must be mistaken in your man."

"You made me a very definite promise and I am sorry to say you have broken faith with me."

"I don't know what you're talking about. You must be crazy. I never saw you before in my life."

Lake turned away. He did not propose to be bothered by this old lunatic any longer.

"I'd like to say one thing more to you," urged the old man.

Lake wheeled and faced him angrily. "I don't know you, I tell you. Who the hell are you?"

"I am Joaquin Murrieta. I told you I would kill you if you betrayed me and I have come to keep my word."

The old man spoke very quietly. Not a flicker of change crossed his countenance. He looked feeble and doddering and perfectly harmless.

Lake's anger grew hotter. He shrugged contemptuously. This old fool evidently was trying to play a joke on him. An incredulous sneer was still on Lake's face as he fell dead.

Hornitos was one of the wildest and toughest towns in the mining country. It had 5,000 people in gold rush days—though to-day only twenty live among its ruins—and $50,000,000 in gold was taken from its mines. It was a main place for Mexicans and a favorite rendezvous of Murrieta and his men who found many pleasant ways there for spending their stolen money. Drinking and gambling were in riotous swing night and day and the saloons and dance halls swarmed with dusky sirens.

Juan Berreyesa was an old time member of the outlaw band but was now acting as a spy in Hornitos where he made his home. Cunning, bold and suave, he was regarded by Murrieta not only as an efficient confederate but a friend. Joaquin was living for a while beneath Berreyesa's roof. The two sat talking one evening in the front room.

"Town seems pretty quiet," remarked Joaquin.

"It's dead. Only two men shot last night and not a necktie party in a week."

"Guess I'll stroll down to Pedro's place and take a whirl at monte."

"Feeling lucky?"

"Let 'em break my way and I'll clean out the bank."

While Joaquin sat at the monte table he happened to drop his hand to his gun holster. It was empty. Strange. What had become of his revolver? Any minute without his weapon might prove fatal to him. He hurried back to Berreyesa's house and entered by the rear door. While fumbling in the dark for a candle, he heard voices in the adjoining room. One was Berreyesa's, the other evidently that of an American.

"One thousand dollars—that's my price."

"Bird in hand or no pay?"

"Do you take me for a fool? Cash down in advance."

"How do we know you'll not give us the slip once you've got your fingers on our money?"

"I'll play square with you."

"You're betraying him. You may betray us."

"I'll put him before your guns. That's all I can do."

"He might beat us at our own game."

"Then you lose both ways—your money and your man."

"Where'll it be?"

"Here in my house two hours from now. But I must

not be known in the affair. If his men learn I have betrayed him, my life will not be worth a red copper."

"I'll go get your money right now."

"Then we'll consider the deal closed."

When Joaquin heard retreating footsteps on the front walk, he opened the door between the two rooms and stood face to face with Berreyesa.

"So this is how you betray my friendship."

"Don't kill me Joaquin. On my knees I beg you not to kill me."

"A thousand dollars! Is my blood slough water?"

"Spare me—for the sake of our old friendship—spare me!"

"You traitor!"

"Spare me!"

Murrieta leaped at him like a tiger and buried a dagger in his heart.

Riding through the San Joaquin valley south of Stockton, with some of his followers, Murrieta spied two travelers ahead jogging in the same direction.

"I'll see how much money those *hombres* have in their pockets," he said and spurring his horse, quickly caught up with them.

"Hands up!" he cried with his six-shooter at a level.

"Why, hello, Joaquin," said one of the travelers laughing. "What's all this? You wouldn't rob an old friend? Don't you remember Bill Miller?"

"Of course I do," replied Joaquin. "I didn't get a good look at you."

Murrieta and Miller had been friends in old days in Murphy's Diggings.

"How are you, Bill?"

"Broke."

"You're riding a pretty good horse."

"But without a nickel in my pockets."

"How does that happen?"

"I heeled my last stack from the queen to the ace in Mariposa and the cards fell the wrong way."

"Will a hundred dollars do you any good?"

"I've got a long distance to go and I wouldn't mind a bite to eat on the way."

"Here you are. You've always been a good friend of mine. *Vaya con Dios.*"

Murrieta with several of his men arrived one night at a ferry on the Tuolomne river near Big Oak Flat. Thumping on the door of a cabin with the butts of their pistols, they aroused the ferryman.

"We want to get across," said Joaquin. "But first we would like all the money you have."

"You are robbers?" spluttered the frightened ferryman.

"O no," replied Joaquin. "We merely wish to borrow the money. We'll pay you back some day—maybe."

"We've got no time to lose," snapped Three Fingered Jack drawing his bowie. "Shell out quick or I'll work on you."

The ferryman handed over a purse containing a hundred dollars which he had concealed beneath his pillow.

"You'll have to dig up more than this," snarled Three Fingered Jack.

"That's all I've got."

"All?" asked Joaquin.

"Every cent in the world. I'm very poor. I make a bare living out of my ferry."

"Take back your purse then," said Murrieta. "There are plenty of rich fellows to rob. I don't need a poor man's money."

James J. Perry, one of the proprietors of the Sperry & Perry hotel in Murphy's Diggings, was a fighter and afraid of nothing that ever wore hair. He had been a bartender in early days when the price of a drink of whiskey was a pinch of gold dust taken from a buckskin pouch between the thumb and forefinger and when all bartenders, before being hired, were asked the stock question, "How much can you raise at a pinch?" Having large hands and being an expert pincher, Perry had been regarded as an ideal gold camp bartender, and in effete later times, when drinks were paid for in coin of the realm, he always acted as bartender in the hotel saloon.

When one day Joaquin Murrieta, Three Fingered Jack, Valenzuela, Vulvia, Claudio and Pedro Gonzalez —as hard a bunch of *hombres* as could have been raked together in California with a fine tooth comb—dismounted in front of the Sperry & Perry hotel and stalked into the saloon, there was Perry in his white apron behind the bar, beaming welcome and smiling in anticipation of the neat sum he would drop into his money drawer. For several hours the outlaws stood at the bar having a high old time over their liquor, and Perry, being a jovial person himself, told as many jokes and laughed as boisterously as any of them.

"Well, boys," said Murrieta at last, "we've had enough. Let's go."

The genial Perry set out the bottle for a last drink on the house. With a cheery chorus of *"Buena salud!"* the outlaws downed their liquor and started out of the saloon.

"Just a minute," said Perry. "How about paying for these drinks?"

"I am Joaquin," replied the robber chief drawing himself up proudly. "Joaquin never pays for drinks."

"Well, this is one time he does," roared Perry and stooping beneath the bar, he came up with a double-barreled shotgun at his shoulder.

Joaquin looked for a moment into the muzzle of the

gun and broke into a laugh. "You win, Jim," he said. Perry figured up the account in the expert way that had won him fame as a bartender in old days and Joaquin paid the bill to the last penny.

Mrs. Jennie Weslow of Sacramento owns a dagger given by Murrieta to her mother. The knife has a bone handle without a cross-guard and its blade is ten inches long. The lower part of the blade to an inch above the tip had once been poisoned, as was determined by a chemical test, and the stain on the steel left by the poison is still plainly visible.

"William and Maria Calloway, my father and mother," said Mrs. Weslow, "came to California across the plains from Kentucky in 1852, and lived at Simpson's Crossing on the Yuba three miles from Marysville. My father ran a pack train and was off in the mountains much of his time and my mother was often left at home alone. Mexicans had a bad name in those parts and not many people would take them in even for a night. But one day when a Mexican rode up to the house and asked if he could get board and lodging for a few days, my mother let him stay.

"He was a handsome young man, nicely dressed, and with the polite manners of a gentleman. His horse had the clean lines of a thoroughbred; the saddle was of carved leather and must have cost at least a thousand dollars, and saddle and bridle were richly ornamented with silver. He kept much to himself in his room and his horse always stood saddled and bridled in the barn. Though she was a little suspicious of this mysterious stranger, my mother, who was very young and very pretty, tempted his appetite with her best cookery and did all she could to make him comfortable.

"The day after he arrived, several swarthy men rode up and held a conference with him in his room. Soon after they left, he paid his bill and told my mother good-bye. As he sat on his horse at the door, he drew a dagger from his sash and presented it to her.

" 'I appreciate the courtesy you have shown me,' he said, 'and I want you to have this dagger to remember me by. I would advise you always to wear it. In this rough country you never know when you may be called on to defend your honor.'

"Then tipping his hat gallantly, he rode off and my mother never saw him again. He had not been gone half an hour when Sheriff Buchanan of Yuba county galloped up to the house with a posse. When my mother described her guest to him, the sheriff became quite excited. 'That's the fellow I'm looking for,' he said. 'That's Joaquin Murrieta.' "

At Martinez, some miners heard a cry of "Murder!" and hurrying to a cabin, found a German with his throat slashed and his pockets emptied. Two Mexicans seen running away were pursued but got into the brush and escaped. Shortly afterwards, Luis Vulvia rode to a saloon in town and was seized by a crowd while drinking at the bar. The miners were not sure of his guilt but, declaring he looked like one of the Mexicans who had fled from the cabin, they made preparations to hang him. Justice Brown, however, prevailed on them to turn him over to the civil authorities and Vulvia was locked in the calaboose to await legal trial. Vulvia owed his life only to the fact that he was not known in that vicinity. If the mob had been aware he was one of Murrieta's most famous captains, he would have been given short shrift.

While Vulvia was being tried next day before Justice Brown, a well-dressed man, speaking good English and apparently an American, walked into court.

"Your honor," he said, "you undoubtedly have the

wrong man under arrest. I would like to be heard in his behalf."

The justice took a long squint through his spectacles and being impressed by the stranger's prosperous appearance, told him to take the witness stand.

"What is your name?"

"Samuel Harrington."

"Very well, Mr. Harrington, proceed in your own way and tell what you know about this case."

"I am, your honor, a merchant of San Jose. I am on my way home from a freighting trip into the mountains and am camped five miles from here. Last night I sent one of my Mexican packers to town for some provisions and, much to my astonishment, he failed to return. Hearing by chance a Mexican was under arrest here for murder, it occurred to me that in some unaccountable way my hired man might have fallen into the clutches of the law. When I entered your court room, I saw at a glance this was true. The prisoner at the bar is my packer. He did not leave my camp until after dark and could not possibly have had any part in the murder. He has been in my employ for four years and I can vouch for his character. All his life he has been an honest, sober, hard-working fellow."

"Have you any way of proving your own identity, Mr. Harrington?"

"I happen to have some letters that I am sure will establish my identity to the complete satisfaction of the court."

The witness presented five or six letters to Justice Brown who read them carefully. All were addressed in a different hand to Mr. Samuel Harrington at San Jose and bore post-marks from various parts of the state.

"These letters, I may say, Mr. Harrington," declared Justice Brown, "are in every way convincing. There is no question in my mind that you are exactly what you represent yourself to be and that your testimony given under oath in this case has been the unvarnished truth. The evidence against the defendant was in the first place purely circumstantial. You have proved his innocence beyond all reasonable doubt and I hope you will accept the apologies of the court for the unfortunate mistake that has been made. The prisoner is discharged."

Murrieta and Vulvia rode out of town together and had a good laugh behind the first hill.

"But for you, Mr. Harrington, I undoubtedly should have stretched hemp," chuckled Vulvia. "But how did it happen you arrived just in the nick of time?"

"I struck your camp last night by accident," replied Joaquin. "Soon after I arrived, two of your men rode in with the news you were in trouble in Martinez. Then as luck would have it, I thought of the ruse that saved your bacon."

"But how did you come by those letters?"

"I killed this Samuel Harrington near Jackson a few days ago and took the letters from his pocket. If I had not had the good sense to keep them, you, Señor Vulvia, would be swinging from a live oak at this very minute. How much money, by the way, did you find on the German?"

"Not much. I had an idea he was well fixed but he turned out a sad disappointment."

"Well, better luck next time."

"You pulled the wool over the eyes of that wise old owl of a justice very neatly. Padre Jurata himself could not have done better. That bold rascal scrupled at nothing. Sometimes he saved a member of his band from the rope by appearing on the witness stand in his priestly robes and swearing to an alibi or he presented in court a forged pardon for some scamp to which he had signed the name of the governor of the state. When he was not robbing travelers at pistol's point on the highway, he was telling his beads in cowl and cassock. He heard so many scandalous secrets in the confessional he had no trouble in levying blackmail in huge sums on some of the wealthiest and most aristocratic men and women in Mexico. One of the cleverest rogues that ever took a purse or slit a throat was that Padre Jurata. God rest his soul!"

A physician of San Andreas was summoned by a Mexican to visit a patient in the country who had been shot. Taking his surgical case and saddle-bags, the physician rode with the man to Bear Mountain and came at length to a small waterfall in a wild cañon. Here a heavily armed man stepped from the brush.

"I will act as your guide now," he said. "But from here on, you must be blindfolded."

"I will submit to no such indignity," declared the physician.

The fellow waved his arm about his head. A dozen swarthy bravos rose from the chaparral with a loud cocking of six-shooters and the doctor was blindfolded. A few miles farther on, the bandage was removed and he found himself at the mouth of a cave high on a mountain. In an open space sheltered by a projecting rock, a man lay on some blankets suffering from a dangerous bullet wound through the lungs. Having dressed the wound, the physician told the outlaws grouped about that it would be impossible for two or three days to determine whether the patient would survive. Then he started for his horse."

"You will remain here, doctor," said his guide, "until the crisis is past."

"Impossible. I have other serious cases requiring my attention. But to satisfy you, I will pledge my professional honor not to reveal your hiding-place."

As half a dozen revolvers slid out of their scabbards, a

young man of striking appearance stepped from the cavern. He wore a white shirt, black pants and half-boots and a scarf of deep scarlet was twisted around his waist. The doctor noted with a touch of admiration his clean-cut features and flashing black eyes.

"I am Joaquin Murrieta," said the young man, pausing a second to note the effect of the name. "I see the justice of your refusal to remain here. I will trust in your honor. Come again day after to-morrow. I myself will meet you at the waterfall."

The blindfold having been adjusted again, the doctor was conducted back to the San Andreas trail. On the second day, he rode to the trysting place. But he was met, not by a handsome young man, but by a brutal looking Mexican with unkempt whiskers who saluted him with a grunt as he bound his eyes. Arrived at the cave, the doctor found his patient much improved.

"It seems," said the doctor to his guide, "your leader is not a man of his word. He did not keep his promise to meet me at the waterfall."

The guide made a few quick movements with his hands. In an instant he had changed into the youthful Murrieta. The transformation seemed magical. Murrieta laughed at the doctor's amazement.

Twice again in the next few weeks, the physician visited the cave. By that time the patient was making a rapid recovery.

"My services are now at an end," the doctor said to Murrieta on his last visit. "I have done my duty as a physician. Now I must do my duty as a citizen. So far I have kept my word with you. But to-morrow I will report your whereabouts to the authorities. In fairness to you I give you this warning."

It was past midnight when the doctor was called to the bedside of a girl known in San Andreas as Joaquina. She was at the time Murrieta's sweetheart and the doctor had attended her a number of times before. He found her in a violent state of hysteria and under the care of a rather prepossessing Mexican girl. The physician gave her an opiate and she soon fell into a quiet sleep. The good looking attendant accompanied the doctor to the door.

"I am Joaquin Murrieta's sister," said the girl.

"Ah, I thought I detected a resemblance."

"I will tell you a secret if you will promise me to keep it for only half an hour."

The physician looked at his watch. It was 2 o'clock in the morning.

"I will give you my word."

"Joaquin is in San Andreas. He has been to see Joaquina and has told her you have sworn to report him to-morrow. Her alarm for his safety brought on her attack."

"Joaquin is bold. Venturing into San Andreas is like putting his head into a lion's mouth. Since I have become acquainted with Joaquin, I am willing to admit—at least to his sister—that I rather like him. If you could arrange it, I would like to see him to-night for the last time and tell him good-bye."

"You would not recognize him. He is in disguise."

"Absurd. I would know him at once. He tricked me the first time. But I made it a point to study him. I have impressed every detail of his face and figure on my mind. He could assume no disguise that I could not instantly penetrate."

"You seem quite sure of it."

"Of course I'm sure. He could never fool me again."

"Come with me, doctor," said the girl and she led him into an inner room where a lamp was burning. There with lightning-like rapidity she passed her hands over her face and hair, threw off her garments, rolled down the legs of a pair of pants that had been hidden beneath her skirt and rose before the astounded physician a smiling, handsome young man with clean-cut features and flashing black eyes—Joaquin Murrieta.

When he had returned to his office, the doctor heard the tattoo of a horse's hoofs in the street and looking from the window saw a cloaked figure, leaning forward in the saddle, go flying past. It was 2:30 by his watch. The time limit of his silence had expired. He hurried to the residence of Deputy Sheriff Charles Ellis and thumped loudly on his door.

"Come quick, Ellis," he said in great excitement. "Joaquin Murrieta has this minute ridden out of San Andreas. We have a fine chance to capture him."

The deputy sheriff yawned. "The same chance a stump-tailed bull has in fly time. Go on home, doc, and go to bed." *

* This story, written as a personal experience by the doctor himself, appeared in the Argonaut in 1876. It was signed "B. R.," whose address at that time was given as Healdsburg.

CHAPTER X.

HARVARD MAN.

CALEB DORSEY, who practiced law with a six-shooter buckled around him and was not averse to enforcing the statutes with the noose of a good hemp rope, was a graduate of Harvard and a member of a distinguished Maryland family. Belmont, the ancestral estate of the Dorseys in Maryland, was originally a land grant from George II of England to Caleb and Priscilla Dorsey, the first American forebears of the family. When Caleb Dorsey went to California by way of the Isthmus of Panama in the gold rush of 1849, he took a law library with him with the intention of setting up in practice in San Francisco. But the lure of gold laid its hold upon him and he followed the stampede into the foothills.

At Shaw's Flat where he first located, he went into mining with a Swede sailor who had run away from his ship in the Bay. Dorsey was taken down with typhoid fever and while he was being nursed through a long illness by Tom Gilman, the former slave, his jack-tar partner dug $25,000 in gold from a pocket on their joint claim. As Dorsey had taken no part in the mining operations, he waived his claim to a share in the treasure but the Swede, being a square buddy, divided it with him. With this stake, Dorsey and two partners went into the lumber business and started a saw mill at Saw Mill Flat under the firm name of Dorsey, Jacobs & Smith. He moved later to Sonora where he settled down permanently to the practice of law. He built in 1850 the first brick residence in Sonora, in which still live his two daughters, Miss Elizabeth M. Dorsey and Miss Anita E. Dorsey, cultured and charming ladies of the old school. He died in 1885.

"For a Harvard man, my father had some rather startling adventures," said Miss Elizabeth Dorsey. "He had two personal encounters with Joaquin Murrieta who at one time had marked him for death. He camped one night with a band of Murrieta's outlaws who had sworn to kill him but did not suspect his identity. As a member of a vigilance committee, he assisted in the capture of the celebrated Claudio and as a lawyer he defended him after his capture. He led a fight against crooked gamblers in Sonora, forced them to surrender after they had barricaded themselves in a building on the site of the modern Sonora Inn, and with the vigilance committee at his back, marched them to the county line at Knights Ferry. He was in five stage coaches when they were robbed by highwaymen. The famous Black Bart officiated with a shotgun in three of these hold-ups, twice near Copperopolis and again on the trail between Sonora and Brown's Flat.

"My father knew all the famous characters of this part of the country in early days and had many entertaining anecdotes about them. Some of his choicest stories concerned Justice Barry, the autocratic old curmudgeon and ignoramus, whose high-handed methods would have been a joke if they had not been a tragedy. When Barry finally wearied of Sonora and Sonora wearied of him, he sailed from San Francisco for his former home in the East taking with him a large amount of gold in a carpet bag and a magpie that he had taught to speak a few words and of which he was immensely fond. During a storm at sea when the ship's company had to take to the life boats, Barry had his choice of saving his gold or his magpie. Without hesitation, he saved the magpie and let the gold go to the bottom."

Black Bart, incidentally, has but three rivals among the traditional heroes of the mining country—Bret Harte, Mark Twain and Joaquin Murrieta. He had no confederates in his crimes; he operated entirely alone. Of the twenty-eight stage coaches he robbed, he held up the first near Copperopolis in 1873 and the last at exactly the same spot in 1883. After robbing a stage, he used to leave in the looted treasure box, some doggerel verses scribbled in pencil on a Wells-Fargo way-bill and signed "Black Bart, PO8." One of his poetic effusions, for example, ran thus:

> I've labored hard for daily bread
> For honor and for riches.
> But on my feet too oft you've tread,
> You fine-haired sons of bitches.

He accidentally dropped a silk handkerchief and a linen cuff in leaving the scene of his last robbery and was traced by a laundry mark on the cuff and arrested in San Francisco. During the ten years of his criminal career he had lived quietly in that city. He was fine looking and affable, had a wide acquaintance and was generally supposed to be a mining man in easy circumstances. He dressed in expensively tailored clothes, wore a derby hat and carried a light walking stick. He had blue eyes, iron gray hair, mustache and imperial, and at the time of his arrest was forty-five years old. He never drank, smoked or chewed tobacco. He was a great reader. A number of books rated as literary classics were found in his room, and a well-thumbed bible.

He was convicted at his trial in San Andreas and sent to San Quentin penitentiary. Through the influence of the Wells-Fargo Express Company, whose strong boxes he had made a specialty of plundering, he was pardoned after serving three years and was taken into the company's employ. He drew a fine salary and had nothing to do but report at the San Francisco office for a few minutes every day and refrain from robbing stages. But after his life of romantic adventure, this monotonous routine palled upon him and he suddenly and mysteriously vanished. No one knows what became of him. He was never heard of again. His real name was Charles E. Bolton.

Caleb Dorsey was a man of great courage and a stout champion of law and order. While living at Shaw's Flat, he acted as prosecutor at the lynch court that tried Janori and Antonio Cruz for the killing of Snow and took part in hanging the two murderers. When he located his saw mill at Saw Mill Flat, Murrieta and his band were holding high carnival in the surrounding country, and Dorsey lost no time in organizing a vigilance committee with the announced intention of exterminating the outlaws. He led a number of posses into the hills on the hunt for them and his determined war upon them brought on his head the wrath of Murrieta, who swore to kill him and hunted Dorsey as relentlessly as Dorsey hunted him.

Word reached Dorsey one night that Joaquin was at that moment present at a dance at a fandango house in Martinez half a mile from Saw Mill Flat. With a dozen men, Dorsey hurried to Martinez. The possemen filed into the dance hall so unobtrusively that the dance, then in full swing, was not interrupted. From positions along the walls, they scrutinized the crowd but saw no one resembling Murrieta. When the music ceased, they drew their six-shooters and began to question the dancers. All denied the outlaw leader had been there. A bearded Mexican, rather cheaply dressed and smoking a cigarette, spoke to Dorsey.

"Who are you fellows looking for?" he asked. "Joaquin Murrieta? Ho, ho! That's a good one. What would he be doing here? Do you think that robber with a price on his head would attend a public dance? Not he. That fellow is too wise to take a chance like that. He knows on which side his bread is buttered."

"We had reliable information that he was at the dance," said Dorsey.

"Somebody must have been having fun with you."

"Hasn't he been here to-night?"

"That's a joke. He hasn't been here and I'd like to gamble he hasn't been within twenty miles of here."

"Have you any idea where he is?"

"No more idea than you. But out in the hills somewhere and safe wherever he is. You can bet on that. You see what a fox he is? If he had come to the dance to-night, he would be a dead man at this minute or you fellows would have had a pair of handcuffs on him."

"That's the truth if you ever told it. If he'd been here, we'd have taken him or killed him."

"He's a pretty dangerous fellow. I wouldn't want to crowd him too close. I don't think you'll ever take him alive."

"It would suit us just as well to take him dead."

"Do you know him?"

"No, I've never seen him but some of the fellows with me know him."

"They could identify him as soon as they saw him?"

"No doubt about it."

"They say Joaquin can disguise himself so his best friends can't recognize him."

"Bosh."

"Well, that's what I've heard."

"Don't believe any such nonsense."

The music started up. "There's my girl over there,"

said the Mexican, and he strolled across the room and whirled off in a waltz with a pretty señorita.

Some of his Martinez friends surprised Dorsey next day by telling him that the Mexican with whom he had been talking at the dance was Joaquin Murrieta himself.

Dorsey's saw mill was burned to the ground a few nights later and his horses and cows were found dead in his corral. A spring that supplied the drinking trough with water had been poisoned. Murrieta sent word to Dorsey, Ira McRae and John Turner that they would be killed within three weeks. McRae kept the largest store in Saw Mill Flat and Turner was a saw mill owner. Both had been active in Dorsey's campaign. Turner was frightened into leaving the country. Dorsey and McRae refused to be terrorized.

Saw Mill Flat's population had dwindled to a few hundred since boom days. When a citizen announced he had received secret information that Murrieta was preparing to sack the town and massacre the inhabitants, wild excitement prevailed which grew into panic when it was reported McRae's merchandise establishment was to be robbed and burned on a certain night. In its desperate situation, Saw Mill Flat appealed to Columbia for assistance. Columbia dispatched its company of militia under Captain Tom Cazeneau. The soldiers with feathers in their caps marched into town, laughing and shouting as if on a picnic and dragging along a small brass cannon used on great days for firing salutes. This formidable piece of ordnance having been planted in a commanding position where, if the occasion arose, it could rake the main street with withering broadsides, McRae's store was strongly garrisoned, a line of pickets was thrown around the town and squads with fixed bayonets patrolled the streets.

The night of the expected attack passed without incident. Two more nights came and went and the threatened outlaw invasion failed to materialize. In the meantime, the town's defenders must eat. As no civic arrangements had been made for their sustenance, they solved their own problem. They had been called out on this warlike expedition primarily in the interest of McRae. What more logical than that he in his gratitude should fill their stomachs? Before their ravenous onslaughts, everything edible in the store disappeared and was washed down with every drop of liquor behind the bar. When finally the troops marched gayly out of town, McRae viewed his empty shelves sadly but was thankful he had a few stray yards of dry goods left in stock. Saw Mill Flat had been saved but, according to a historian, it remained doubtful in the minds of the citizens, especially McRae, whether it might not have been better to be robbed by Joaquin than protected by the soldiery.

Soon after he had moved to Sonora, Dorsey rode one day through Calaveras on his way home from a trip into the high country. Some men in the town who knew him stopped him.

"Keep your eyes about you, Dorsey," they said. "Murrieta knows you are out alone in these parts and he's got a bunch of cut-throats scouring the woods for you. Better nor follow the trail. They might waylay you. Cut across the hills. That'll be safest."

Dorsey took their advice. He knew he was marked for death and he had grown instinctively wary. Riding across rough country with no landmarks to guide him, he lost his way. Darkness came before he found his bearings and he built a brush fire in the timber and prepared to camp for the night. He had nothing to eat. While he sat smoking his pipe and meditating sourly upon his hard-luck day and supperless evening, six Mexicans rode up and went into camp near him. Their flashy dress and the rich accoutrements of their handsome horses led him at once to suspect they were outlaws and doubtless the ones who were hunting him and meant to kill him.

But if there were such a thing as murder on their minds, it apparently did not in the least worry them. They were as jolly a bunch of Mexicans as Dorsey had ever seen, and when they had cooked supper, they hallooed to him in a blithe, comradely way to come over and share it with them. Dorsey went. Pangs of hunger outweighed his uneasiness. If he were going to be killed, he might as well have the satisfaction of stowing a square meal under his belt before he died. That was the way he looked at it. He did not remember ever having seen any of the Mexicans before and he was greatly relieved to find that obviously none of the Mexicans knew him. After supper, all lounged around on the grass smoking cigarettes and talking in high spirits and Dorsey, who spoke Spanish almost as well as he did English, joined in the conversation.

"Do you know a lawyer named Dorsey in Sonora?" a one-eyed Mexican asked him.

"I know him slightly," replied Dorsey. "I meet him about town every once in a while."

"What kind of a looking fellow is he?"

"He's a very tall man, lean and raw-boned with piercing black eyes and long, coal-black hair."

Dorsey in fact was of medium height, well set up and had brown hair and gray eyes.

"We've never seen him—yet. But when we do see him, something's going to happen to him."

"What?"

"We'll kill him like a dog."

"What's Dorsey done to you?"

"He sticks his nose too much in our business. We'll shoot that nose off of him some day."

The Mexicans burst into loud guffaws at this sally.

"I take it," remarked Dorsey laughing, "you people don't like Dorsey any too well."

"Dorsey," the one-eyed man went on, "is on Joaquin's black list. He'll be scratched off only when he's dead. When Joaquin says a man must die, he dies."

"Dorsey's not a bad fellow."

"Do you know how many men have taken an oath to kill him?"

"How many?"

"Not fewer than twenty. Do you think with twenty men sworn to kill him, he can escape? He's got no more chance than a rabbit."

"Have you any objections to my telling Dorsey this?"

"Tell him the first time you meet him, if you like. It won't do him any good or us any harm. We'll get him sooner or later and no doubt about it."

This interesting little colloquy having ended, the Mexicans sang songs for a half hour or so. They had good voices and filled the pine woods with such lively airs as *"El Grullo," "La Vaquilla," "El Tuza," "El Maracumbe,"* and other popular songs of old Mexico. The one-eyed cut-throat, Dorsey noticed, was the loudest singer of them all.

Dorsey went back to his own camp and everybody curled up in his blankets and went to sleep. Next morning, the genial scoundrels invited Dorsey to have breakfast with them. When he had eaten, he mounted his horse and rode off for Sonora.

"Adios," the Mexicans called after him cheerily. *"Vaya con Dios."*

A Mexican arrested as a horse-thief was lodged in jail in Sonora. He asked for a lawyer and Dorsey was called. When Dorsey arrived and peered through the cell bars, he saw a one-eyed Mexican, thunder-struck with astonishment, staring back at him.

"Are you Dorsey?" exclaimed the one-eyed prisoner.

Dorsey laughed. "Yes, I'm Dorsey."

"Valgame Dios!"

"What's the matter?"

"So you're Dorsey?"

"Nobody else."

"Well, Dorsey, if you're as good a lawyer as you are a liar, I want you to take my case."

"But you're one of the men sworn to kill me."

"Under the circumstances, we'll forget that. But if we'd known who you were when we had you out in the woods all by yourself, I'd have to find another attorney."

"My services come high. Have you any money?"

"Don't worry about your money. I have plenty and my friends have plenty more."

"That being the case, I'm ready to defend you."

"Do you think you can clear me? Of course, I'm guilty."

"I always do my best for my clients."

"Clear me, Dorsey, and I'll square you with Joaquin. Everything I told you the other night is true. Every member of the band has instructions from Murrieta to shoot you on sight. But if you clear me, I'll take the curse off you. You can take my solemn word on that. I am strong with the chief. He will regard the promise I make to you as sacred and give orders that it be carried out."

Dorsey handled the case in court and the one-eyed horse-thief went free.

Constable John Leary of Columbia arrested a Mexican in Saw Mill Flat for stealing a pistol. Several Mexicans rushed to the rescue of the prisoner. Leary drew his gun and started shooting. The Mexicans returned the fire. Citizens ran to the constable's assistance, Dorsey among them. A lively little battle developed. A dozen shots were fired at a Mexican who leaped on his horse and galloped out of town. This Mexican was said to have been Murrieta. Another of the Mexicans was wounded. He ran into the brush and trudged weakly up a hillside. At the top of the hill he fell. The citizens closed in on him. Lying on the ground, the Mexican emptied two six-shooters at them as they advanced. When his ammunition was exhausted, Leary and Dorsey rushed upon him. In a murderous rage, the constable stuck a cocked six-shooter in the Mexican's face and in another second would have blown out his brains if Dorsey had not knocked the weapon aside. The Mexican whose life Dorsey saved proved to be Claudio, one of the most noted sub-chiefs in Murrieta's band.

Claudio was taken to a hospital in Sonora where he lay with a dangerous wound for several weeks. When he was sufficiently recovered, he was placed in jail. He sent for Dorsey and engaged him as his lawyer.

"You saved my life in Saw Mill Flat," said Claudio. "Now let's see if you can save my neck. It is true Murrieta has sworn vengeance against you. But if you get me out of this trouble, I promise you that you can ride from one end of this country to the other and no harm shall ever befall you."

"On what security do you make me this promise?" asked Dorsey.

"Sir," responded Claudio proudly, "you have the word of honor of a highwayman."

"That," said Dorsey with a grin, "ought to be good enough for anybody."

"Moreover," added Claudio, "if you win my case for me, I will make you a present of the finest horse you ever owned—a splendid animal with gorgeous trappings."

The grand jury failed to indict Claudio. The Sonora Herald commented on its failure to return a true bill against a notorious robber as an inexplicable neglect of duty. It was whispered that Dorsey could have explained the mystery. But he merely smiled enigmatically and kept his mouth shut.

While on his way to Mariposa to attend a session of court, Dorsey saw some Mexicans camped at noon near the trail where it crossed Moccasin creek. He was riding on past when he heard himself hailed vociferously and saw Claudio coming toward him waving his hand in cordial greeting.

"So it is you, Señor Dorsey," said Claudio beaming joyously. "We are just having dinner. You must stop and take a bite with us. It is a great pleasure to meet you again."

Dorsey had had a long ride and was hungry, and dismounting, he accompanied Claudio into the brush to where half a dozen outlaws were at their meal seated on the grass around a smouldering fire.

"This is my friend, Señor Dorsey," Claudio announced to the band. "I owe him much. He saved my life when, if it had not been for him, I surely would have been killed, and he got me out of jail as slick as a whistle when it looked very much as if I would stretch hemp. Señor Dorsey is the best lawyer in this country and one of the finest men that ever stood in shoe leather. Take a good look at him so you will all know him if you ever see him again. Rob anybody you like at any time. Kill anybody that needs killing. But keep your hands off Señor Dorsey. He must never be molested in any way. That is my wish and it is Joaquin's command."

With this flattering introduction, Dorsey sat down among the outlaws and ate a hearty dinner.

"By the way," he said to Claudio as he prepared to continue his journey, "I have never seen hide or hair of that splendid horse with gorgeous trappings that you promised to give me."

"Ah, Señor Dorsey, I have not forgotten my promise," Claudio answered. "That animal will be munching oats in your barn before very long. We are now on our way south. That is good horse country. When we return, you shall have the finest horse in California."

"With gorgeous trappings and everything?"

"O yes. A saddle and bridle, silver mounted and of the finest leather. Andres Pico himself, that magnificent old peacock, has none better than I will give you."

As Dorsey with his horse at a walk mounted a hill between Big Oak Flat and Mariposa, a Mexican of gallant bearing, dressed in gay vaquero costume and superbly mounted, came cantering toward him along the road. Something about the face and figure reminded Dorsey vaguely of the Mexican he had met at the fandango in Martinez and he quickly drew his six-shooter. He sensed rather than knew that the horseman was Murrieta and the recognition was mutual. Within a few paces of him, the outlaw chief drew rein and gave him a friendly salute.

"Put up your gun, Señor Dorsey," he said. "You are in no danger. Pass in peace. Joaquin Murrieta never breaks his word."

Claudio found his "good horse country" a few weeks later. With six of his men—the same six doubtless with whom Dorsey ate dinner on the Mariposa road—he raided many ranches in the Salinas valley and seriously depleted many herds of horses. His ravages were so bold and extensive that John Cocks, justice of the peace at Salinas, raised a posse and started out to run the outlaws down. Cocks was a lion of a man. All he wanted was seven other men as stout-hearted as himself to go after seven horse-thieves trained in Murrieta's cut-throat school, and that was all he took along. He had an advantage over the outlaws of only one man.

On the Salinas river near Cooper's Crossing, a man named Balder lived in an adobe house under some cottonwood trees in an unfrequented part of the valley. Balder's ranch was known as a shelter for criminals of all sorts and Balder himself had a shady reputation. To this thieves' rendezvous, Squire Cocks trailed Claudio's band. It was night and a full moon hung over the mountains. Taking off their spurs so the jingle of the rowels would give no alarm, the Americans silently surrounded the house. But a watch dog stirred uneasily. "Woof!" said the watch dog tentatively. That dog thought he heard something suspicious but was not quite sure. He would test the matter out. "Woof, woof!" he remarked again in a conversational tone. That did the work. He not only heard something but saw something. He was certain this time. Then came a rolling thunder of barks that ran the gamut of canine menace and viciousness. Boo—woo—boo—woo—woo! The hullabaloo could have been guaranteed to awaken every outlaw sleeping within ten miles.

Throwing precautions to the wind, Cocks stepped boldly to the door and hammered upon it with the butt of his six-shooter. The door flew open. Out came rushing Claudio and his six followers with a rattle and blaze of guns. The Americans welcomed them with a deadly six-shooter blast. Several of the outlaws went down. Crouching for a moment in the deep shadow of the adobe wall, Claudio emptied his revolver. Without a shot left in its cylinder, he made a dash to break through the ring of fire. But he blundered straight into Squire Cocks' arms and was held helpless in a grasp of steel. Claudio dropped his useless weapon to the ground.

"Estoy dado, señor," he cried. *"No tengo armas."* (I surrender, sir. I have no arms.)

Cocks, official bulwark of law and guardian of the

peace, did not wish to kill him. Content to take him prisoner, he released his hold. Claudio sprang back. Stooping quickly, he jerked a huge knife from one of his leggings and made a savage lunge. Cocks dodged nimbly aside. At the same moment, his six-shooter spurted fire and Claudio fell dead at his feet.

The door yard of Balder's house had been turned into a shambles during the sharp little battle. Six outlaws sprawled lifeless in the moonlight. None of the Americans was injured. One of the robbers escaped. Zigzagging among the cottonwoods, he struck across the river that was shallow and full of sand bars and lost himself in the hills. He was captured later and sent to San Quentin penitentiary. Soon after his release from prison, he was taken in a crime and hanged by a mob.

So farewell to Claudio, youthful desperado, handsome, dashing and of fiery courage. He is known in tradition as one of the smartest and most daring of Murrieta's lieutenants and as the well-beloved friend of the outlaw leader. Claudio in death kept his record clear. Bold, resourceful and treacherous he had been in life, and bold, resourceful and treacherous he remained in his last tragic moment. He fought until he could fight no longer. Fate, the remorseless and inevitable, caught him as Squire Cocks' arms closed about him. He tricked Squire Cocks but he could not trick fate. His hour had come and his last desperate stratagem was in vain. *"Es destino,"* the Mexicans say when misfortune comes to them. It was destiny.

"I would be willing to wager a small sum," remarked Caleb Dorsey in Sonora, "that Claudio got himself killed by hunting a little too eagerly for the splendid horse with gorgeous trappings that, on the honor of a highwayman, he had promised to give me."

CHAPTER XI.

HANG TREE.

HANG trees were peculiar to the gold camps of early California. Every camp, that had any civic pride about it, had its hang tree. If a hang tree stood on the main street, it gave a town class. The citizens swelled out their chests with a sense of superiority and expressed condescending sympathy for less fortunate villages. It was too much trouble to drag a man into the hills merely to hang him. With a hang tree conveniently located in the heart of town, a criminal could be swung off between drinks with hardly an appreciable interruption to a poker game. Since the men of gold rush days must drink and gamble and occasionally hang one of their fellow men, the hang tree ranked with saloons and faro banks as a public necessity.

The psychological effect of a hang tree was not to be denied. It was a moral and restraining influence. It stood as a monumental warning to men to tread softly and be good, decent citizens. It seemed to say: "Watch your step or the hang tree will get you." It destroyed evil doers that the good might enjoy normal conditions of life. It was like the hair-trigger marshals of the old frontier who established peace by shooting a town full of law and order.

But despite its important civic duties, the hang tree was a tree of sinister import. Its very aspect seemed clouded by the tragedies in which it had taken part. It was a tree apart—a tree that had fallen into wicked ways and become malign and venomous. Those who viewed it as a necessary evil held it in secret dread and loathing. Its status was like that of Samson, the old-time headsman of the guillotine, of whom all people stood in horror while they recognized the value of his cold-blooded and atrocious efficiency. The hang tree's leaves twinkled as merrily as those of other trees; its massed foliage held the same sunny gleams and cool shadows; it crooned the same lullabies when the breeze stirred its branches. But men who admired its beauty, crossed the street to avoid walking beneath its haunted shade. When the stars sparkled in the sky, it stood in the clear darkness like a grim specter seemingly ready to reach out a skeleton hand and clutch those who ventured near it. On a night of storm, its weird and dismal creaking was like the wail of lost spirits. The hang tree was a living gallows. It was a green, umbrageous drama whose big climaxes were dead men.

The three most famous of the hang trees were at Jackson, Second Garrote and Placerville. The one at Placerville was a white oak; the other two were live oaks. Only the one at Second Garrote is still standing. Placerville's hang tree was felled to make way for a business building. The one at Jackson was so badly burned in a fire that almost destroyed the town in 1862 that it was cut down. Three men were hanged on Placerville's tree, six on that at Second Garrote and ten on the one at Jackson. The first man was hanged on the Jackson tree in 1850, the last in 1855.

The Placerville tree figured as a hang tree on only one occasion when three men were hanged who had murdered a Frenchman who kept a trading post in Log Cabin ravine. This was the first hanging in the mining country. It took place February 12, 1849, and gave the new camp its name of Hangtown by which it was known for several years. The hang tree stood at what is now the corner of Main and Coloma Streets. The three men hanged on it were buried on the north bank of Hangtown creek and over their graves was erected the plant of the Mountain Democrat which was published there for twenty years.

The hanging of Richard Crone, known as Irish Dick, in October 1850 was another of Placerville's famous affairs. If the citizens of those days had realized the publicity value of a hang tree to a town in modern times, they would have built up the record of the original hang tree, but they overlooked an opportunity and strung up Irish Dick on another tree.

Irish Dick, a dapper young gambler who dealt monte in the El Dorado saloon, killed a miner in a quarrel over a wager on the layout. Two thousand miners swarmed into town from the diggings to avenge their comrade's murder. Court was held in the middle of the main street, Justice Humphreys presiding, and the prisoner was sentenced to death. As Uncle Billy Rogers, the sheriff, was preparing to take him to jail at Coloma, the county seat, the mob dropped the noose of a lariat over Irish Dick's head and dragged him to an oak that stood near the site of the modern Presbyterian parsonage on Coloma street. With the crowd roaring around him, the young gambler said coolly: "Don't be impatient, gentlemen. I'll soon give you a good layout." He asked to be permitted to climb the tree and jump down to make sure his neck would be broken instantly. But the privilege was denied him and Irish Dick was lifted into eternity.

The record of the hang tree at Second Garrote is vague. The tree flings its branches across the road near the house in which, according to Bret Harte's famous story, Tennessee and his partner lived. The names of the six men hanged on it, the dates of their execution, and the crimes for which they died, seem to have been forgotten. Old timers will say nonchalantly, "Six men were hanged on that tree," and that is all they know about it. But the record of Jackson's hang tree, the star hang tree of the mining region, is definitely authentic.

The Jackson tree had two branching trunks and one of its limbs, on which all ten men were hanged, stretched half across the highway. It stood on the main street in front of the Astor House near Louis Tellier's saloon. The spot is now unmarked. It is just off the curb opposite the old Pioneer saloon across whose bar soft drinks are sold in this prohibition era. Jackson is to-day a town of three thousand people. An engraved picture of the hang tree adorns the official seal of Amador county.

Here is the tree's record:

1. Coyote Joe, an Indian who killed a blacksmith. Hanged 1850.

2. A Chileno, who stabbed an old man to death and was hanged a half hour after the murder. (1850).

3. Jose Cheverino, who killed two Frenchmen at Squaw Gulch. (1851).

4. Cruz Flores, Cheverino's accomplice. (1851).

5. Antonio Valencia. (1853).

6. A Mexican of unknown name who robbed a Chinese camp at Cook's Gulch and killed a Chinaman. (1854).

7. A Swiss named Schwartz, a horse thief. (1854).

8. A Mexican captured by Chinese while plundering their camp. (1855).

9. Manuel Garcia. (1855).

10. Rafael Escobar. (1855).

Of these men, Antonio Valencia, Manuel Garcia and Rafael Escobar were veterans of outlaw service under Joaquin Murrieta. Garcia and Escobar paid the penalty at a rope's end for their part in a massacre at Rancheria in which six white men, a woman, and an Indian were murdered. Escobar, the hang tree's last victim, went to his death August 15, 1855.

Cheverino stabbed two Frenchmen to death at Squaw Gulch while robbing their store. He was arrested in Sacramento by Sheriff Waterman H. Nelson and was taken back to Jackson handcuffed to another Mexican suspected of stealing a horse. A mob took the two prisoners from the sheriff. When Blacksmith Martell had cut the chain of the handcuffs, the Mexican suspect was led apart by Allen, proprietor of the Union hotel.

"Did you steal that horse?" Allen demanded.

"No," replied the Mexican.

Allen pointed to the road leading out of town. "You *sabe este camino?*" he asked.

"Si, señor."

"Then git."

Cheverino was tried before Justice Bruce Husband and found guilty. The mob marched him to the hang tree. Twice the rope was placed around his neck and twice it was cut by Sheriff Nelson after it had been thrown over a limb. At the third trial, the Mexican shot into the air. But the crowd had neglected to bind his hands. Catching the rope, Cheverino loosened it from about his neck and fell to the ground. He had stoutly maintained his innocence before but now, facing certain death, he confessed his guilt. Again he was strung up. This time his hands were tied behind him.

Cruz Flores, a lad in his teens, was arrested a month later and tried before a lynch court. His guilt was not satisfactorily proved and he was turned over to the civil authorities. As he was being taken to jail, several hundred French miners, armed with shotguns and pistols, made a rush for the prisoner. During the struggle, the boy's arm was broken. The Frenchmen got him into their custody in the end and he was strung up. As he twisted in the noose, one of the Frenchmen hung on his legs till life was extinct.

Murrieta and his band raided a Chinese camp near Jackson early in 1853, killed five Chinamen and rode off with $7,000. In the pursuit of the robbers, Antonio Valencia was wounded and later captured at Lancha Plana where a Mexican woman betrayed his hiding place. Valencia, a grim fellow, refused the ministrations of a priest and refused to confess. A mob took him from the Jackson jail and hanged him.

Schwartz, a native of Switzerland, stole a horse from Evans & Askey's livery barn. Captured at Bridgeport, he was brought back to Jackson by the sheriff. As the prisoner rode into town at the sheriff's side at sunrise, a dozen citizens who had been playing poker all night, dragged him from his saddle and tried him on the steps of the Louisiana House. In ten minutes he was found guilty.

"You are sentenced to be hanged," said the judge of the court of twelve poker players.

Schwartz did not understand. He spluttered something in German that was equally incomprehensible to the court. But the noose of a hemp rope, it seemed, needed no interpreter and Schwartz went to his doom on the hang tree. Then the court adjourned to Louis Tellier's saloon and played a jackpot for a gold ring taken from the dead man's finger.

Two Mexicans had hard luck in attempting to rob a Chinese camp four miles from Jackson in 1854. One was stunned by a blow from a Chinaman's hatchet and was captured. The other escaped. Wildly excited and jabbering crazily, the Chinamen wound a rope about the prisoner from head to foot so that hardly an inch of his body was visible between the coils, and then sent to Jackson for help. When a force of whites arrived they found the Mexican so rigid in his bonds that he could not bend and with ropes stretching tautly in a circle around him and made fast to stakes driven in the ground. The Americans took the Mexican to Jackson and the hang tree was his gallows.

The Rancheria massacre in August 1855, aroused intense excitement. Twelve Mexican bandits took part in it, all of whom, it was established, had been members of Murrieta's band. The robbers were first seen at Hacalitas. They were well mounted and each carried two six-shooters at his belt. They were a hard-looking outfit and made no pretense of being anything but robbers. From Hacalitas they moved leisurely to Drytown, plundering several Chinese camps on the way. They rode into Drytown at nightfall and had supper in a Mexican restaurant in Chile Flat. Terrified by the invasion of these armed strangers, a Mexican woman hurried to Deputy Sheriff George Durham. "The town is full of robbers," she said, "and if something is not done we will all be murdered." Durham gathered together a squad of citizens and, locating the bandits in the restaurant, opened fire on them. A lively skirmish followed in which forty shots were exchanged without damage to either side, and the Mexicans rode off in the direction of Rancheria. It was believed this attack upon them saved Drytown from the fate that a few hours later befell Rancheria.

When the Mexicans had departed, Robert Cosner set out across country to warn Rancheria of impending danger. When he arrived, the little mining village was dark and apparently deserted while the rumble of galloping hoofs was fading in the distance. The silence of the place seemed ominous. Cosner gave a loud halloo. For a time there was no answer. Then Dave Wilson crept from a ditch where he had been hiding in terror.

"The whole town has been slaughtered," exclaimed Wilson. "I don't know how many are dead."

Cosner hurried to Francis' store, the principal business house of the settlement. He found Dan Hutchinson, a clerk, Sam Wilson and two other men dead on the floor. Francis with both legs broken was stretched on the ground at the rear of the store. A dead Indian lay near him. At Dynan's hotel near by, Mrs. Dynan was dead and her husband dying.

"The Mexicans," said Francis, "came into the store as if to make some purchases. Hutchinson and I went behind the counter to wait on them. Sam and Dave Wilson and two of their friends, whom I did not know, lounged about, talking. An Indian stood near the back door. Suddenly the Mexicans drew their revolvers.

" 'Open that safe,' said one.

"Covered by a six-shooter, Hutchinson obeyed. I had $20,000 in the safe and I did not propose to lose it without a fight. I jerked a six-shooter from a drawer and started shooting. In my excitement my bullets went wild. All the Mexicans fired and Hutchinson fell. The Wilson boys and their two friends made a break for the front door. All were killed except Dave Wilson who escaped. As I ran toward the back door, a volley broke both my legs but I managed to crawl outside before I toppled over in a faint. The Indian dropped dead beside me."

Having looted the safe of $20,000, the robbers went to Dynan's hotel. There they obtained several hundred dollars. Though neither Mrs. Dynan nor her husband made any show of resistance, the bandits shot them without mercy. Then they swung into their saddles and galloped out of town. Francis died the next day.

Five hundred armed miners swarmed into Rancheria as soon as the news of the atrocity spread over the country. The first thing they did was to round up every Mexican they could find and burn every Mexican house in the village. They soon had thirty-five Mexican prisoners corraled in a rope enclosure under heavy guard. Three, who talked defiantly and seemed to know more about the massacre than they would tell, were marched to a tree and incontinently hanged. The remainder were released and fled from the country never to return. Indians, in revenge for the death of their tribesman, killed eight of the fugitives. The mutilated bodies of some were found in old prospect holes. Others lay near springs of water to which they had crawled when wounded. Hogs had devoured a number of the slain.

Sheriff W. A. Phoenix with a strong posse set out in pursuit of the robbers who crossed the Mokelumne river at Diamond Bar and headed south. At Chinese Camp beyond Sonora, inhabited almost exclusively by Mexicans, the sheriff and his men went into a dance hall at night to look the crowd over. Scowls of hatred greeted them. A Mexican girl ran to the back door and waved her hand in warning to some men outside. Sheriff Phoenix and his deputies rushed out and were met by a blast of gunfire from half a dozen Mexicans only dimly visible in the darkness. The sheriff was killed instantly. The outlaw believed to have been his slayer was brought to his knees mortally wounded by the bullets of the posse, but he continued firing. George Durham put him out of the fighting with a blow from an ax that split open his skull. A wounded Mexican crawled into a canvas hut. The house was set on fire. The Mexican staggered out again with his clothes and hair in flames but pumping bullets from two six-shooters. He died in a rain of lead.

One of the robbers wounded in the battle at Chinese Camp made his way to Algerine. There he asked a Mexican whom he knew to hide him in the shaft of an abandoned mine.

"The Americans will kill me if I hide you," said the Mexican.

"I will kill you if you don't," replied the robber.

Sheriff's men trailed the bandit to Algerine and were told of his hiding place. They dropped blazing brush down the shaft to smoke him out. They stood at the mouth of the shaft with their guns cocked to kill him as soon as he appeared. They waited a long time in vain. When the smoke had cleared from the shaft, they went down. They found the outlaw lying dead on a ledge. He had sent a bullet through his brain.

Sheriff William A. Clark of Calaveras county, Paul McCormick and Six Fingered Smith of Campo Seco had a fight with three of the robbers at Texas Bar and wounded and captured Manuel Garcia. With a rope about his neck, Garcia was driven to Jackson in a buggy. On the road, he made a full confession of his part in the Rancheria murders and named all his accomplices. A crowd of Jackson citizens met the buggy as it came into town. Sheriff Clark, sitting beside the prisoner, tossed the crowd the loose end of the rope. The crowd threw it over the outflung limb of the hang tree. As the buggy, without stopping, passed slowly beneath the bough, Garcia was lifted out of his seat by a pull on the rope and his lifeless body was soon swaying in the breeze.

Sheriff George Wood of Tuolumne county arrested forty Mexicans in Sonora and summoned George Durham to see if he could identify any of them. Durham recognized Rafael Escobar who had been implicated in the massacre by Garcia. Escobar was a well dressed, well educated young man who formerly had lived in Drytown. When questioned, he pretended he could not speak English. An interpreter was called. Escobar protested he knew nothing of the Rancheria atrocity. He had been in Sacramento, he declared, at the time it occurred and he had been greatly shocked when he heard of it. He lied plausibly and with cool assurance. But when Durham told him Garcia had named him as one of the murderers, the man, who knew no English, made the air blue with Anglo-Saxon curses and denounced Garcia as a traitor and a coward in fluent and forcible English. He was taken to Jackson and died in the usual way on the usual bough. With the hanging of Escobar, the hang tree's record was closed.

Sing ho the hang tree of Jackson! Vampire of trees. Beautiful in its evergreen garments as it choked out the life of its victims. Purring softly in the breeze as corpses dangled beneath it. For years it had lived in the peace of the wilderness. It had been a playfellow of the elements, singing and laughing as the winds tossed its branches, shouting joyously in the storms like a light-hearted boy. It had been kindly, friendly, beneficent. It had furnished shade for the deer and the grizzly. It had given the birds shelter in which to build their nests and hatch their broods. Upright it stood in its comely strength as if proudly conscious of virtue. But an evil change came over it with the coming of the white man. To the race that conquered the hills and looted them of their gold, its surrender was abject. The tree that had been all kindliness was transformed into a demon. It held out its arms for the hangman's rope. It became the agent of man's murderous passions. It flourished on hatred and vengeance. The stir of its leaves was a devil's hiss. It glowered in dark menace as mobs stormed around it, thirsting for blood.

But its end came in a tragedy as remorseless as that of any of the poor devils who had died on its merciless bough. Fire enwrapped it as if it had been doomed to be burned at the stake for its crimes. Flames writhed and coiled about it like fiery snakes crushing out its life.

From its blazing tortures, it emerged a ghastly skeleton, its limbs gaunt talons, its twin trunks pillars of blackness. The verdure that had masked its cruel malevolence had been stripped from it and it stood in ugly nakedness as a tree of death. The ax that finished it seemed the last stroke of retributive justice. Sing ho the hang tree of Jackson!

CHAPTER XII.

THE BLACK KNIGHT.

HARRY LOVE was born a frontiersman, for the greater part of his life he lived among frontier conditions, and though civilization closed about him in his later years, he remained a frontiersman until he died. He was born in Texas when it was still under the Mexican flag; he lived in Texas when it was a republic under the flag of the lone star; and he continued in Texas after it became a state under the stars and stripes. He was a boy when Crockett, Bowie, Travis and their fellow patriots died at the Alamo and when old Sam Houston won the independence of Texas at San Jacinto. He grew up with a rifle in his hands. The buffalo still blackened the Llano Estacado and the dead bodies and burned homes of pioneer settlers marked the war trails of Kiowas and Comanches.

When the Mexican war broke out he crossed the Rio Grande with a company of Texas Rangers in the army of Gen. Zachary Taylor. Though there is no definite record of his services in the war, he is said to have taken part in the battles of Palo Alto, Resaca de la Palma, Monterey and Buena Vista. For two years he was on active duty in northern Mexico and for much of the time was employed as a scout and express rider. In this capacity he had to ride alone for hundreds of miles across deserts and mountains to carry messages from army headquarters to distant outposts. No service in the war was more dangerous. The country swarmed with guerilla bands who watched every mountain pass and desert water hole and many an American scout or small detachment of troops fell before their onslaughts, and left their bones to be picked by the buzzards and coyotes. Padre Jurata and Vincente Gomez, "the Fra Diavolo of Mexico," were the most famous leaders of these wandering free lances and Love used to tell of the desperate rides he had across lonely stretches of wilderness to escape with his life from these murderous devils. Joaquin Valenzuela and Luis Vulvia, Murrieta's captains, served with these banditti and it is possible that these two men in those days pursued Love as relentlessly as Love in after years pursued them.

At the close of the war, Love, like many another Texas Ranger, went to California in the first gold stampede. For a time, he was a miner. But he seems to have had little success with a rocker and, abandoning it for a six-shooter, became a peace officer. For several years he was a deputy sheriff, first at Santa Barbara and then at Los Angeles, and finally made his place in history as a captain of State Rangers. Covered with glory by his achievements, he settled at Santa Cruz. He resided later at Santa Clara near San Jose and there in 1868, his romantic career came to a tragic conclusion.

Harry Love's personal appearance was the subject of argument in early California newspapers. Some writers declared he looked like a gorilla. Others said he was of the dashing cavalier type. A contemporary newspaper picture of him has come down but whether it was a sketch from life or a copy of a daguerreotype is not known. It is a crude picture but enough of a portrait to settle the old debate. Love looked neither like a gorilla nor a cavalier. He was sometimes called the ugliest man in California and he, good naturedly, owned the soft impeachment. The charge was—perhaps—a slight exaggeration but, judged by the newspaper cut and by authentic descriptions, Love was anything but a handsome man.

He was, however, a strikingly picturesque figure. His fair skin emphasized the startling blackness of his hair, mustache, beard and eyes. As black as the plumage of a cornfield crow and showing the same glints of metallic luster, his hair fell upon his shoulders in a bushy mass. His black mustache drooped around the corners of his mouth. His black beard covered the edges of his jaws and ended in chin whiskers. His deep-set black eyes snapped and sparkled under rugged brows and were surrounded by a network of fine wrinkles caused doubtless by squinting with habitual alertness into wind, rain and strong sunlight. His face was full and placid and might have been considered a little pasty, and his expression was rather quizzical and good humored. He was of medium height but his tremendous shoulders, deep chest, and massive legs and arms gave an impression of herculean strength. He looked poised, unafraid and imperturbably calm. He was heavy in his movements—no lightness or grace in him. He suggested a grizzly bear, good natured while feeding in a berry patch on the mountain but savage when disturbed and carrying death in a swipe of its paws. Something of the inevitability of the man was written in his face. Danger not only did not daunt him but did not ruffle his cool serenity. He was not to be swerved from a purpose. Once he fixed his eye upon a destination, he moved toward it with plantigrade clumsiness, but with steady, crushing momentum.

Love used to visit Monterey occasionally in his later years from his home at Santa Cruz across the bay, and the visits of "the Black Knight of the Seyante," as he was called, were always chronicled in the one newspaper of that ancient capital. He wore on these state occasions a fringed buckskin coat while a long sword with a gold hilt clanked against his roweled boots. The sword was the old warrior's proudest possession and had been presented to him by some grateful *hidalgo* whose life he had saved in the Mexican war. It made the old fellow look perhaps a trifle absurd but whenever he appeared in public with his good Toledo blade dangling at his side, he strutted with his chest out and his head held high, with all the dignity of the most pompous old grandee that ever ruled in the governor's palace when California was an appanage of the Spanish crown.

To Love, his visits to Monterey were royal progresses, and right royally he celebrated them. Having received the plaudits of an admiring public, he used to retire to a snug tavern whose vine-draped windows overlooked the bay, and there, with a worshipful group about him, ensconce himself in a comfortable chair by a table and hold high revel as befitted majesty. His favorite tipple was grog, and over the glasses he would recount with naïve boastfulness his many adventures and hair-breadth escapes. As the bumpers were filled and refilled he became more and more boastful, and his deep voice rumbled among the smoke-stained rafters. He did all the talking and if any of his companions ventured a remark, Love, it was said, would frown portentously upon the bold knave who had dared to interrupt him and roar him down with an outburst of piratical profanity. When in the small hours of the morning the carousal ended, the Black Knight staggered off to bed as drunk as a lord.

It was this tough, seasoned frontiersman who was to take up the trail of Joaquin Murrieta and follow it to the end. A thrilling chase it was to be—a wily quarry, a relentless huntsman. Unknown to each other, of different races, with no cause of quarrel between them, one came from Texas, one from Mexico—from the ends of the earth—to meet in mortal combat at a certain spot in California where one was to triumph and the other die. Why? For the same reason that the king at faro loses when it loses and the ace wins when it wins. Love was the symbol of law, Murrieta the symbol of lawlessness, and both of their kinds were unique examples. Murrieta was the master criminal; Love the master policeman. As far as the poles apart in character—Murrieta, daring, quick-witted, murderous; Love plodding, methodical, stolid, but equally deadly. The odds seemed all on the side of Murrieta. Any shrewd gambler who knew both men would have bet his money on the outlaw. But Murrieta's time had come. His courage, resourcefulness and brilliant strategic ability could not save him. His fate was written in the stars. Destiny crooked its finger and Murrieta answered the summons. Love's six-shooter was a mere detail in the final tragedy.

Deputy Sheriff Harry Love of Los Angeles county was cruising alone in the region between Los Angeles and San Buenaventura on the lookout for horse thieves. Remarkably bold in the deputy sheriff was this one-man expedition, for Joaquin Murrieta was known to be in the southern country and his band was busy rustling horses among the ranches in the San Fernando and Simi valleys and in the snug coves locked among the Santa Monica, Santa Susana and San Gabriel mountains. But in his trip up the coast from Los Angeles, Love had seen no horse thief to arrest or shoot at and, as he jogged into San Buenaventura, he felt a little discouraged and also a little dry. San Buenaventura in those days was a small adobe village that had grown about the old Mission founded by Father Junipero Serra's companions in 1782 and was shut in against the sea by a semi-circle of mountains. To a little *cantina* where he had often drunk before, the deputy sheriff steered as straight as he could lay his course and refreshed himself with a glass of grog.

While in casual converse with the bartender he learned that two heavily armed Mexicans had been carousing for a day or two in San Buenaventura and had ridden off toward the south only an hour or so before Love arrived. From description, Love believed these two men to be Pedro Gonzalez and Juan Cardoza. Love had known Gonzalez personally several years before when that young rascal was hanging around Nigger Alley in Los Angeles as a gambler. Since those days, Love had won a certain fame as a peace officer and Gonzalez had launched upon a career as an outlaw and had become known throughout California as the most daring horse thief in Murrieta's band. Cardoza, unknown to Love except by reputation, was Gonzalez's intimate associate and had become almost as expert at stealing horses as the master thief himself. He was, incidentally, to fall heir not only to Gonzalez's glory as a horse thief but to his prestige in love. It was Cardoza, it will be recalled, who a little later was to succeed Gonzalez in the affections of Mariquita Vasquez and meet his death in Tejon Pass beneath the dagger thrust of that little tigress.

The bartender's information was welcome news to Love and he climbed into his saddle and headed south. The fact that he was alone and the two men he was after were among the most desperate cut-throats in Murrieta's band made no difference to him. The deputy sheriff had a child-like faith in his ability to take care of himself, and the odds of two to one against him gave him no anxiety. As he turned a bend in the mountain road, he saw two Mexican horsemen dismount and enter a wayside tavern and identified one as Gonzalez. After their spree in San Buenaventura, the two outlaws felt the need of a drop of liquor to brace them up for their journey to San Gabriel, where they had had word Murrieta was awaiting them.

Luck seemed playing into Love's hands. Hiding his horse in the chaparral, he made his way on foot to within a short distance of the tavern and went into ambush in a position commanding the front door. He had not waited long when Cardoza came out and looked up and down the trail to make sure no enemies were about. He saw nothing to alarm him and turned to go back inside when Love's six-shooter barked and a bullet cut a groove along one side of Cardoza's head and knocked off his hat. Forgetting suddenly that a jolly horse thief was waiting at the bar to click glasses with him, Cardoza darted around a corner of the building and ran up a hill at the rear. One fleeting glimpse Love had of him as he dodged among the rocks and trees and sent a second bullet after him but failed to hit him. Rushing from his hiding place, Love met Gonzalez rushing out the door.

"Hands up!"

Love had the drop. To disobey that command would have meant death and Gonzalez was no fool. Up went his hands and Love quickly disarmed him.

"Well, Pedro," said Love coolly. "It's quite a while since we met. We'll take a drink for old time's sake. There's a rope waiting for you in Los Angeles and we've got a hard ride ahead of us."

Gonzalez took the affair with a nonchalance equal to that of the deputy sheriff.

"So you think they will hang me?" he remarked, pouring out his liquor.

"You can bet the bank roll on it," replied Love.

For a moment Gonzalez looked a shade thoughtful. Then he shrugged cheerfully.

"Buena salud, señor," he said, lifting his glass.

"Here's how."

They drank like two old friends.

The sun was declining as Love and Gonzalez mounted their horses and started for Los Angeles. Love had been in the saddle all day but, if he was to land his prisoner in the Los Angeles jail, there was nothing for it but an all-night ride. Cardoza would carry the news to Murrieta and Murrieta undoubtedly would attempt a rescue. Good luck and a hard ride were now Love's only hope.

Night fell. The moon rose over the mountains. Love and his prisoner rode in silence, Gonzalez unfettered, Love a little in the rear, his keen eyes watchful. There were stretches along the trail where all Gonzalez would have had to do to escape was tumble from his horse and dodge into the brush. But he was afraid to risk it;—he knew Harry Love. Over the hills, across the valleys, they went, now within sight of the white surf breaking on the ocean beaches, now inland among the mountains and pine woods. Always the trail was rough, climbing steeply, falling abruptly. Speed was impossible. A white streak glimmered over the eastern ranges. The morning star hung in the sky. Mountains and valleys began to unfold in shadowy perspective in the dim light of dawn.

Meantime, Cardoza was doing exactly what Love had supposed he would do. On a stolen horse, he was riding at breakneck speed for San Gabriel to carry the news to Murrieta. Over the Simi hills, he sped, across the level plains of the San Fernando valley, over Cahuenga Pass. With his horse marbled with foam and ready to drop from exhaustion, he dashed into San Gabriel shortly after midnight. He aroused Murrieta. The outlaws of the band were hastily rounded up from their sleeping quarters in adobe huts about the village. No time to lose. Love might be intercepted before he reached Los Angeles. Gonzalez might yet be saved from the gallows. Boots and saddles and away! Out of the slumbering village, galloped Murrieta, Three Fingered Jack, Valenzuela, Luis Vulvia, Cardoza and Mountain Jim Wilson. The old Mission church faded behind them in the moonlight. Across country, through woods and thickets, by cow paths and brush trails known only to themselves, they made their way through the darkness on their mission of rescue and vengeance,—rescue for Gonzalez, death for the man who had captured him.

The sun was rising over the Simi hills as Love and Gonzalez with their jaded horses at a walk were climbing the long mountain slope known as the Cuesta del Conejo. Through the dewy stillness of the morning, came a sudden sound like the growl of distant thunder. They shot a quick glance behind them. Out of a tumult of dust, six horsemen were bearing down upon them at a mad rush, yelling like devils and with revolvers blazing. Gonzalez thrilled with hope. Visions of the gallows faded from his mind. Rescue seemed certain. He drew a handkerchief from his pocket and waved it joyously. At this signal to the enemy, Love glowered ominously. The fire of the outlaws became a fusillade. The air was vibrant with the whine of bullets. Puffs of dust flew up along the trail as if from thunder drops heralding a breaking storm.

Love's case seemed suddenly hopeless. He might save himself by flight. But he would lose his prisoner. Must he lose this man after risking his life to capture him? Here was a problem for Love to solve in a fraction of a second or he would lose both his prisoner and his life. A fraction of a second was all Love needed to make his decision. He drew his six-shooter instantly and sent a ball through Gonzalez's heart. As the outlaw toppled out of his saddle and thumped upon the ground, Love put spurs to his horse.

The outlaws reined to a halt beside Gonzalez but only

long enough to see that he was dead. Then they swept on in pursuit of Love. But their halt had balked them of their kill. Love was traveling like the wind. He made the summit of the Cuesta del Conejo. He went dashing down the long slope on the other side. A few bullets from his pursuers pattered about him. The fire of the outlaws slackened and ceased. Murrieta glared with rage as Love dwindled in the distance and disappeared behind the shoulder of a hill. A few hours later, the deputy sheriff, safe and unscathed, rode at an easy gallop into Los Angeles.

The outlaws did not return to where Gonzalez lay. He had been their comrade for years but why waste time on a dead man? Good-bye and good luck to him on the out-trail but they had other things to think about. Turning from the road into the brush, they took up their journey back to San Gabriel. On their way they stopped at the hut of a peon and told him of the dead man lying on the highway. The peon found the body and buried it. The grave in a little while was obliterated. The site of it passed out of memory. All that was known was that the famous Pedro Gonzalez, who in his busy life as an outlaw probably had stolen more horses than any man that ever lived in California, slept his last sleep somewhere in the Cuesta del Conejo.

A merry company set out on a holiday journey from the Arroya Cantova. Business was slack, robbery had fallen off, murder was in a slump. So to relieve the dreary monotony, Murrieta had decided upon a picnic jaunt to San Luis Gonzaga rancho a hundred miles or so to the north. With him went the bewitching Maria Ana Benites, Reyes Feliz and his Carmelita, Juan Cardoza and the lovely Mariquita Vasquez, who had taken Cardoza for her lover as soon as she had ceased weeping for her lost Pedro Gonzalez. As gay and light-hearted as children they rode along across the level reaches of the San Joaquin valley in the pleasant sunshine of a day in May. Ahead of them, the Coast Range lay dim and blue along the horizon. Pacheco Pass was plainly visible and at the mouth of the pass was the old Spanish rancho at which they planned to spend a few weeks of leisure among friends.

It happened that at that time Albert Ruddle, on his return trip from Stockton fifty miles away, was also heading for Pacheco Pass with a wagonload of provisions. Murrieta, the eagle eyed, spied him from afar off.

"My funds are running low," remarked Joaquin to his companions. "Here is a chance to replenish my purse. I will ride ahead and overtake that young man. He looks as if he might have money."

"Fine," exclaimed Maria Ana Benites enthusiastically. "We'll play audience."

"Give us a good performance," echoed Mariquita.

Off he dashed in jovial mood and presently drew alongside Ruddle who was riding the near wheeler of his four-horse team.

"Good morning," Joaquin saluted cheerfully.

"Howdy," returned Ruddle sourly.

"I would like to borrow what money you have," said the affable outlaw.

Ruddle stared at him in amazement, not sure whether he was a humorist, a maniac or a bandit.

"I've got no money for you," he replied.

"I need it," urged Joaquin. "I'm broke."

"What the hell do I care?"

"Will you not accommodate me?"

"What lunatic asylum did you escape from?"

"What you have in your pockets will satisfy me."

"All you'll get off of me you can put in your eye."

"I see," said Joaquin, "I will have to explain. I am a robber of whom you have doubtless heard. But I am in earnest when I say I wish to borrow the money. I will regard it as a loan pure and simple and I will pay you back as sure as my name is Joaquin Murrieta."

"Your name don't scare me," Ruddle retorted. "You'll borrow no money off of me and you'll have a tough time robbing me."

Ruddle was mad all the way through and his courage was clean strain. He reached for his six-shooter. Murrieta threw up his hand in an amiable gesture.

"Don't be foolish," he said. "Give me your money and let's get this matter over with. I have no desire to kill you."

"If there's any killing to be done," shouted the enraged Ruddle, "I'll do my share. You're fooling with the wrong man."

Out came his gun. With a sweeping overhand movement, he was throwing it down to a level, when Joaquin jerked a knife from his sash and slashed him across the throat. Ruddle fell out of his saddle dead.

Joaquin dismounted, coolly turned the body over, and rifled the pockets of three hundred dollars. When he had counted the money and dropped it into his pocket, he wiped a few splotches of red from his fingers with his handkerchief. He was sitting calmly on his horse as his companions rode up smiling.

"It was as entertaining as any show I ever saw, Joaquin," said Maria Ana Benites. "You did splendidly."

"A rope dancer in a *maroma* could not have done better," declared Mariquita.

"I had not intended to take the poor fool's life," said Murrieta. "He insisted on being killed."

Leaving the dead man lying beside the team and

wagon, the party rode on, as gay and light-hearted as children, toward San Luis Gonzago rancho.

News of the murder of Albert Ruddle traveled quickly all over the state. He was not prominent in any way, but he was honest, intelligent and industrious and a fine type of citizen. The cold blooded killing of such a man aroused intense bitterness against Murrieta and had as much to do as any one incident in starting the final drive that eliminated him from California's criminal problems. Murrieta later expressed regret at having killed Ruddle but his regret had no effect in tempering the indignation of the people or in weakening their determination to exterminate the murderous robber who for years had terrorized the state.

As soon as information of the tragedy reached Los Angeles, Harry Love again took the trail. But he did not go alone. He had narrowly missed disaster in one brush with Murrieta and this time he prepared for emergencies and set out on the hunt with a dozen good fighting men at his back. The posse followed the Camino Real up the coast to Pacheco Pass. There Love learned of the presence of Murrieta and his party at San Luis Gonzaga rancho. Pacheco Pass, forty miles south of San Jose, was a deep gap in the Coast Range mountains, twenty-five miles through, and in those days was the main highway between the coast and the southern section of the Sierra mining country. At the western entrance was the immense landed estate of the Pacheco family that gave the pass its name and at the eastern end where the pass opened into the San Joaquin valley was San Luis Gonzaga rancho, which had long been a harboring place for the outlaws and which in later years was a refuge for Tiburcio Vasquez and his gang.

Since the Ruddle murder, Murrieta, Reyes Feliz, Juan Cardoza and their three women companions had been quartered in a tent house on the ranch. These tent houses were common at that period, especially in the mining region. They had doors and windows and their frame work was like that of ordinary houses, but their walls, and often their roofs, were of canvas. Slipping through Pacheco Pass one dark night, Love and his men arrived at San Luis Gonzaga rancho and saw the tent house, lighted from within, glowing like a huge lantern in the darkness. Leaving their horses some distance away, they approached the house on foot. As they drew near, a Mexican woman stepped from an adobe hut and screamed an alarm. Instantly the lights in the tent house went out. Rushing to the door, Love hammered upon it. A woman opened it. He and his companions brushed by her and quickly lighted the lamps again. The place was plainly furnished with beds, a washstand, table and chairs. Three women were the only inmates. They were Ana Benites, Mariquita and Carmelita though Love did not know them.

"Where's Joaquin Murrieta?" Love demanded brusquely.

The women looked astonished. They spread their hands. They shrugged.

"Joaquin Murrieta?" said Ana Benites blankly. "I do not know him."

Love glared at her savagely. "You know him well enough. He's been here. Don't deny it. Where is he?"

"No, señor, I have never heard of such a man."

Love caught her roughly by the arm. "Don't lie to me. Everybody in California has heard of Joaquin Murrieta."

"But, señor, you see I have been in this country only a very little while. I am just from Mexico. Who is this Joaquin Murrieta?"

"The greatest thief in the state."

"Thief? Then of course I do not know him. I do not associate with thieves."

"Murrieta and two of his men have been living here with you."

Ana Benites was scandalized. "No, no, no," she exclaimed indignantly. "You wrong us, señor. We are good, honest women. We live here quietly all alone."

Love had shot his way out of many difficulties but this stone wall of polite mendacity was too much for him. In his helplessness, he was ready to concede that the suave tongue of a pretty woman was a better weapon than a six-shooter.

"Why did you douse the lights when you heard that woman scream?"

"Because we were frightened. We did not know what might happen to us. They tell us this is a dangerous part of the country. Many bad men come and go through Pacheco Pass."

"Humph."

"You doubt my word, señor?"

"I'd be a fool to believe it."

"That is unkind, señor. I speak only the truth. But if you still think the man you seek is here, why do you not search the house?"

"There's nothing to search. Everything here is in plain sight. Murrieta can't hide in a band box."

That struck Ana Benites as a very good joke and she laughed merrily.

Love's information had been positive. Murrieta had been there that night and he knew it. He felt sure, moreover, that Murrieta had been in the house when the lights went out and the posse was within a few feet of the door. But what had become of him? In what mysterious way had he vanished leaving no trace behind him? Love saw no way out of the muddle. He was wasting time trying to learn anything from such a charming liar as Ana Benites.

"Let's go, boys," said Love finally. "We might as well give it up. You young ladies," he added gallantly, "will have to excuse us for breaking in on you like this."

"Por supuesto, caballero. Como no?"

Ana Benites bowed the posse out graciously. Then doubtless she and Mariquita and Carmelita had a good laugh. If Love had looked behind the washstand, he would have found a long knife slash in the canvas wall of the house through which Murrieta, Reyes Feliz and Juan Cardoza had escaped.

After Murrieta's attempt to rescue Pedro Gonzalez, Valenzuela and Mountain Jim went to San Diego to steal horses. While prowling about the country they dropped into a roadside dram shop fifteen or twenty miles out of town. They had had several glasses of brandy when four or five heavily armed Americans rode up and stalked into the bar. These gringos were hunting for horse thieves and, suspecting very strongly they accidentally had found two, they looked them up and down in a bold way that embarrassed Valenzuela, who was sober, but did not feaze Mountain Jim, who was quite drunk. Valenzuela drew Mountain Jim outside.

"I size those fellows for sheriff's men," said Valenzuela. "The best thing we can do is to climb on our horses pronto and get out of here."

"Pshaw, them fellers ain't sheriff's men," replied Mountain Jim thickly. "They're all right. Come on back in. We'll buy 'em a drink."

"They don't like our looks."

"Well, we ain't none too purty. But them boys don't mean no harm. I know nice, sociable lads when I meet 'em."

"Come on with me. Get on your horse."

"Wait a while. What's your rush? I've got to have a few more drams. That's the best brandy I ever tasted."

"You'll be tasting lead if you don't watch out."

"Who, me? Say, I'm a pretty rough fellow in a ruckus myself."

"You're drunk. If trouble started, you wouldn't have a chance. They'd kill you like a rabbit."

"They'd play hell killin' me. But if you're scared, ride along. I'm stayin' here until I get good and ready to leave. I ain't afraid o' nobody and no bunch o' men that ever wore hair can run me out."

"All right," said Valenzuela. "Stay here and get killed if you want to. As for me, I am taking it on the run."

Mountain Jim swaggered back inside. His jovial, booming voice came out to Valenzuela as that crafty *hombre* swung into his saddle. "Have one on me, fellers," roared Mountain Jim. "Mr. Bartender, fill 'em up."

A dozen horsemen came round a bend. Valenzuela sank his spurs into his horse's flanks and went bounding away at top speed. The horsemen thundered in pursuit, their bullets buzzing about him. But Valenzuela drew away and the hills swallowed him.

Mountain Jim had just tossed off his drink and was wiping his mouth with the back of his hand, when he was startled into sudden sobriety by this unexpected uproar. The Americans, who had just clicked glasses with him, covered him with their six-shooters.

"That was good brandy," remarked one with his gun at a level.

"The best I ever tasted," said Mountain Jim, throwing up his hands.

The citizens of San Diego took Mountain Jim from jail next day and hanged him on a cottonwood tree. He looked a little downcast as he stood with the rope around his neck.

"This ain't right, boys," he said. "All I done was buy a round o' drinks. This ain't no proper reward fer good intentions."

But somehow the citizens failed to look at it that way and strung Mountain Jim up on the cottonwood tree, not for hospitality, but for stealing horses. Mountain Jim was as amiable, genial, kind-hearted and generous as any horse thief that ever lived. Everybody said so.

Pedro Obiesa and Juan Graciano—their names were Spanish but the men were French—bought up a drove of cattle around San Luis Obispo and started north to sell them in the San Francisco market. They camped the first night of the drive on the road north of Paso Robles at the mouth of the Nacimiento in a country known as "the dark and bloody ground" because of the many murders that had been committed there. They awoke next morning to find that their horses had been stolen and went out to look for them. They never returned. Their skeletons, identified by their clothing, were found a few weeks later with bullet holes through the skulls. The men had been robbed of $3,500.

Two months later, Bartolo Baratie and M. J. Borel, well-to-do Frenchmen, bought the San Juan Capistrano ranch forty-five miles from San Luis Obispo. Soon after they had established themselves there in the cattle business, eight Mexican bandits swooped down upon the ranch. Borel was shot and killed as he was drawing water from a well. Baratie was wounded and escaped into the brush but was pursued and slain. After the two murders, the bandits ransacked the ranch house and stole $2,700. The money was piled on the floor and, in the presence of the wife of one of the slain men, Rafael

Herrada, known as El Huero (The Blonde) divided it among the murderers.

Both these crimes were committed by the same band of outlaws under the leadership of Pio Linares. Two posses under Captain David P. Mallagh and Captain John Wilson were organized in San Luis Obispo and took the trail of the robbers. Pio Linares, Miguel Blanco and Desiderio Grijalba were surrounded in the brush. Linares was shot to death but not before he had killed John Matlock, one of the posse. Blanco and Grijalba were captured, taken to San Luis Obispo and hanged by the vigilance committee on a gallows erected in the public square. Santos Peralta and Luciano Tapo were taken and hanged on the same gallows a little later. Nieves Robles was tried legally and acquitted. On the jury that freed him was one of the murderers, while another member was a slayer who was a fugitive from justice. Jose Antonio Garcia was caught at his home in Santa Barbara, taken to San Luis Obispo and hanged. He was a small merchant and had shared in the loot of the Nacimiento atrocity but had not actually participated in the crime. When his companions showed him the dead bodies of the two Frenchmen, Garcia, it was said, was stricken with horror and fainted. Pio Linares and Rafael Herrada, Garcia confessed, killed Obiesa and Graciano. El Huero was never captured.

Jack Powers, it was established, was the brains of the gang and shared in all the money obtained in its criminal operations. Hunted by the vigilance committee, he narrowly escaped the gallows by fleeing from the state. Powers was a noted character. He lived in Santa Barbara for years and later became the king-pin gambler of Los Angeles and boss of the underworld. He was a power in politics and, as the friend of a succession of governors, made his political influence felt in the state capital. For months, he shielded from arrest the notorious Ned McGowan when that former member of the state judiciary, charged with wholesale corruption and bribery, was hiding from the vigilance committee that cleaned up San Francisco. Lordly, genial, wealthy, immaculately dressed and with the manners of a gentleman, Powers lived in princely style, owned a fine ranch, maintained a stable of thoroughbred horses, and hunted behind a pack of imported fox hounds. But at the height of his prosperity, he was in close alliance with half the thieves and cut-throats in California and Joaquin Valenzuela and Solomon Pico took his orders. When he left the state, he settled in Northern Mexico. There a band of Yaqui Indians in his employ, after a bitter quarrel, lassoed this genial, lordly gentleman, dragged him to death at their horses' heels and, having slashed his body into pieces with their machetes, fed it to their hogs.

In an account of the work of the San Luis Obispo vigilance committee written by Walter Murray, one of its leading members, and embodied in the History of San Luis Obispo County, we find this interesting paragraph:

"The men that went in pursuit of the Nacimiento slayers spent a week in fruitless search in the hills. The murderers, being well mounted, easily eluded them. At the Rancho San Emilio, however, they took one, Joaquin Valenzuela, known also as Joaquin Carrillo, Joaquin Ocomorenia, and Joaquin Bottilier, who was identified by several persons who had known him. This man was an old accomplice of Jack Powers and spoke of him as his patron and was a man steeped to the lips in guilt. He was well known at the mouth of the Merced river and on the San Joaquin and owed justice a score which fifty lives could never pay. He was hanged in full sight of the whole people of San Luis Obispo in broad daylight by the voice and assistance of all the respectable men of the county and died acknowledging his guilt, asking pardon of his friends, and warning all malefactors not to tell their secrets even to their most intimate friends. '*Porque asi se pierde,*' said he. That is, 'For in that way you doom yourself.' "

So Joaquin Valenzuela, Murrieta's gaunt, hollow-eyed, Mephistophelian captain who had learned his trade of robbery and murder under Padre Jurata, came to the end of his crimson trail. A criminal from childhood, this strange man mapped out his crimes, as an architect plans a building, with meticulous, blue-print craftsmanship. His cunning foresight enabled him to last on earth more than forty years, which is a long time for one who faced death every day and might logically have expected a bullet or a dagger thrust at any minute. The posse that captured him was not looking for him. The vigilance committee hanged him, not for any particular crime, but as an incidental detail in its campaign for law and order. His death was an afterthought of fate. Fate had forgotten him and passed him by; then suddenly remembering a duty unperformed, turned back and remedied its oversight.

CHAPTER XIII.

THE CITY OF THE ANGELS.

LOS ANGELES was the capital of California under Governor Pio Pico. Gen. John C. Fremont and Gen. Stephen W. Kearny made their headquarters there during the American conquest. The battle of San Pascual, the most important engagement fought on California soil during the Mexican war, took place to the south and at Cabuenga Rancho near by, Gen. Fremont received from Gen. Andres Pico the surrender of the last remnant of the California army and signed a treaty of peace that ended hostilities.

Los Angeles with fifteen hundred people was the largest town in California when the era of Arabian Nights development dawned with the discovery of gold. It was hardly an impressive metropolis. But its site was a wilderness when Portolá, leading the first white men into the unknown land of California, camped there in 1769. All California had only three thousand white inhabitants at the end of the Spanish régime in 1821. In 1842, Monterey, the capital, had two hundred people and Los Angeles two hundred and fifty, while San Francisco was a cluster of nondescript cabins dignified by the name of Yerba Buena. With the tremendous inrush of settlers during the gold excitement, Los Angeles grew rapidly and Americans became influential in business and public affairs.

Among the Americans four-fifths were Southerners. They gave society and public sentiment its dominant tone. Steeped in the traditions of the South, they were brave, proud, hot-tempered, generous and quixotic. Slavery and state rights were national issues; secession was already being discussed; the first lightning flashes of the Civil war were on the far-off horizon. The growing bitterness between the North and the South divided the population of California in which the Southern element was strong. Political campaigns were characterized by flaming intensity of feeling and by savage personal attacks. Political rivals not infrequently appealed their quarrels to the Code Duello which, with its tragic silliness, was a recognized institution; and many men died on the field of honor, including some of brilliant abilities and national fame. In a state that seethed with rabid politics, Los Angeles was a stronghold of political fire-eaters. Secessionist sentiment was paramount and the so-called "bowie knife chivalry" was in the saddle.

The pueblo of the early fifties retained the physical characteristics of its Spanish and Mexican origin. The Plaza, dominated by the Cathedral, was the center of the town's bustling life. The houses, for the most part, were one-story, flat-roofed adobes, many of which were calcimined in white, pink and blue. Residences of the rich were sheltered in walled gardens. Main, Aliso and Los Angeles streets constituted the shopping district and were busy thoroughfares. Nigger Alley—Calle de los Negros—was the rendezvous of the underworld. The streets were alive with horsemen in gay Spanish costume, ponderous wagons of freighters, mule teams, burros of vegetable peddlers, ox-drawn *carretas* with huge wheels of solid wood. Emigrant trains were constantly rolling in from the desert trails across Arizona and New Mexico. Every day the six-mule stage from San Pedro came into town at a gallop and, in front of the Bella Union hotel, unloaded its passengers newly arrived by steamer or sailing vessel from San Francisco, San Diego, Santa Barbara and Monterey.

There was much wealth and much pretentious elegance. The Spanish gallants thought nothing of appearing in clothes that cost $500 or $1,000. Pedestrianism was at a discount. Everybody went about on horseback. Saddles costing $2,000 and $3,000 were not uncommon. Andres Pico's saddle cost $5,000. The girls were noted for their beauty and vivacity and affected the picturesque styles of Mexico City and Havana. Society was a gay whirl of routs and balls. Wine and liquor were the symbols of hospitality in every home. In the saloons of the better sort, the dandies sipped juleps, cocktails, punches and all the fancy mixtures known to the bibulously fastidious. Gambling houses had a tremendous patronage. A player lost caste who wagered less than a slug, which was an octagonal gold piece minted in California and current as $50. A stack of twenty slugs was frequently bet on a turn of the cards at faro. On fiesta days, which were innumerable, flags fluttered from the houses and religious processions moved through the streets with solemn pomp. On Sundays and holidays, rich and poor thronged to bull fights, bear baitings, cock fights, and horse races on which immense sums were won and lost.

From all over California came, with retinues of servants and chests of gold, the men and women of the rich old *hidalgo* families to enjoy the polite pleasures of the gay southern metropolis. Here met the Picos, Carrillos, Bandinis, Arguellos, Sepulvedas, Castros, Ortegas, Norriegas, Vallejos, Lugas, Vacas, Pachecos, Yorbas, Alvarados, and Peraltas. Aristocrats to their finger tips, ceremonious, gravely dignified, courtly in manner, bred in all the punctilios of charming courtesy. Their fathers and grandfathers had come to California with Portolá, Rivera y Moncada, Serra and Crespi. As for their lineage, the Norriegas dated back to the Moorish wars in Spain and retained family traditions of knightly deeds of arms under Ferdinand and Isabella before the walls of Granada. An Arguello had fought as a captain under Cortez in the conquest of Mexico. The Peraltas bent their warrior knees to Phillip II, when half the western hemisphere acknowledged the sovereignty of Spain. Don Alonzo Vallejo commanded a company of soldiers on the ship that sailed to Santo Domingo with Bobadilla, who sent Christopher Columbus home in chains.

More murders were committed in California in the early fifties than in all the United States besides, and more were committed in Los Angeles than in all the remainder of California. Two sheriffs were killed within a year and for a time the office with an annual income of $10,000 went begging. "How many men were killed last night?" was a common question over the breakfast coffee. Times were dull when murders did not average one a day. Robber bands under Solomon Pico, Luis Vulvia and Senate harried the neighboring country, and Joaquin Murrieta carried on his bold maraudings at the very gates of the city.

The town was prolific in bad men with notched gun handles. Cherokee Bob had killed six men in single handed combat. Crooked Nose Smith came from the northern mines with a reputation of having slain half a dozen and was not permitted to remain until he had given his promise to refrain from murder. Just before his departure he killed a gambler. His hand was growing rusty, he explained, and he needed practice. But as a fighting man, Ricardo Urives outshone them all. Urives was well-born and his sister was married to Señor Ocampo, owner of the Rancho de los Coyotes. After Jim Irving with thirty cut-throats had plundered the ranch and driven off many fine horses, Urives with a band of Cahuila Indians ambushed the robbers in San Gorgonio Pass and slaughtered them to the last man. When attacked by a dozen men in Nigger Alley, Urives killed five, put the others to flight and bleeding from many knife and bullet wounds, rode his horse up and down Main Street for an hour, defying the gringo police to arrest him.

The Los Angeles vigilance committee was organized in 1851 as a voluntary police force at a meeting of citizens authorized by the city council and held in the office of Mayor B. D. Wilson. It was paradoxically a lawless body legally constituted and continued in existence for more than a decade. Under its régime, hangings were so numerous that one-man executions aroused little interest. Double and triple hangings were numerous. On one occasion four men were lynched, and on another five.

David Brown, who had killed a man named Clifford, was convicted after a legal trial and sentenced to the gallows. But when the Supreme court granted a stay of execution, Mayor Stephen A. Foster resigned his office, led an attack upon the jail, and Brown was hanged to the cross-beam of the jail yard gate. A few days later, Mayor Foster was reëlected by a unanimous vote of the citizens.

Manuel Ceredel, arrested for the murder of John Rains, stoutly maintained his innocence. But, while in jail awaiting trial, he was taken down with the smallpox. Believing his last moment had come, he confessed his crime and was greatly disgusted with himself after he had recovered. Sentenced to ten years in San Quentin, he was taken in custody of the sheriff aboard the steamer Cricket for the voyage to San Francisco. While the vessel swung at anchor in San Pedro harbor, a crowd put off from shore in small boats, took Ceredel from the sheriff and strung him up to a yard-arm. When taken down, iron weights were fastened to his feet and he was thrown overboard.

Charles Wilkins, most heartless of murderers, gave a knife and pistol to a disreputable young fellow named Woods. "You ought to be ashamed of yourself," said Wilkins, "to do nothing but hang around brothels and live off of women. Take these weapons and go out on the road and earn your living like a man." Woods was caught in his first robbery and hanged by the vigilance committee. Wilkins, who preached honor to Woods, murdered John Sanford for twenty dollars. It was such an atrocious crime, that the jailer asked him if his conscience did not bother him. "No," replied Wilkins. "I have killed eight other men and think no more of killing a man than a dog." Wilkins was the seventh man hanged by the vigilance committee within a week.

Derasio Berreyesa, executed during the clean-up of the Manila gang of which Juan Flores and Pancho Daniel were the leaders, had the singular distinction of having been hanged before. He was strung up first in Santa Clara county but was resuscitated by his friends to whom his body was turned over for burial. He had been pronounced dead. No sign of life remained. He had passed into the timeless void known as eternity and if he had been allowed to rest in peace, he undoubtedly would have continued his dreamless sleep forever. But somewhere deep within him still smoldered a spark which in some strange way was fanned into life and Berreyesa arose, as it were, from the dead, as strong and healthy as he had ever been. But his cataclysmic experience taught him nothing and his sojourn in eternity meant no more to him than a tipsy jaunt through the dives of Nigger Alley. No sooner had he returned to life than he plunged again into crime. He was captured by the vigilance committee and headed straight back along Dead Man's trail. This time he must have kept right on traveling and arrived at whatever place this road leads to, for he never came back. The marks left by the rope at his first hanging were still fresh on his neck when he was hanged the second time.

Ignacio Ygarra, Manuel Obbus, Ramon Espagnol and Octaviana Espagnol, his sister, were arrested on word from San Luis Obispo that they had murdered and robbed a French peddler. Two thousand dollars worth of shawls, silks and trinkets that had belonged to the peddler were found in their possession. Don Abel Stearns, richest Yankee in Los Angeles, who had married into a wealthy Spanish family and was one of the most influential citizens of the town, presided at the people's court that tried them. The evidence against them was conclusive and they were sentenced to death. But a question of etiquette arose. The crime had been committed in San Luis Obispo. Would it be polite for the people of Los Angeles to deprive the people of San Luis Obispo of the pleasure of hanging them? It was unanimously decided that such a proceeding would be a marked discourtesy and the four criminals were put on board a schooner and sent up the coast to San Luis Obispo. A delegation of the prominent citizens of that town met the schooner at the *embarcadero* and, in appreciation of the gracious honor accorded them, hanged the culprits, including the woman, to the nearest tree.

So, you see, the drowsy peace that usually gives a delightful charm to old Spanish towns was wholly lacking in this picturesque pueblo by the southern sea. The City of the Angels was a lively village.

Deputy Sheriff Robert Wilson of Santa Barbara was an apostle of the strong arm. He had courage without discretion. Of tireless energy and great physical strength, he was just the man to ride for days and nights on end on a trail that was easy to follow. But when the trail was lost, he was lost also. He attempted to solve all problems with a bludgeon. If force failed, he had nothing left. He had no finesse, no wit, no shrewdness. He could not mask a deadly purpose beneath a smile or worm out a secret by suave diplomacy. He was blatant when secrecy was required; bold when he should have been cunning. He would have made a good roughneck harness bull on a modern police force. As a detective, he was a total loss. A poor sort to set out on the hunt for such a daring and resourceful rogue as Joaquin Murrieta. But with superb confidence in himself as a man hunter, this tough young bull-head undertook the task, and headed as straight as he could ride for Los Angeles when he learned the outlaw was secretly quartered there.

Murrieta and Reyes Feliz, in fact, were at that time at the Mission San Gabriel, where after a hard campaign in the north country, Joaquin was enjoying a period of voluptuous repose with the charming Maria Ana Benites. The outlaw lived with little attempt at secrecy. His identity was known only to a few Mexicans who were his friends and regarded him as a hero, and he danced at the fandangos, and drank and gambled with no fear of betrayal.

No sooner had Wilson arrived in Los Angeles than everybody in town knew what he was there for. He became a familiar figure in the saloons and gambling houses and the resorts of Nigger Alley as he stalked about, looking grim and dangerous with his bold, keen eyes, and his six-shooter buckled around him. Who was this Joaquin Murrieta? Just an over-rated thief. Man to man, he, Bob Wilson, was not afraid of any outlaw that ever wore hair. He could shoot as straight and was as quick on the trigger as any of them. Just let him get one glimpse of Murrieta and that was all he asked. A six-shooter made all men of one size and the tougher they were, the harder they fell. That's all there was to that.

Wilson stood talking casually with a group of men in front of the Bella Union in the Plaza one hot July afternoon. Few people were abroad. A Mexican woman padded along with a basket of groceries on her arm and a black shawl over her head. Some peons in steeple hats squatted on their heels along the shady side of a building puffing at their cigarettes. A fat tradesman mopped his red face in the door of a shop. The gray Cathedral, that was a thing of beauty in the dusk or the moonlight, looked bare and ugly in the glaring sun. From the open windows of the Bella Union came the droning voices of the gamblers—"Keep the little ball a-rolling," "Make your game, gentlemen."

Through the heat waves trembling over the square came a solitary horseman, riding at a walk. He slouched in his saddle. His bridle reins hung carelessly on his horse's neck. His lazy figure was in keeping with the quiet scene and he looked at peace with all the world.

He straightened suddenly as he stopped his horse beside Wilson. His face hardened. His white teeth gleamed in a snarling smile.

"I understand you're looking for me," he said, a shade of menace in his tone.

"Who are you?" asked Wilson in surprise.

"Joaquin Murrieta."

"Yes, I'm looking for you."

"Well, you've found me."

Wilson reached for his gun and was not slow about it. But he was not prepared for the lightning-like draw of his antagonist. Wilson's six-shooter was not more than half out of its holster when Murrieta's bullet struck him between the eyes.

The tragedy was over so quickly, the men with whom Wilson had been talking stood in stunned bewilderment. They saw as in a daze the dead man crumpled at their feet. They looked up blankly. On the far side of the Plaza where a street came in, a cloud of dust was hanging. The horseman had vanished.

The vigilance committee met this murderous challenge by prosecuting the war against crime with renewed vigor. In the drastic operations launched against the outlaws, Gen. Joshua H. Bean took a prominent part. Gen. Bean was known throughout Southern California as a public spirited citizen. He had been the last *alcalde* and the first mayor of San Diego in 1850, and in the Guerra insurrection he had been major general of state militia. He moved to Los Angeles in 1851, became identified with the progressive American element, and was held in high esteem by business men and public officials. He was now living in San Gabriel, where he kept a general store and saloon. He was a man of the pioneer type, honest, outspoken, and fearless.

Gen. Bean was assassinated on the night of November 21, 1852. He had attended a performance of a *maroma,* or Mexican circus, in San Gabriel, and was riding to his living quarters in the Mission building, when two shots were fired at him. One struck him in the breast and he fell from his horse. Drawing his six-shooter, he fired three shots at his assailants. Then as he staggered toward the house of Juan Rico, another shot was fired at him but missed him. Gen. Bean said he did not know who had shot him or how many men were engaged in the attack. He was waylaid in the darkness, he declared, and was shot before he was aware of any danger. The only bullet that struck him ranged upward through his breast and passed entirely through him. He died next morning.

The murder has been credited by Murrieta's biographers to Murrieta and Three Fingered Jack, and was believed to be the bandit leader's vengeance upon Gen.

Bean for his part in the Los Angeles vigilance committee's relentless campaign against the outlaws. This theory was never definitely substantiated, but later developments indicated quite clearly that either Murrieta directed the crime or was himself the assassin. Three Fingered Jack, the arch villain of Murrieta's organization, apparently had no part in the tragedy. Through Maria Ana Benites, the mistress whom he unsuccessfully attempted to kill afterwards in the Mariposa hills, Murrieta made a determined effort to fasten the crime on Cipriano Sandoval, an inoffensive cobbler who was in no way concerned in the murder; and, acting unquestionably under his orders, the woman gave false testimony on which this innocent man was hanged. Maria Ana, it was reliably reported, told her friends later that Murrieta was the murderer. A few days after the crime, Murrieta left for the north.

The verdict of the coroner's jury after an investigation of two weeks read: "We the jury find as our verdict that Gen. J. H. Bean came to his death by a shot received from some person or persons unknown to the jury."

Ana Benites and seven men were arrested and turned over to the vigilance committee. The men were Reyes Feliz, Felipe Read, Cipriano Sandoval, Benito Lopez, Juan Rico, Jose Alviso, and Jose Eleuterio. Rico, Alviso and Eleuterio were released. Felipe Read was surrendered to the civil authorities. The others were tried before a citizens' court.

Ana Benites, called before the investigating committee of the vigilance organization, made a long statement which was for the most part false, as it was afterwards proved. The portions given here are verbatim:

"There was a performance of the *maromas* the night Gen. Bean was killed," she said. "I was present with Joaquin Murrieta. I left the *maromas* with him and returned to the house of Juan Rico and went immediately to bed. Rico, his wife and family, a certain Sancedo and his woman, slept in the house. Myself, Joaquin Murrieta, Juanito Rico and another young lad, whom I do not know, slept in the *rama dita*. Late at night I heard two shots and loud and excited voices. A moment later I heard several other shots. The shots were fired between the houses of Rico and Peña. As Gen. Bean came crying out toward Rico's house, another shot was fired at him. He was dragging his cloak when he arrived at Rico's door and cried, 'Rico! Rico! Rico!'

"I sat up in bed and saw him. When Señora Jesusita Rico opened the door, her son Juanito already had him in his arms. 'Mother,' the boy said, 'it is Gen. Bean.' I asked Gen. Bean who had shot him. Señora Jesusita took me by the shoulders. 'You meddle in things that do not concern you,' she said. A moment later a man drew near the house and stood looking in. Then he turned and hurried away. I recognized him. It was Cipriano Sandoval. He killed Gen. Bean. There is no doubt about it.

"This took place Sunday night. Next day Murrieta and I came to Los Angeles and as we passed the little ditches close to the Mission, Cipriano Sandoval overtook us. He wore his serape over his shoulders and had his six-shooter in his waist band. He said to Murrieta: 'Hombre, I confide to you the secret of what I have done and I ask you to direct your woman to keep it to herself in order that the Americans may get nothing against us.' Then Cipriano, who was very much excited, told the whole story of the crime. After he had gone away, I said to Joaquin, 'Is that the one who killed Gen. Bean?' 'Yes,' he answered. 'And why?' I asked, 'Because,' he said, 'Gen. Bean, who was very much intoxicated, had beaten an Indian woman.'

"Murrieta then told me never to reveal the secret. 'If by chance the Americans should call you as a witness,' he said, 'I charge you to say nothing. If I ever learn that you have said the least thing, I will be your worst *knue*. If you should hide in the very guts of the Yankees, I will drag you out. They will not be able to take from you what I will do to you.'"

As Maria Ana Benites sat in the witness chair she afforded an opportunity for a close-up view of the woman whose fascinations had brought the young outlaw chief to her feet. She was, as they say, easy to look at—rosy, dusky, with snapping black eyes and a figure beautifully symmetrical. She spoke rapidly and clearly, with an appearance of honesty. But as she sat coolly betraying her friends and swearing away the life of an innocent man, there was at times a certain suggestion of furtiveness and icy coldness about her that gave some faint inkling of a soul as black as her eyes. With glowing beauty masking a character that sounded the depths of moral turpitude, it was not difficult to understand that she could easily lure men to love her and as easily, if she chose, lure them to their ruin.

Certainly Maria Ana Benites was a clever actress. The artful way in which she depicted a harmless cobbler as a desperate assassin was convincing. The pretended glimpse of Sandoval as he stood in the darkness peering into the Rico home after the murder and then stole silently away was an impressive detail. The poor shoemaker had probably never carried a weapon in his life but the woman's description of him, wrapped grimly in his serape and with "a six-shooter in his waist band," made him appear a villain capable of any atrocity. But at least one part of Ana Benites' story rang true. That was the threat she declared Murrieta had made. That threat was unique and it might seem to have come straight from the heart of such a murderously vindictive man as Murrieta. "I will be your worst *knue*"—a relentless demon of Indian myth and an eloquent symbol of Murrieta's character. "If you should hide in the very guts of the Yankees I will drag you out." The phrase drips blood. It is the quintessence of cold-hearted malevolence. But the probability is that Murrieta threatened Ana Benites with horrible death, not if she betrayed Sandoval, but if she betrayed Murrieta himself.

Reyes Feliz, who had just recovered from wounds received in an encounter with a grizzly bear, was placed on trial immediately after his arrest before a citizens court that sat in the Los Angeles court house. He declared he was a member of Murrieta's band but denied having had anything to do with the murder of Gen. Bean. His statement was printed verbatim in the Los Angeles Star. Reading it to-day, we seem to hear the voice of Murrieta's boyish brother-in-law and sense a touch of pathos in him as he faced his judges and fought for his life in his stupid way, blundering along with artless and hopeless simplicity.

"My name is Reyes Feliz," he said. "I am fifteen or sixteen years old. (He was eighteen.) I was born at the Real de Bayareca in Sonora. I live at San Gabriel. I did not know Gen. Bean. I do not know who killed him. Here in Los Angeles, I heard some gentleman whose name I do not know, say that Murrieta's woman had said Joaquin Murrieta killed him.

"It is true that I asked Pilinguije for a dagger and I told him I was going to gamble with two Americans and that in case I should lose, I would take their money from them. I do not own but one murder. The man I killed was Antonio Marias. I killed him with a shot in Sonora Camp. It is a year since I committed this crime. I killed Marias because he was threatening to kill an American who was a *padrino* of mine.

"I belonged to the company of Joaquin Murrieta and

Pedro Gonzalez who was killed by Americans at the Cuesta del Conejo. I was not then with Gonzalez. I was ill at the time from the bites of a bear. Joaquin Murrieta, Gonzalez and myself robbed twenty horses in Avisimba at the *orilla de las sierras* (foot of the mountains) near the Pueblo of San Jose. We brought the horses to the Tejon mountains where the Indians took them from us. I don't know the name of the man from whom we robbed the horses. He was a Mexican. I have not robbed any more. I know nothing about the death of Gen. Bean."

Cipriano Sandoval and Benito Lopez were tried next day. Ana Benites had "laid the finger" on both of them.

"When I was on my way home from the performance of the rope dancers at 11 o'clock at night," said Sandoval, "I heard shots and a man came running up to me. It was Felipe Read. Felipe said: 'Cipriano, I have just shot Gen. Bean. Here is five dollars. Say nothing. When you want money, come to me and get it.' I understood that Gen. Bean had been too attentive to Felipe's mistress."

Benito Lopez admitted he had operated as a bandit with the gangs of both Joaquin Murrieta and Solomon Pico. He denied complicity in the Bean murder but confessed another murder more atrocious.

"On my way to Los Angeles from the northern mines where I had been with Joaquin Murrieta," he said, "I killed an Indian named Sosa and his woman. Sosa had recently murdered two Americans near Coloma and had robbed them of a mule, a mare, a rifle and two pistols. To gain possession of this property I killed Sosa with a club. His woman seized a rifle and I killed her also. It was twelve days ago that I did this and the bodies may still be found. I left them lying in the brush at the Cabuenga Rancho. I have known for some time that

Ana Benites belonged to Murrieta's gang of robbers. She herself told me she was Joaquin Murrieta's woman."

A squad of citizens took Benito Lopez to the Cabuenga Rancho twelve miles out of town. Two skeletons lay in the brush. "That's them," said Lopez without the flicker of an eyelash, pointing at the ghastly relics. "That one's Sosa and this one's the woman." The woman, it was established, had been a mulatto slave named Mary, owned by a Mr. Thompson who lived in the northern part of the state.

With the evidence all in and much of it conflicting, the presiding judge of the trial court laid before the citizens the question of what should be done with the three prisoners.

"Gentlemen," said the judge, "the court is now ready to hear any motions."

"I move," shouted a gambler, "that Feliz, Sandoval and Lopez be taken to Fort Hill and hanged."

The motion was carried with vociferous acclaim. Next day was Sunday. A herald marched through the streets ringing a dinner bell. "Hear ye, hear ye," he shouted, "three men convicted of robbery and murder by the citizens of Los Angeles will be hanged at high noon on Fort Hill."

As it happened, Pedro Lubrigo while on his way to church that morning had been murdered. He had been walking arm in arm and conversing pleasantly with a man he believed to be his friend when without a word of warning or explanation, the fellow drew a *puñal* from his belt and plunged the blade into Lubrigo's heart. As four men could be executed at the same time on the gallows that had been erected, the citizens decided it would be convenient to hang Lubrigo's murderer with the others.

Rain—rain—pouring in torrents. Four men in line on

the death-trap of a gallows. Half Los Angeles—men and women—standing deep in mud staring silently at four sodden figures bulking darkly high against the gray sky. Hands bound behind them. Straps around their ankles. Ropes about their necks. An abyss of death beneath their feet. To four hopeless wretches, Father Anacleto, in surplice and stole, speaking hopefully. And rain—rain. It drenched the hangman and his assistants. It danced whitely on the bare, pine floor of the gallows. It beat upon Father Anacleto's gray poll and soaked his priestly robes. It swept in windy gusts into the white faces of the men about to die and trickled down their cheeks like tears while they waited stolidly to drop from the misty dimness of the storm into the empty blackness of oblivion. Was ever such dismal death scene?

"I was betrayed by the mistress of my best friend. I warn all that hear me not to place faith in a woman." It was Reyes Feliz speaking.

"I am justly punished for my crimes. God have mercy on me." That was Benito Lopez.

"I die innocent. But it is my fate and I am content." Cipriano Sandoval kissed devoutly the crucifix Father Anacleto held to his lips.

The murderer of Lubrigo kept silent, his mouth curled in a silly, unchanging smile. He was believed to be insane.

Father Anacleto spoke solemnly. "Dear God, forgive them their transgressions. Wash them clean in the blood of Christ." Solemnly the responses came. "God have mercy on me." "Holy Mary pray for me." A heavy thud struck upon the ears of the crowd as the trap fell.

Felipe Read was released from custody and never brought to trial. He was half Scotch and half Spanish and had rich and influential family connections. He died five years later after making a death bed confession of his complicity in Gen. Bean's murder. It was generally believed that both he and Murrieta participated in the crime.

After Gen. Bean's death his San Gabriel drinking place known as the Headquarters saloon passed into the hands of his brother Roy Bean. The younger Bean went to Texas and opened a saloon on the west bank of the Pecos where a cattle trail crossed the river. A few settlers built cabins near him and his five or six neighbors unanimously elected him justice of the peace. He became known as "The Law West of the Pecos," a sardonic title not wholly devoid of truth. His caustic wit, bizarre decisions and rough-and-ready justice gave him a national reputation as one of the original and picturesque characters of the Southwest. The collection of shanties was still nameless when a transcontinental railway was built through it. A limited express developed a "hot box" one day and stopped there. Who should step daintily from the platform but Lily Langtry, English stage beauty. Justice Bean strolled up. For ten or fifteen minutes the famous actress and "The Law West of the Pecos" chatted pleasantly. Bean fell hard. He never ceased to talk of the Jersey Lily's charm and loveliness. He had found at last a name for the village that had grown about his frontier groggery. It was Langtry.

A certain Los Angeles madame gave a ball at her establishment on upper Main street in celebration of the arrival of a bevy of girls of the half-world from San Francisco. It was an elaborate event attended by the sporting elite. After midnight while champagne corks were popping and the revels were at their height, twelve Mexican bandits stalked into the place with drawn six-shooters. They lined men and women against the walls, emptied their pockets, stripped them of their diamonds and jewelry and ransacked the house to the last trunk and dresser drawer. Their business accomplished, they took part in the festivities. They drank many bottles of the madame's most expensive wines and ate heartily of the costly viands spread on the banquet table. "Give us some music," shouted the leader full of the spirit and spirits of the occasion. As the orchestra struck up a dance, the gallant robbers with their arms encircling the silk and satin waists of decollette fair ones whirled about the hall with jovial whoops and spurs jingling. Then having pledged the company in a final bumper of champagne, they kissed the landlady and the beauties of her menage good-bye, and took their departure. *"Buena noche,"* they called back jovially as they passed out the door, taking with them loot valued at twenty or thirty thousand dollars.

Immediately after this exploit, they robbed the residence of a wealthy French vintner on New Aliso street. But by this time the news of their depredations had reached the police, and City Marshal Jack Whaling with a squad of deputies encountered the bandits as they were riding out of town. In a battle that followed, Whaling was killed. It became known in a short time that the leader of the robbers was Luis Vulvia and the man who killed the city marshal was Senate. The murder of Whaling aroused intense excitement; posses took the field; and a reward of $1,500 was offered for Senate dead or alive.

A bull cart driven by an Indian lad, its immense wooden wheels wobbling and creaking, halted in a drizzle of rain in front of the jail on Fort Hill. A Mexican horseman, who had been riding beside it, dismounted. Sheriff Thompson, the jailer, and a few guards looked from a window curiously. Filling the bottom of the cart was something covered by a blanket. Some suburban truck gardener, the officers supposed, bringing vegetables for the prisoners. But the covering with its peculiar undulations did not suggest a cargo of market produce, and a human leg, booted and spurred and visible from the crook of the knee, dangled from the rear of the cart as a ghastly hint of what was hidden beneath the blanket. No, it was not roasting ears and turnips for the jail inmates, but a cartload of dead men.

The horseman introduced himself as Atanacio Moreno. Our old friend Atanacio Moreno, who had been Joaquin Murrieta's secret confederate while keeping store in Yaqui Camp and who had guided Deputy Sheriff Ellis on a false scent when that officer was hot on the outlaw's trail. When the sheriff and jail guards came out to investigate, Moreno coolly removed the blanket and exposed to view five bodies that evidently had been tossed into the cart like sticks of fire wood. They lay sprawled in confusion, rigid in fantastic attitudes, glazed eyes staring wide. One of the dead men, Moreno explained, was Senate and another, Luis Vulvia. The names of the other three, he said he did not know. Moreno had killed them all and he told the story of the single-handed massacre boastfully and dramatically.

"These fellows," said Moreno with a wave of his hand to the five corpses, "captured me as I was riding along the road and held me for ransom at their camp in a wild cañon near La Brea rancho. Luis Vulvia, as you know, was one of the most desperate cut-throats that Joaquin Murrieta ever numbered among his followers and Senate was little inferior to him in boldness and cunning. I laid myself out to ingratiate myself with these hardened rogues. They soon regarded me as they might a harmless and entertaining companion and relaxed their vigilance over me. Once when Vulvia and three others had gone off on a marauding expedition, I was left alone in camp with Senate. Catching him off guard, I snatched his own six-shooter from its scabbard and killed him. Two of the other bandits rode in and I shot them out of their saddles. In a short while Vulvia and a companion arrived and I also killed them. I hired an ox-cart in a neighboring Indian village and brought the bodies to Los Angeles to prove my story and claim the reward."

As soon as Moreno's story had spread through the town, he became the hero of the hour. Every one wanted to shake his hand and buy him a drink. Nothing was too good for him. Crowds followed him. He was pointed out as the bravest man in Los Angeles. The $1,500 reward offered for Senate, dead or alive, was paid to him at a banquet given by the mayor and town officials at which he was the guest of honor. His heroic courage was extolled on all sides.

While Moreno basked in glory, Charles Ducommon, a store keeper, reported to Captain A. W. Hope of the Los Angeles Rangers, that Moreno had offered to sell him an imported gold watch stolen from the French vintner. Moreno was arrested with the watch in his possession. Both the vintner and the half-world madame identified him as one of the band that had robbed them. With the evidence against him overwhelming, Moreno confessed that he had been a member of Luis Vulvia's banditti and had murdered his five comrades while they slept to obtain the Senate reward. The great hero, who stood suddenly revealed as one of the most atrocious scoundrels, was given a legal trial and sentenced to fourteen years in San Quentin but was pardoned after serving only four years. Upon his release he disappeared from California and all trace of him was lost.

CHAPTER XIV.

THE LAST STAND.

THE pioneer age, the pastoral age, the age of gold, the age of lawlessness,—through all these phases California had passed in less than three-quarters of a century. The age of law was dawning in 1853. For more than three years, the state had endured Joaquin Murrieta's reign of rapine and devastation. Now the Days of the Terror were drawing to a close. The state had grown weary of the red nightmare; and the weariness of the state was a menace of death. Heretofore communities, countrysides, counties, had fought Murrieta. For the first time he was to feel the crushing power of the state as a state. The ultimate result was a foregone conclusion. The mighty forces of organized society were marshaling to annihilate the individual pigmy. The whirlwind was gathering to sweep him to destruction.

Governor John Bigler in May 1853 offered a reward of $1,000 for Murrieta dead or alive. The Legislature, sitting at Benicia, passed a bill authorizing Harry Love to recruit a company of mounted men to hunt down the bandit. The company was to number "not more than twenty men" and was to be known as the California Rangers. Enlistments were limited to ninety days. The pay was to be $150 a month. Love began at once the work of organization. By the first of June the company was ready to take the field. Love had selected his troopers with care. They were all men of proved courage, inured to frontier hardships and dangers, good marksmen, hard riders, and as wise in the craft of woods and plains as the outlaws themselves. They were equipped with rifles, shotguns and six-shooters and their horses were animals of speed and stamina.

John R. Ridge, a pioneer California editor, who wrote the original biography of Murrieta which was first published in 1867, gives the names of the men as follows: Bill Byrnes, William T. Henderson, Patrick Edward Connor, Lafayette Black, John S. White, George and John Nuttall, C. F. Bloodworth, G. W. Evans, C. V. McGowan, Robert Masters, W. H. Harvey, Col. McLane, D. S. Hollister, P. T. Herbert, Willis Prescott, James W. Norton, Coho Young, E. B. Van Dorn and S. K. Piggott.

William J. Howard, in a sketch of his life entitled "The Last of the California Rangers," lists the men in this way: Bill Byrnes, William T. Henderson, Patrick Edward Connor, Augustus Black, John White, George and John Nuttall, Charles Bludworth, George Evans, George Chase, Robert McMasters, William and Edward Campbell, Doc Hollister, James Norton, Nick Ashmore, Ned Van Buren, William J. Howard and his brother, Thomas J. Howard.

Howard was a Virginian of fine family. For years he lived on a ranch near Mariposa where he bred thoroughbred horses which he raced in later years at Tanforan and the Bay District tracks near San Francisco and on other race courses in the West. He was at one time sheriff of Mariposa county. He died in Portland, Oregon, in 1924 at the age of ninety-seven and claimed to be the last surviving member of Love's posse. Though Howard was not included in Ridge's list and his account of the pursuit and death of Murrieta is widely at variance with the commonly accepted versions, his claim has never been disputed. Howard furnished most of the horses for

Love's company which for a time camped at his ranch. He knew Love intimately and a number of the Rangers were his neighbors in the Mariposa country.

Of the Rangers, Bill Byrnes alone knew Murrieta or had ever seen him. Dead-shot, dare-devil, adventurer and desperado, Byrnes was a quiet man with a gray eye, sub-zero blood and a face like marble. He started out in life in Missouri under the impressive name of William Wallace Byrnes and studied for the priesthood in a college in St. Louis. At twenty, he went to Texas. Indians were on the rampage in northern Mexico and were spreading terror throughout the country with endless pillage and murder, and the Mexican government offered a bounty of fifty dollars a head for dead Redskins. To Byrnes, who had a shrewd business head on his shoulders, the bounty proved alluring, and with Jim Beckwith, Bob Carson and Jim Lansing, he trekked across the Rio Grande and hunted scalps for the market. Killing Indians, the four partners found, was not difficult once they got the hang of it. The only trick seemed to be to keep their own scalps on while taking the scalps of their victims, and they reduced the danger involved to a minimum by stealing upon encampments by night and killing the Indians while they slept. Throwing themselves into the work with enthusiasm, they filled their pockets with bounty money on two hundred and fifty dead Indians before the trade slackened.

Bob Carson was said to be a relative of Kit Carson, the famous scout. Beckwith was a noted plainsman who lived for years among the Crow Indians and by prowess on the war path in inter-tribal clashes rose to be a sub-chief in the tribe. Lansing had sailed as a pirate under Jean Lafitte, terror of the Gulf of Mexico in the early part of the century, who with his freebooters fought under Gen. Andrew Jackson against the British at the battle of New Orleans. In retaliation for an insult, Lansing murdered fourteen trappers of a fur brigade in the Rocky mountains and fled to Arizona where he found refuge among the Apaches and married a squaw. He was killed in Contra Costa county, California, in 1849. The authority for this hectic period of Byrnes' career was Byrnes himself.

Upon his return to Missouri, Byrnes enlisted for the Mexican war under Col. Sterling Price who became a general in the Confederate army during the Civil war. He saw hard service with Gen. Zachary Taylor's army and was taken prisoner by the Mexicans at the battle of Buena Vista.

"While my father was a prisoner of war," said Mrs. Nellie Abbott, Byrnes' daughter, "he was confined at a Mission town in Sonora. When the priests learned he had studied for holy orders, they became interested in him and he was allowed to attend divine services at the Mission and study Spanish in the Mission school—a language in which he soon became remarkably proficient. It happened that at the time Joaquin Murrieta, then sixteen years old, was a pupil at the school. My father warmed to the bright, handsome lad and, as they were able to converse in the boy's native tongue, they became fast friends. With six or seven other American prisoners, my father finally escaped and made his way to California. One of the party became ill and was left behind at San Bernardino. Another who had fought in the war as a soldier and who begged to be left behind with him, turned out to be his sweetheart. She and the invalid were married upon his recovery."

After his arrival in California, Byrnes shared pot luck as a prospector with Peg-Leg Smith who won his pseudonym by amputating his own leg with a sheath knife and a hack saw after he had been wounded in the knee by a poisoned Indian arrow. Peg-Leg Smith was the reputed discoverer of a gold mine of fabulous riches in Death Valley. He died without revealing its location and the fame of the lost Peg-Leg mine still lingers in romantic California legends.

After trying his hand as a miner at Placerville, then known as Hangtown, Byrnes was a gambler and saloon keeper in the mining camps and, falling in again with Murrieta, became his partner in a monte game in Murphy's Diggings. Byrnes ranched in Carson valley, served as a captain of guards at San Quentin penitentiary, and took part in a campaign against the Piute Indians under Chief Winnemucca in Nevada. He was a desperate gun-fighter and killed a number of men in personal encounters and was himself shot thirty-two times, having had seven bullets removed from his body on one occasion in a San Francisco hospital. The suffering caused by these old wounds, one of which had fractured his skull, eventually drove him crazy and in 1873 he was confined in the asylum for the insane at Stockton and died in that institution in 1874.

While Byrnes and Murrieta were gambling partners in Murphy's Diggings, Byrnes acted the part of a friend and did his best to save Joaquin from being flogged and his brother from being hanged by Bill Lang and his crowd. Nothing had occurred since then to break the friendship between the two but now as a member of Harry Love's Rangers, Byrnes, in cold blood, was engaged in hunting his old-time friend to his death. Whatever Byrnes' feeling may have been for Joaquin in an earlier day, it is certain that Murrieta had been warmly attached to him. On more than one occasion the outlaw had said that, of all the Americans he had ever known, Byrnes was the only one for whom he had a genuine affection. But Byrnes was a strange composite of ice and iron, and in the light of his amazing career, the unutterable horror of certain of his exploits when he had come to the end of his former comrade's last trail, is not wholly inexplicable.

Love's campaign opened when he received word that Murrieta was in the neighborhood of Hornitos; he led his posse south from Stockton, scouting the country on the way. It was not long before the Rangers had an opportunity to demonstrate their mettle and give the public an idea of what might be expected of them. On the lower Merced, they captured two Mexican horse-thieves known to belong to Murrieta's outlaws and started to Quartzburg to lodge them in jail. On the road, the two prisoners attempted to escape and were riddled with bullets by their captors.

At Quartzburg, Ranger Connor wrote: "We have taken the horse which Mr. James Welsh rode when he was shot between San Jose and Santa Clara two months ago and we are now in pursuit of the Mexicans who sold the animal in this place."

At Hornitos, Love found no trace of Murrieta but learned that Albino Teba, a Spaniard, had killed Pedro Sanchez of Murrieta's band at a fandango at Martinez.

While camped at Howard's ranch near Mariposa, Love wrote to Dr. D. S. Clark of Columbia: "So far we have recovered thirty-one stolen horses." Here Love received information that Murrieta had left the hills, heading for the Santa Clara valley, and the Rangers took the trail for San Jose.

Murrieta had kept fully informed of the new power organized to destroy him and realized clearly that the crisis of his life had arrived. He was too wise to think he could cope for any length of time against the state's forces and he made up his mind to withdraw from California forever. But he proposed to himself one final coup that would crown his career and leave his name a symbol of terror for all time among the gringos. He had operated as an outlaw on a magnificent scale, and not for nothing had he raided and plundered and murdered throughout the length and breadth of the state. On many occasions he had sent sums of money ranging from $25,000 to $50,000 to his family in Mexico to hoard against the time when he should return to his native land. He was a rich man at twenty-three. He had had his fill of hardships and dangers. Now he could go back to his boyhood home and live in peace and plenty for the remainder of his days. But he would strike one more blow before he departed and make a bonfire of gringo homes to light him on his final journey.

To carry out this grandiose scheme, he sent couriers to the southern country with orders to his scattered bands to assemble as quickly as possible at the Arroya Cantova and prepare for the stroke that was to wind up his career as an outlaw in a blaze of glory. Meanwhile, to allow time for his instructions to be carried out, he planned to travel down the coast in leisurely fashion and join his followers at the appointed rendezvous. As Love and his posse moved upon Hornitos, Murrieta took the westward trail never to return to the Hills of Gold that had been the scene of so many of his romantic crimes and daring achievements. Death was waiting for him at the end of the road. The Hundred Days were upon him and Waterloo was close at hand.

Murrieta arrived early in June at the ranch of Joaquin Guerra near San Jose and remained in concealment for two weeks. Francisco Sicarro, foreman of the ranch, was secretly connected with his band and guarded him against danger. Two incidents broke the monotony of his sojourn. While drinking in the Tivoli Gardens in the outskirts of San Jose, he was recognized by a Frenchman, the proprietor of the place, and shot him for fear he would betray him. Again he sent an Indian to San Jose to bring him a jug of whiskey, but learning from Sicarro that the fellow suspected who he was and was not to be trusted, Murrieta mounted his horse, overtook the Indian and killed him. The two murders indicated plainly that in his crucial situation Murrieta's nerves were tensed to the breaking point.

Toward the middle of June, Murrieta with fifteen men left the Guerra ranch and started south along the coast road. He traveled with great secrecy, camping by day and riding by night. Occasionally, the country people had fugitive glimpses of ghostly horsemen wrapped in serapes slipping silently past in the moonlight. Exciting little items in the San Francisco and Los Angeles papers bulletined the outlaw's progress.

"Murrieta is known to have passed through Monterey county."

"Murrieta's band rode through San Luis Obispo at midnight. The outlaw leader was identified by several men who knew him."

"Joaquin, it is believed, is bound for Lower California and probably will sail from the old Mission town of Loretto on the east coast of the peninsula, across the Gulf of California to Sonora."

"That Joaquin passed through Los Angeles is certain. Many men of veracity assert positively that he and his band are now somewhere between San Juan Capistrano and San Diego."

"Deputy Sheriff Bors of Santa Barbara arrived in Los Angeles at the head of a posse in pursuit of Murrieta whom they had trailed to within four miles of town. They continued their search at Mission San Gabriel and San Juan Capistrano but without success. It is altogether probable the villain is somewhere in the vicinity of Los

Angeles and it is also probable that he will soon be taken."

"The citizens of San Diego while in pursuit of Joaquin came so near the rogue as to stampede a dozen of his horses. An advertisement in this paper describes four for which owners are wanted."

"Joaquin has executed a surprise movement. He has halted his march toward the southern border and is heading back north. He recently stole more than sixty head of horses near Los Angeles from the ranch of Gen. Andres Pico, brother of Pio Pico, the last governor of California under Mexican rule. He is said to have passed north over the Tehachapi mountains through Tejon Pass and is now believed to be in the Tulare Basin of the San Joaquin valley."

Love and his posse spent several days in San Jose where they had difficulty in picking up Murrieta's tail. When at last they found it and headed south, they were at least two weeks behind the outlaw. This in the end proved fortunate. Murrieta had in truth turned in his course and was traveling north on the east side of the Coast Range while Love was moving south on the west side. Eventually they came abreast of each other and less than a hundred miles apart.

For a day Love camped at San Juan Bautista or San Juan as it is now known. There he had his midnight interview with Antonia La Molinera, Murrieta's former mistress, who had deserted him for Pancho Daniel, and to murder whom the outlaw chieftain had sent Pedro Vergara and Juan Borilda to Los Angeles. Through her underworld associates, this embittered woman had kept posted on Murrieta's movements and had definite information that he was now at the Arroya Cantova. There, she told Love, he would find him. La Molinera was at last to have her revenge.

Love determined to act at once upon this secret information but to mask his plan, he gave it out that he proposed to continue on his way down the coast to Los Angeles and hunt for the outlaw in the southern part of the state. As a ruse to deceive Murrieta's spies with whom the country swarmed, he moved south from San Juan and at the end of a day's march, went into camp on the Salinas plains. But as soon as it had fallen dark, he doubled back on his trail to the neighborhood of San Juan, where at dawn he camped in a secluded cañon and remained concealed all day. At night he headed directly east. That way lay the Arroya Cantova.

After a forced march of fifty miles, he lay up in camp for a day on San Benito creek in the heart of the Coast Range. One more night of travel brought him to Chico Panoche Pass and he sent out scouting parties in an effort to locate the outlaws, who, he knew, were somewhere in those mountain fastnesses. His next camp was at Grande Panoche Pass. From this point, he could look out over the San Joaquin valley and had his first distant glimpse of the narrow cañon leading into the Arroya Cantova.

In Arroya Cantova on the east flank of the Coast Range, Love expected to surprise Murrieta and his band. There was, however, only one entrance to the outlaw stronghold and that was through the tortuous cañon opening into the San Joaquin valley. A surprise attack by night, Love figured, would prove a failure. If Murrieta were in hiding there he undoubtedly would have lookouts posted at the cañon's mouth. Love's only hope of success, as he saw it, lay in a dashing charge into the valley in daylight, with horses at top speed and guns roaring. Though his plan had obvious disadvantages and might result in a number of empty saddles, Love adopted it.

Trusting to luck and their six-shooters, the Rangers went storming into the valley in the early morning. But instead of surprising Murrieta, they were themselves surprised. They found, not a small band of outlaws, but seventy armed Mexicans in charge of several hundred horses. It was too late to retreat and with a bold front, the company rode into the encampment. Love decided to bluff his way through. There was nothing else left to do.

"What are you fellows doing here?" he demanded.

"Hunting mustangs," replied one of the Mexicans.

"You seem to have had pretty good luck."

"We've not done badly. Plenty of wild horses in these parts."

"Seems to me I see brands on some of those animals."

The Mexican shrugged and offered no explanation. Love and his men moved off nonchalantly to the herd and scrutinized the horses closely. They found eight or ten bearing the brands of private ownership and, in a cool, business-like way, cut the animals out of the herd. This took at least a half hour, which was a long time in such dangerous circumstances. When the job was finished, they rode back to the Mexicans who had been watching them in dour silence.

"Those horses were stolen," said Love as brusquely as if he were addressing some cowering thief instead of a crowd of hostile Mexicans. "We'll take 'em along with us."

Sour looks were his only answer.

"We're driving them to San Juan," Love went on with diplomatic mendacity. "If you can prove ownership, you can recover them there."

Then Love and his men rode away, driving the horses before them. Without a single glance behind them, they sat in their saddles as calmly as if engaged in a job of humdrum routine. Seventy armed men could have annihilated them at a single volley but nothing happened. Their exhibition of cold nerve left the Mexicans dumbfounded.

Love went into camp ten miles away in the mountains. Convinced he had nothing to fear from such a cowardly crowd, he sent off two of his men with the horses to Mariposa. Since he had taken the trail, he had arrested a number of horse thieves and recovered many stolen horses and it had been necessary from time to time to use some of his men as guards to escort prisoners and horses to various towns. These duties had seriously reduced his company. Though the absentees were expected to rejoin him as quickly as possible, he now had only seven men left with him. These were Byrnes, Henderson, Black, White, George Nuttall, George Chase and William Howard.

Love sent spies from his camp on July 24 to see what had become of the mustang hunters, and was surprised to learn they had disappeared. This intelligence was not reassuring. If the Mexicans were outlaws, as he suspected, they surely had gone to join Murrieta, who undoubtedly was in the vicinity, and if seventy Mexicans should return with Murrieta at their head, Love would be in a pretty pickle. That night Love saw signal fires burning in the mountains. Having failed to find Murrieta in the Arroya Cantova, he determined to search the neighboring parts of the San Joaquin valley; and he and his men saddled their horses at 3 o'clock in the morning of July 25 and rode to the edge of the hills.

By the time they had arrived on the heights above the mouth of the Arroya Cantova, day was breaking. The illimitable levels of the San Joaquin valley spread out before them, dim in the matutinal twilight, silent, empty, without sign of life. Against the red eastern sky, the far-off Sierra Nevadas were deeply purple. The land at the foot of the hills was rolling and covered with sage brush and scrub-oak. A strip of timber marked the meandering course of Cantova Creek flowing through a deep arroya with steep earth banks.

Suddenly a thin spiral of smoke rose into the sky. In the still air, it stood like a tall blue column above a spot three miles out on the plains in the fringe of trees bordering the arroya. It was evidently the smoke of a camp fire. How many men or what kind of men were about that camp fire, no Ranger could guess. They might be harmless mustang hunters. They might be Murrieta's band of outlaws. All that seemed certain was that at the bottom of that column of smoke, a pot of coffee was boiling and a pan of bacon frying on the coals. Love was a direct man. He dealt straight with his fellow men, he shot straight, he looked straight ahead of him. No beating around a bush for him. No strategy in him. There was the pillar of smoke and he rode straight toward it as if he feared he might be too late for breakfast.

With the column of smoke to guide them, it was not difficult in the broken country for the Rangers to keep under cover. They dodged behind hills, they wound through gaps, they sheltered themselves in rain-washed gullies. The daylight grew clearer. The shadowy heights behind them took definite shape. On the ridges, the pine trees that had been formless blurs came out in green distinctness. Gray ghosts about them became clumps of sage brush. The last stars faded out. The sky above the distant Sierras changed to burnished gold. The world was ready for the sunrise.

The hoofs of the horses made little noise on the sandy loam and the Rangers made their way to within two hundred yards of the camp without being discovered. They filed down then through a side ravine into the deep *arroya* of Cantova creek and, hidden by the embankment, rode rapidly. At a break in the line of mud cliffs where a declivity led down to the creek, they rode up again with weapons drawn and horses lunging, and took the camp by surprise as they burst over the top of the embankment directly upon it.

Seven Mexicans were about the camp fire. One was busy cooking. Another—a swarthy, villainous-looking fellow with a broadcloth serape drawn about his shoulders—squatted on his heels smoking a cigarette and waiting for breakfast. Four were still asleep in their blankets. Off a little distance to one side, a slender, handsome young man, in pants, leggings and white shirt, with a pan of water in his hand, was washing the legs of a bay horse that stood, as if trained, without bridle or saddle. At the opposite side of the camp, six other horses were tethered to picket pins.

As the Rangers closed about the camp fire between the Mexicans and their horses, the one smoking a cigarette arose, the four sleepers sprang to their feet fully clothed and armed, the cook stood blinking through the smoke with a slice of bacon on his fork, and the young buck washing the horse turned and stared in blank astonishment.

"Good morning," said Love cordially with a cocked six-shooter in his hand.

"*Buenas dias,*" returned the ugly customer.

"Where you fellows from?"

"Los Angeles."

"What are you doing in this part of the country?"

"Hunting mustangs."

"Address your questions to me," called out the *caballero* beside the horse. "I am captain of this company."

"Mind your own business," Love shot back. "I'll ask questions where I please."

With a casual air, the young bravo moved toward a brace of six-shooters lying on a pair of blankets near a saddle that glittered with silver mountings close by the fire. Love guessed his purpose and threw his revolver down on him.

"Stop where you are," Love commanded. "Move another step and I'll kill you."

The young dare-devil's eyes flashed angrily and his hand went as if by instinct to the ivory handle of a poniard—his only weapon—sticking from the scarlet sash about his waist. But he went back to his horse and stood with his hand resting on the animal's neck.

"Watch that fellow and keep him covered," said Love to Henderson, and Henderson coolly moved the muzzle of a cocked shotgun over in the Mexican's direction.

Bill Byrnes, Murrieta's old friend, who had lagged behind the posse, now came galloping into camp. His face lighted up as he caught sight of the young man standing beside the horse.

"That's Joaquin," he shouted, pointing his finger. "We've got him at last."

"The hell you say," roared Love who had had no idea who these Mexicans were. "Kill that man." And aiming at the bandit leader, he let fly a shot from his revolver.

Murrieta flung himself on his bareback horse at a bound. "Save yourselves if you can," he cried in Spanish to his men as he dug his heels into the animal's flanks and went racing away at breakneck speed along the *arroya* embankment. Throwing his shotgun to his shoulder, Henderson fired, but his shot went wild and, with Byrnes and White at his heels, he dashed after the outlaw.

As Love fired at Joaquin, Three Fingered Jack Garcia —he of the villainous face—fired at Love, the bullet clipping a few strands of hair from the captain's head. Cut off from their horses, all the Mexicans broke for the brush on foot, firing as they fled toward the hills with the Rangers in pursuit pumping lead from their six-shooters.

With bullets raining about them, two of the fugitives threw up their hands and surrendered before they had run a hundred yards. Marched back to camp, they were bound hand and foot and left lying on the ground while their captors rejoined the chase. Three others, whose identities were never learned, jumped into the creek bed and clambering out on the other side escaped into the foothills. Three Fingered Jack was left to flee and fight alone.

Three Fingered Jack, here in his last extremity—the renowned Three Fingered Jack who loved the sight and smell of blood and had slashed the throats of so many helpless Chinamen in the old, wild days—knew that his plight was hopeless. But no trace of fear was in the black soul of this strange monster, who was as deadly as a cockatrice and as merciless as a tiger, but who, throughout a life of blood curdling horrors, had remained as light hearted and carefree as a boy. A devil from hell in fiendishness, he was a lion in courage.

Converging toward him, the Rangers centered their fire on Three Fingered Jack. Ponderous, ungainly, his long black hair shaking over his shoulders, he bounded through the sage brush on his bandy legs with the clumsiness of a great ape but with the speed of an antelope. Over the uneven ground, criss-crossed by gullies, streaked with chaparral and tangled brakes, he made at times better speed on foot than his foes on horseback. He darted through thickets that the horsemen could not penetrate. When it seemed he must be overtaken, a deep ravine intervened to save him. While his pursuers hunted for a place to cross, he leaped into the ditch and climbed out again with simian agility and left them far behind. If they drew dangerously near him on unbroken ground, he wheeled and sent a ball from his six-shooter whistling about their ears. On three occasions when he turned and fought, Black, Nuttall and Chase had their horses shot from under them and were put out of the hunt. For more than three miles, the bandit ran with an amazing vigor that seemed tireless.

Leading the chase, Love rode hard on his heels. One of Love's bullets winged him. The outlaw shook his shaggy head and kept on with undiminished swiftness. A second bullet struck him. He tumbled to the ground, bounced up like a rubber ball and continued to run. Love was firing rapidly. He emptied one six-shooter and drew another. Three Fingered Jack's trail showed spots of blood. His speed slackened. His tremendous strength was playing out under the effects of his wounds. He began to waver and stumble crazily. The end was near. He stopped dead in his tracks and, swaying for an instant, turned at bay. His savage face writhed with hatred. His eyes glared like those of a jungle beast. Love galloped to within a few yards of him. It was man to man at last. Love had one bullet left in his revolver, Three Fingered Jack, one left in his.

"Throw up your hands," shouted Love, with his six-shooter at a level.

"I will throw up my hands for no gringo dog." The outlaw's voice was like the snarl of a panther.

With his expiring strength, the bandit brought up his six-shooter for his last shot. The weapon aimed at Love's heart, wobbled feebly from side to side and sagged slowly downward. Love fired. The ball crashed through the robber's brain and Three Fingered Jack pitched headlong at full length and lay sprawled with arms out-flung and his blood-smeared face half-buried in the loose sand. Merciless he had been in life, and in death he received no mercy. The same bitter draft he had held so often to the lips of others he was compelled to drain to the lees. One of the Rangers slipped the noose of a lariat about the dead man's neck and dragged him back to camp at his horse's heels.

Meanwhile with Henderson, White and Byrnes in relentless pursuit, Murrieta was fleeing for his life with bullets whispering death around him. Riding like an Indian warrior with his arms locked about his horse's neck and one leg hooked over its shoulders, the outlaw hung at his horse's side and was shielded from the shots of his foes. He kept for a while to the top of the *arroya* embankment. Mounted on one of Howard's thoroughbred racers, Henderson began to gain on him. In danger of being run down and captured, Murrieta headed his horse for the brink of the cliffs that walled the creek. A plunge of fifteen feet was ahead of him. With reckless daring, he took the leap. Out into the air shot his steed. Down it fell with a thundering crash at the bottom of the *arroya* and plunged over in a headlong somersault while the outlaw went flying to the ground. When the horse rose, Murrieta, springing on its back, rose with it and sped down the cañon like a whirlwind as buckshot from the second barrel of Henderson's shotgun rattled about him.

Henderson did not care to risk his neck in such a foolhardy venture and he continued the pursuit on the bank above. But he could catch only occasional glimpses of the bandit and the interminable windings of the ravine retarded his speed. He must at all hazards get to the bottom of the *arroya*. Fortune favored him and, coming to a place where the wall was low, he jumped his horse into the cañon without accident. But the leap brought the animal to a dead stop. Seconds were precious. Joaquin drew out into a long lead and disappeared around a bend. A few more lost seconds and the outlaw would escape.

Into the sides of his horse, Henderson drove his spurs.

The blood of sires that had raced to glory on the turf was in this thoroughbred and, straining every nerve, it responded to the call for speed as if in a desperate home-stretch drive. On it flashed among the cottonwoods and live oaks along the creek, slipping around the curves, hugging the cliffs, dashing across the shallow stream from side to side, flinging the water high in sparkling rain, while the cañon echoed to the drumming thunder of its hoofs. Foot by foot, it cut down the distance. Henderson raised a view-halloo when Murrieta at last came in sight again.

Henderson's six-shooter flamed. This time he shot, not at Joaquin, but at his horse. The animal stumbled as the ball crashed into its thigh. Again he fired. The horse floundered and nearly went down as the second shot struck almost in the same spot. Blood gushed from the wounds, leaving a trail like a broad crimson ribbon. The bullets evidently had cut an artery. As if it knew its master's life depended upon its speed, the courageous animal, dying on its feet, struggled onward. Quick to realize the crisis, Murrieta straightened upright and urged on his steed with voice and heels.

For the first time, Henderson, a crack marksman, had a fair target. He planted a ball in the small of the bandit's back that dropped him over on his horse's neck. White and Byrnes, who had found a place where they could ride down into the *arroya,* caught up with the chase. As he drew abreast of Henderson, White sent a second bullet into the outlaw. Byrnes galloped up and fired a third shot. Murrieta pitched to the earth with a heavy thud. His horse in its last throes gave a few violent lunges beyond him and fell dead.

Getting to his feet with a painful effort, Murrieta ran unsteadily in a desperate effort to escape. To the last heart-beat, the human creature was fighting instinctively for its life. But nothing could save him. All hope was gone. Henderson pulled his horse to a stop and drew a steady bead. His six-shooter spouted fire. The bullet passed through the outlaw's body and narrowly missed his heart. Wounded to the death, Murrieta turned with quiet acceptance of fate, and facing his enemies, raised his right hand.

"Es bastante," he said in a clear voice. *"No tire mas. El trabajo se acabo. Ya estoy muerto."* (It is enough. Shoot no more. The job is finished. I am dead.)

As he stood there in his last thirty seconds of life, a spot as deeply scarlet as his sash showed on the bosom of his white shirt over his heart. An ashen pallor overspread his bronze face. A look of weariness came into his eyes. His head drooped forward. He dropped to his knees and, leaning over for a moment on one hand, sank on his side. It was as if death had gathered him in its arms and laid him gently down. With his face pillowed on his arm, he lay as if in peaceful sleep.

As the outlaw died, the sun rose over the distant Sierras, and plains and mountains were bathed in the radiance of the morning. For California, a new era came with the sunrise—an era of law and order.

CHAPTER XV.

HEADING WEST.

CAPTAIN HARRY LOVE was in a quandary. He pursed his rugged brows as he sat by the camp fire among his Rangers and drank a cup of coffee.

"It would have been better," he said, "if we could have taken Murrieta alive. We want that reward offered by Governor Bigler but now that Murrieta's dead, how are we going to prove we killed him? I'm wondering if the governor will pay us unless we produce proof."

Well, that was worth thinking about. The captain's astute observations made the Rangers a trifle uneasy.

"Don't you think the governor will take our word for it?" asked Henderson.

"I'm not so sure about it. The governor's foxy. If he disbelieved our story or pretended to disbelieve it, he'd save himself a thousand dollars. That reward is to come out of his own pocket—if it comes."

"Seems to me he ought to take the word of eight men."

"He might and he mightn't."

"What're we going to do about it?"

Captain Love for a moment sipped his coffee in silence.

"I'll tell you what I think we'd better do. We'd better cut off Murrieta's head and take it to Benicia and show it to Bigler."

"That would be proof enough for anybody," laughed Henderson.

"If we showed him Murrieta's head, he'd have to pay us and no doubt about it."

"There's no other way out of it," declared Bill Byrnes. "But while we're about it, we'd better cut off Three Fingered Jack's head too and his three-fingered hand. They'd be what you might call corroborative evidence."

"We'll do it," declared Love. "If we can show down two heads and a hand, we ought to win the pot. A couple of you fellows go and attend to the job. You might begin on Three Fingered Jack. You'll find him lying right over yonder under that cottonwood tree."

But no man moved to obey the order.

"What's the matter?" asked Love. "Didn't you hear me?"

"I don't want the job."

"Me neither."

"Same here."

"I wouldn't do it for pay."

"The governor can keep his money if it's left to me."

"I didn't know you fellows were so lady-like," said Love. "How about you, Byrnes?"

"Sure, I'll do it," replied Byrnes coolly.

So equipped with a hatchet and sheath-knife, Byrnes, the emotionless man of frozen blood, rode down the *arroya,* cut off his old friend's head and brought it back to camp. Then he sliced Three Fingered Jack's head from his shoulders and hacked off his right hand. Voila! The proof was ready for the governor.

The two Mexicans that had been taken prisoners gave their names as Antonio Lopez and Jose Maria Ochova, though the latter was identified later by another Mexican in Mariposa as Salvador Mendez. Ochova made oath to the identity of Murrieta and corroborated the report that the outlaw leader had been preparing to pillage and burn on a wholesale scale before he said good-bye to California and retired permanently to Sonora. Lopez, a grim-faced, athletic man, steadfastly refused to talk.

"I'll make him talk," said Love and he held up Murrieta's gory head by the hair and shook it before the prisoner's face. "Answer our questions or we'll treat you to a dose of the same medicine."

"I can die but once," said Lopez. "Do what you please. You will get nothing from me."

Byrnes and Black took the two heads and the hand in a gunny sack to Fort Miller ninety miles away across the San Joaquin valley. There they obtained from Dr. Edgar Leach, the post surgeon, a keg of alcohol in which Murrieta's head and Three Fingered Jack's hand were placed to preserve them. Three Fingered Jack's head had been so badly disfigured by Love's last shot that it was thought inadvisable to preserve it and it was buried. With the gruesome relics, Byrnes and Black rejoined the posse in Mariposa.

Spoils of the victory that fell into Captain Love's hands were six fine riding horses, seven costly saddles and bridles, a brace of holster pistols, and a number of six-shooters and broadcloth cloaks. All the horses had been stolen and were later restored to their owners. No money was found. Ochova declared Three Fingered Jack had flung away a purse full of gold during the chase and it was thought possible Murrieta had done the same. The headless bodies of Murrieta and Three Fingered Jack were left unburied for the buzzards and coyotes.

While the Rangers were crossing Tulare Slough on their way to Mariposa, Lopez committed suicide by plunging headlong from his horse into six feet of water. He did not come up and George Chase, an expert swimmer, dived after him. Chase grasped him about the waist under water and tried to pull him to the surface, but Lopez, determined to kill himself, hung on tightly to the stems of the tules at the bottom and Chase could not break his hold. During the excitement, the horse Lopez had been riding backed into deep water where it became entangled among the rushes and was drowned.

When the Rangers arrived at Mariposa, Ochova was placed in jail. He was subsequently transferred to the jail at Martinez where, in the hope of saving himself from the gallows, he made many startling disclosures regarding the secret affiliation of Mexican citizens of the town with Murrieta's outlaw organization. The night after he had made his confession, he was taken from jail by a mob, composed exclusively of Mexicans, and hanged to a tree on the main street in front of the office of Judge Holton, a brother-in-law of Benjamin F. Butler, afterward a distinguished general in the Union army during the Civil war. He was hanged to silence him, and his executioners were supposed to have been Murrieta's former spies and undercover allies and their friends.

In Mariposa and in a number of towns through which the Rangers passed on their journey to the state capital, Murrieta's head was placed on public exhibition and was identified by many. Seventeen affidavits were obtained by Love from persons who had known the outlaw. Among those who signed affidavits were, Father Domnic Blaine, Caleb Dorsey, Ignacio Lisarrago, Henry C. Long, Pedro Manka, Jose Maria Vaga, Stephen Bond, Susan Banta, Juliet G. Sharp, the prisoner Ochova and Bill Byrnes of the Rangers. When Love and his men reached Benicia, which was then the state capital, Governor Bigler was satisfied with the proof submitted to him and paid the reward of one thousand dollars. This money was divided among the Rangers who also received $450 each for their services in the field. Believing Love had not been sufficiently rewarded, the Legislature in May, 1854, passed an act granting him an additional sum of $5,000.

But the adventures of Murrieta's head and Three Fingered Jack's hand were not ended. Henderson and Black exhibited them in towns up and down the state. The public interest in the ghastly trophies was intense, crowds flocked to see them, and the showmen cleared large profits on their venture. Here is a copy advertising the exhibit in San Francisco:

JOAQUIN'S HEAD
Can Be Seen At King's
Corner Sansome and Halleck Streets
Opposite The American Theater
Also Hand of Three Fingered Jack
Admission One Dollar

Head and hand were displayed in glass jars filled with alcohol. "The head," said the Alta California, "does not appear natural, being discolored by the blood that has settled in the face and about the mouth. It is readily recognizable, however, by those who knew the bandit by the deep scar that marks the right cheek." Many superstitious persons, it was said, were "seized with a kind of terror to observe that Murrieta's mustache had grown longer since his head was cut off and the nails of Three Fingered Jack's hand had lengthened almost an inch."

The head and hand were sold in 1855 for $36 "to satisfy an execution" at an auction ordered by Sheriff David Scannell. J. V. Plume bought the head and Dennis Lyons the hand. "How much am I bid for the head of the celebrated Joaquin Murrieta," shouted Auctioneer John Harrison. "So it's selling a human head, you are," spoke up an Irishman. "As sure as the saints will judge you, you'll never have anything but bad luck for the rest of your life." Harrison committed suicide a few weeks later. Plume sold the head to a noted character known as Natchez, who kept a gun store and shooting gallery and furnished the pistols for many duels, including that between U. S. Senator David C. Broderick and David S. Terry, associate justice of the California Supreme Court, in which Broderick lost his life. Soon after Natchez acquired the head, he accidentally killed himself while handling a pistol. These two tragedies gave rise to a superstition that ownership of the head carried with it the dead bandit's curse.

Head and hand eventually passed into possession of Louis J. Jordan and for many years were exhibited at his Pacific Museum of Anatomy and Natural Science, originally located on Pine street between Montgomery and Sansome but later on Market street. They disappeared mysteriously in the late 1890's. What became of them no one ever knew. As an easy solution of the enigma, it became customary in later years to say they were lost in the earthquake and fire of 1906.

Who killed Murrieta was for a time a moot question in the public mind. Henderson, White and Byrnes were each credited with having fired the fatal shot.

"Murrieta," said Henderson, "probably would have died either from my first shot or from White's bullet. It was, however, my second shot that killed him. I don't think Byrnes hit him."

Mrs. Nellie G. Abbott, Byrnes' daughter, who had the story of Murrieta's death from her father, said: "It was because of my father's modesty and Harry Love's boastfulness that Love was popularly believed to have killed the outlaw. Love admitted he had nothing to do with it. My father was one of the best revolver shots in California and Murrieta fell before his six-shooter. It was my father's shot at about thirty feet that knocked Joaquin off his horse. With his dying breath, Joaquin said: 'To think, Byrnes, that you should kill me—the only American I ever regarded as my friend.' "

Harry Love, when asked to decide the controversy, said: "I don't know who killed Murrieta. It was either Henderson or White. Both were shooting at him. I myself killed Three Fingered Jack. There's no doubt about that. I singled out Three Fingered Jack because he was the ugliest man in his crowd and I was the ugliest man in mine. We were about even-up on beauty. But I had a quicker trigger-finger. When he made his last stand, Three Fingered Jack would have killed me if I had not killed him first."

For years, according to his own story, Henderson was haunted by Murrieta's ghost.

"I was riding at dusk one day from Los Angeles to my ranch," said Henderson, "when a headless horseman wrapped in a black serape suddenly appeared at my side.

" 'Who are you and what do you want?' I demanded.

" 'I am Joaquin,' replied the phantom, 'and I want my head.'

" 'Joaquin,' I said, 'your head passed out of my possession long ago and I do not know what became of it.'

" 'I hold you responsible for my head,' said the apparition. 'I can have no peace without it and I will never let you rest until you restore it to me.'

"Then it vanished. Many times after that it appeared to me as I rode along some lonely road and always with the same plaintive refrain, 'Give me back my head.' At night I would awake to hear a voice calling to me in the darkness, 'I am Joaquin and I want my head.' Often too in broad daylight, the sorrowful voice that no one else could hear would ring in my ears—'Give me back my head. Give me back my head.'

"These strange experiences did not frighten me. I was no more afraid of Joaquin dead than I had been of Joaquin living. I would gladly have restored the head if it had been in my power. I felt deeply sorry for the poor, unhappy ghost that seemed doomed to wander forever up and down the earth seeking its head and seeking it in vain." *

Henderson, a native of Tennessee, was a veteran of the Mexican war. While ranching in California, he captured a Mexican who had stolen one of his horses and hanged him to a tree single-handed as a one-man lynching party. He was genial, sober, moral and urbane and became moderately wealthy. He fell dead from a heart attack at Coarse Gold Gulch near Fresno on Christmas day, 1882.

Love and ten of his Rangers died tragically. White was murdered at Fort Tejon by Mexicans in revenge for Murrieta's death. Black served as a Union soldier in the Civil war and was killed in action. James Norton and Nick Ashmore were shot in a brawl in Salt Lake City. Chase went to British Columbia in the Frazer river gold stampede and was drowned. William and Edward Campbell lost their lives when caught by a sudden freshet in King's river. Ned Van Buren cashed out in a fight in Contra Costa county when the other fellow beat him to the draw by an eighth of a second. John Nuttall joined William Walker's filibustering expedition to Nicaragua and was killed in battle in that country. Herbert was among the casualties of the Civil war.

Of the others of Love's company in either Ridge's or Howard's list, Bludworth, who became sheriff of Merced county, died at Snelling; George Evans at Santa Cruz;

* In his entertaining volume of reminiscences entitled "On The Old West Coast," Horace Bell tells this story in a slightly different version as Henderson told it to him.

Thomas T. Howard at Galveston, Texas; Doc Hollister at San Jose; Robert Masters or McMasters at Sacramento; and George Nuttall at Stockton. Walter H. Harvey, a brother-in-law of Governor John G. Downey, was at the time of his death in 1861 Commissioner of Immigration at San Francisco. Mrs. Edward Martin and Mrs. Peter Donohue, sisters of Harvey's wife, were in later years, among the leaders of San Francisco society. Harvey was noted as the killer of James Savage, who in 1851 during an Indian campaign discovered the Yosemite valley. The killing was in self-defense and Harvey was acquitted. What became of C. V. McGowan, Col. McLane, Willis Prescott, Coho Young and S. K. Piggott is not known.

Patrick Edward Connor, a native of Ireland, won distinction as a soldier. In his youth he fought in the Seminole war of 1839 in Florida. He was captain in a Texas regiment during the Mexican war and received honorable mention in official dispatches for conspicuous gallantry at Buena Vista. He was severely wounded in that battle but did not retire from the field and only nine of his company were capable of fighting at the close of the day. Gen. Wool, who found him in the midst of this devoted band, supposed the remainder of his company had fled in panic, and said sternly, "Captain Connor, where are your men?" "There, general," replied Connor pointing to the dead.

At the outbreak of the Civil war, Connor became colonel of the Third regiment of California volunteers but never saw service east of the Rocky mountains. He won a decisive victory over the Indians on Bear river in Washington in which Chiefs Bear Hunter, Lehi, and Sagwitch were slain with two hundred and fifty of their warriors. His most notable campaign was against the Mormons in Utah, who, under Brigham Young, had become hostile. He was made a brigadier in the regular army in 1863 and was breveted major general in 1865. He was in command of Fort Douglas near Salt Lake City when he died in 1891 and was buried in the military cemetery at that post.

Philemon Thomas Herbert was a graduate of the University of Alabama at Tuscaloosa where he was said to have killed a fellow student in a quarrel. He was a member of the California Legislature in 1853-54. In a duel fought at the Presidio in San Francisco between James Hawkins and Christopher Dowdigan, he acted as Hawkins' second. The duel was with rifles at forty yards and ended when Dowdigan was wounded. Herbert was elected to Congress in 1855, and while in Washington killed a waiter named Tom Keating in the Willard hotel. This murder brought him national notoriety and alienated many of his friends and political partisans in California, and he moved to El Paso where he practiced law. He was lieutenant colonel of a Texas regiment in the Confederate army during the Civil war and was wounded at the battle of Mansfield in 1864. From the effects of this wound, he died at Kingston, La., three months later.

Harry Love reached the end of the trail in 1868. A great change had come over him since the days when he and his Rangers had driven Murrieta and his outlaws into their last ditch. Old age was upon him. There was still power in his rugged frame but wrinkles were showing in his face, his black eyes had lost their sparkle, and his blue-black hair was sprinkled with gray. He drank rather hard, his temper had grown sullen and morose, and he talked at times in a way that indicated a clouded brain.

Ten years before, he had married Mrs. Margaret Bennett, a widow with a small property and considerably older than himself, who lived in Santa Clara, a small village a few miles from San Jose. The marriage was unhappy. There were many bitter quarrels, separations and reconciliations. The affairs of the couple came to such a pass that Mrs. Love, afraid her husband might do her violence, hired Christian Elversen, a day laborer, to act as her bodyguard. Love grew jealous without reason; —his wife was past seventy and Elversen was comparatively a young man. Threatening to kill him, Love ordered Elversen off the place. There had been a time when Love's wrath made men tremble. Now this hireling defied him. Elversen would remain at the home as Mrs. Love's protector, he declared, as long as Mrs. Love cared to continue him in her employ.

Accompanied by Elversen, Mrs. Love drove into San Jose to transact some business. Love's anger flamed when he saw them together on the street. "That fellow," he said to a friend, "will never enter my home again except over my dead body." He hurried to Santa Clara. At his home he armed himself with a double-barreled shotgun and a six-shooter and lay down behind the front fence to await Elversen's return. But there was evidence of dementia in his preparations. It had been Love's way in former times to confront his enemies boldly. But here he was lying in ambush behind a fence. Strangely enough he had gone out to do battle to the death with his shotgun loaded with harmless bird-shot. Stranger still, he had provided himself with a bag of crackers and a pot of coffee. Plainly the old man was laboring under a crazed hallucination and imagined he might be besieged.

As Elversen and Mrs. Love, driving back from San Jose, approached the house, Mrs. Love's daughter ran out into the road and warned them of their danger. Drawing his revolver, Elversen sprang from the wagon and rushed toward Love. Both men began shooting. Still lying on the ground, Love poked the muzzle of his shotgun through the fence and fired both barrels. A few of the bird-shot peppered Elversen's face but did not stop him. Firing rapidly Love emptied his six-shooter. One of the balls wounded Elversen slightly in the right arm. He coolly transferred his weapon to his left hand and continued to advance. When he arrived at Love's hiding place, he reached over the fence and shot the recumbent Love in the right arm, breaking the bone above the elbow. Love scrambled to his feet. "Murder!" he shouted at the top of his voice, and the hero of other days took to his heels.

Vaulting the fence, Elversen, whose own ammunition was exhausted, picked up the empty six-shooter Love had thrown away and ran in pursuit. Overtaking Love near the house, he struck him over the head with the gun and knocked him down and doubtless would have finished him if a carpenter, working about the premises, had not interfered to save Love's life.

Physicians were called at once and decided it was necessary to amputate Love's broken arm. They administered a large quantity of chloroform and, while Love lay in a coma, removed his arm at the shoulder socket. Love never regained consciousness and died immediately after the operation His neighbors and friends always remained in doubt as to whether his death was caused by chloroform, the shock of the operation, or Elversen's bullet.

So passed Harry Love, frontiersman, adventurer and redoubtable man-hunter. His last unheroic escapade was no gauge of his character. He was undoubtedly a brave man. He had become a pathetic shadow of his former self. His name no longer inspired fear. His trigger-finger had lost its deadliness and his fighting days were over. In his final battle, he was a ridiculous figure with his bag of crackers and his pot of coffee—ridiculous but tragic. The old warrior, it was believed, had gone insane from brooding over his domestic troubles.

CHAPTER XVI.

STRANGE TALES.

JOAQUIN MURRIETA,—so the story ran—long after he was reputed to have been killed, visited San Francisco accompanied by the Mexican sheriff of Monterey county, viewed the head said to be his own on exhibition in Jordan's museum, and enjoyed the joke with a burst of laughter.

It was not the ghost of the outlaw. It was Joaquin Murrieta in flesh and blood, full of health and vigor and with his own proper head on his shoulders. Ridiculous? A fantastic absurdity? Plain, downright lie? Very well. No one has to believe it. But that was the story and many people in California had no doubt of its truth.

Strange tales became rife that the bandit had not been killed but had escaped to Mexico where he was living comfortably on the fortune he had amassed by his robberies. The head exhibited as his was said to be that of Gregorio Lopez or Joaquin Murias or some other member of his band who strongly resembled him. Reputable citizens who had visited Mexico declared they had talked with Murrieta on his own cattle ranch in Sonora. One story had it that he returned to California and dug up a treasure of $18,000 which he had buried in the Sierra foothills. Four years after the outlaw's supposed death, Antonio Murrieta, his brother, living in Los Angeles, said Joaquin was alive and recently had written him a letter. It was asserted in later years that the famous freebooter died near Arispe in Sonora in 1879.

"Joaquin's sister who lived in Marysville," said Bill Mariana of Middle Bar, "pretended to identify the head when she saw it in Stockton. But to her Mexican friends she declared it was not the head of her brother. She visited Jordan's museum later with an old friend of Joaquin's named Cedro, who lived at Jesus Maria. Cedro was as positive as the sister that the head was not Murrieta's. I knew Joaquin myself and know it was not his head. The head on exhibit has thick lips, coarse features and very dark skin and looks like that of a Yaqui Indian. Murrieta's skin was fair and his features were well formed. He was a fine looking man."

John Green, Jr., of Stockton was the son of the John Green who once had entrusted Murrieta to carry $8,000 from Sonora to the Green ranch in the San Joaquin valley. He had known Joaquin for years.

"I knew as soon as I saw the head," said Green, "that it was not Joaquin's. I told the proprietor of the saloon in which it was on view in Stockton to see if there was a scar about three inches long behind the right ear. There was none. Murrieta had such a scar and I have seen it often. Murrieta's wife was standing beside me at the time. 'God bless you, John,' she said. She declared it was not Joaquin's head."

This Mrs. Murrieta was supposed to be Ana Benites, who was known as the outlaw's widow and who lived in San Jose for twenty years after Murrieta had disappeared.

Alfred A. Green, a lawyer, was employed in 1857 by Mayor Burr of San Francisco to go to San Buenaventura to obtain the testimony of Don Gumazindo Flores in an important case then pending before the U. S. Supreme court in which the city was interested. In San Buenaventura, Green met a young priest from Spain who was in charge of the Mission church. They frequently dined together and became very friendly. One evening after supper they strolled to a knoll a little distance south of the Mission buildings. "Here," said the priest, "is where Gen. Andres Pico hanged five robbers and assassins." The priest related some curious anecdotes of the men who were hanged. The conversation turned to noted California criminals and the name of Joaquin Murrieta was mentioned.

"I will tell you something about him," said the priest, "but with the understanding that you do not repeat it for some time. I will leave it to your own discretion when to reveal it."

Green promised secrecy and the priest related this startling story:

"It was not the head of Joaquin Murrieta that was cut off and that has been exhibited all over the state," said the priest. "Only a month ago when I was in Los Angeles, I was called upon to marry a young couple, and the name of the bridegroom was Antonio Murrieta. I was struck with the name.

" 'Are you any relation of the famous outlaw?' I asked him.

" 'Yes, father,' he replied, 'I am his brother.'

" 'Is it true the Americans cut off your brother's head after they had killed him?'

" 'No, father,' he said, 'it is not true. They neither killed him nor cut off his head. But here is a letter I have recently received from my brother. Read for yourself.'

"He drew a letter from his pocket and handed it to me and I read it with great astonishment. It was dated only a few weeks before at Magdalena, Sonora, Mexico, which is a few miles south of the Arizona border, and was signed 'Joaquin Murrieta.'

" 'I am aware,' the letter read, 'that the Americans have a head that is being exhibited as my head. I ask you, my brother, to sanction the story told about my death and I hope all the members of my family in California will do the same. If the Americans hear that I escaped from California and am still alive, they may follow me into Mexico.'

" 'All the family,' said Joaquin's brother, when I had returned the letter to him, 'have invariably told the Americans who brought the head to us to identify that it is Joaquin's head, and we still tell the same story whenever we are questioned about it.' "

Green was living in Tucson, Arizona, in 1879 and when he received information that Joaquin had died that same year he felt absolved from the promise he had given the priest and made the story public.

"When I was in Mazatlan not long ago," he wrote, "I heard that Murrieta had lived there for a while after he escaped from California but later moved to Sonora. I have recently been informed by my brother, Col. George M. Green, who for the past eighteen months has been on an exploring expedition in Sonora, that he visited several towns in that state where Joaquin had lived and that the outlaw died in October, 1879, near Arispe. At the time of his death, he was the owner of a cattle ranch and was in prosperous circumstances."

R. M. Daggett, a widely known San Francisco journalist, had seen Murrieta several times and identified the head.

"Notwithstanding the ugly knife scar across the cheek," wrote Daggett in 1893, "it was believed by many that the head was not that of the noted outlaw but the head of one of his followers who had looked enough like him to be mistaken for him. It was deemed possible that Murrieta had escaped during or just before the attack on his band and made his way back to Mexico. Absurd as this suggestion may seem, several circumstances imparted to it a color of plausibility. Four or five years after the reputed death of Joaquin, Dr. J. B. Trask, for some years state geologist of California, informed me that a reliable friend of his, just returned from Mexico, had conversed with Joaquin in Sonora and from Joaquin's own lips had heard the story of his escape across the international border. Under an assumed name Joaquin had settled in the state of Sonora and was the proprietor of a large cattle ranch. Dr. Trask's friend had known Murrieta in Tuolumne county and recognized him at once.

"Although Joaquin's sister said the amputated head was that of her brother, it was known at the time she was far from positive in her identification. Bill Byrnes, of Love's Rangers, it is said, denied to several of his intimate friends that Joaquin had been killed. Once, in the early sixties, according to report, Byrnes declared, 'Joaquin would have to be killed once more to entitle him to burial.' On another occasion Byrnes is purported to have said, 'One pickled head was as good as another, if there was a scar on the face and no one knew the difference.' "

Byrnes' alleged statement, as quoted by Daggett, would seem difficult to reconcile with the fact that Byrnes claimed to have killed Murrieta and made oath in affidavit form identifying the head. When Byrnes rode into the outlaw camp, he instantly recognized Murrieta and the recognition led to Murrieta's flight and death. If it had not been for Byrnes' recognition, it is possible the bandit might not have been slain.

Frank Marshall of Pleasant Valley is the authority for the following tale of the mysterious hog man and the buried treasure.

A rich Italian who had kept a general merchandise store in Hornitos and who from time to time had dug for the treasure Murrieta was believed to have buried in that part of the country, took a trip to Brazil. On the street in Rio Janeiro, a courteous, good looking young man accosted him.

"I think I have seen you before," said the young man. "Are you not from California?"

"I am."

"A Californian seems like an old friend to me here in this distant part of the world. I once lived there myself. What town are you from?"

"I now live in San Francisco. But I formerly was a merchant in Hornitos."

"Hornitos? Then you must know something of Joaquin Murrieta, the famous outlaw?"

"O yes, Hornitos was one of Joaquin's old stamping grounds."

"Tell me, was he as black as he was painted?"

"No. Joaquin was a fine fellow. He and his men used to trade with me and they always paid me more for their purchases than I asked. When Joaquin was killed by Harry Love and his Rangers, to tell the truth, I felt a little sorry."

"Suppose I should tell you that Joaquin was not killed, what would you say?"

"I would say you did not know what you were talking about. He was killed very dead and I have seen his decapitated head that was exhibited in San Francisco."

"Did you recognize the head?"

"I can't say that I did. I had seen Joaquin only a few times. But there was no doubt it was his head."

"I will tell you something that will surprise you. Joaquin is still alive and I myself am Joaquin."

The Italian was astounded at this announcement and for a time was incredulous but the young man convinced him he was Murrieta and told him how he escaped from

California. After they had talked a long while, the Italian, who had buried treasure on the brain, led the conversation to that subject.

"I have heard you buried treasure of great value in California," he remarked.

The young man laughed. "Have you ever heard of anybody finding any?"

"No but it is generally believed that you buried much gold in the hills around Hornitos and I myself have dug for it."

"If I left any buried treasure in California no one will ever find it but myself," replied the young man. "I may return for it some day."

Toward the end of his outlaw career, Murrieta, with Three Fingered Jack and five or six others, met six Germans near Moccasin Creek on the trail between Quartzburg and Sonora. The Germans were leaving the mining country and were bound for San Francisco where they expected to take ship for their homes in Germany. They were driving mules before them packed with provisions, blankets and personal effects. Murrieta halted the party and while his men sat in their saddles with cocked revolvers, dismounted and began to search the travelers. The first of the Germans whose pockets he attempted to rifle, resisted. Murrieta slapped his face.

"Shell out," he said, "and be quick about it or there'll be a dead Dutchman not a thousand miles from here."

With a six-shooter cocked in his face, the terrified German forked over a buckskin bag filled with gold dust. While this was going on, his companions, desperate at the prospect of losing the treasure for which they had labored so long in the mines, drew their weapons, determined to sell their lives in defense of it. But they had no chance against such adepts in murder. There was a sudden flurry of gunfire and as the smoke drifted away, six

Germans lay dead in the road. Then the outlaws took their time in going through their pockets and ransacking the packs strapped on the mules. The loot of the robbery was said to be $18,000 in gold dust.

Several years after his encounter in Brazil with the young man who called himself Murrieta, the Italian merchant went to Hornitos on a visit and, while there, heard of the arrival on Moccasin Creek of a mysterious stranger, in charge of a drove of hogs, who had dug for treasure and apparently had found it. Very much interested in this report, the Italian rode to Moccasin Creek. There he found an Italian rancher who gave him the details of the hog man's visit.

"When I arose one morning," said the rancher, "I saw a stranger with a head of fifty or sixty hogs in camp a few hundred yards from my house. I supposed he was on his way up from the San Joaquin valley to market his hogs in the gold camps, and I paid little attention to him. But he remained in camp all that day and the next, and I went out to see if any accident had happened to him. The hog man was strong and athletic but he had long white hair and a long white beard that seemed out of keeping with his young looking face and a pair of remarkably keen black eyes. I found that he had dug a number of holes in the ground here and there about his camp and wondered what he was up to.

" 'Prospecting?' said I.

" 'Yes,' said he.

" 'I don't think you'll find any gold around here. This country has been mined out.'

" 'O, I'm just taking a chance,' he replied. 'Whenever I drive hogs to market through these parts, I keep my eyes open and do a little prospecting as I go along. You never can tell what you may find.'

" 'Have you found anything that looks like gold here?'

" 'No,' he said, 'nothing whatever.'

"As he seemed inclined not to talk, I left him and went back to the house. He remained in camp three days. Then I looked for him and could see nothing of him. His hogs were rooting about but he had vanished. As he did not return, I finally took possession of the hogs. I never saw the white-bearded hog man again.

"Among the holes he had dug was a trench about four feet deep and five or six feet long. At the bottom of it lay a canvas sack old and rotting, with particles of gold dust adhering to it, and about it, a sprinkling of gold on the earth. I took the sack and some of the earth that I scooped up with my hands back home with me where I panned them out and recovered eleven dollars worth of gold dust."

From description, the Italian merchant believed that, despite his white hair and beard, the hog man was the young fellow he had met in Brazil. Remembering the young man's remark that he might return to California some day and dig up the treasure he had buried, the merchant jumped to the conclusion that the hog man was no other than Joaquin Murrieta in disguise. The treasure unearthed was supposed to be the $18,000 that had fallen into the outlaw's hands when he and his men robbed and murdered the six Germans on the Moccasin Creek trail.

Stories that Murrieta was alive carried weight in some quarters but the vast majority of the people of California had no doubt whatever that the outlaw died on Cantova Creek under the guns of Harry Love's Rangers. Such skeptical tales have sprung up after the death of a number of historical characters. The story that Marshal Ney did not die before a firing squad in the Luxembourg Gardens in Paris after Waterloo but escaped to the United States and lived to a ripe old age in the Carolinas is one classic example. Another is that Wilkes Booth, after the assassination of President Lincoln, was not killed by a pursuing posse in Virginia but lived for many years under an assumed name in the West and died a natural death as an old man. There were reputable witnesses—and in the case of Marshal Ney, official witnesses—to the killing of Booth and Napoleon's old commander, but the stories of their survival were as circumstantial and impressive as those of Murrieta's alleged escape from death. Among men of lesser note who were known to have been killed, Billy the Kid of New Mexico, Curly Bill of Arizona, and Quantrill the guerilla chieftain of Missouri were all reported alive years after their death.

"Only people who want to believe Murrieta is still alive doubt that he is dead," said Harry Love. "Let them believe what they please if it does them any good. But Murrieta is as dead as lead can make him and he will stay dead until Gabriel blows his horn. All those who signed affidavits and many more who saw the head had known the outlaw well and all were absolutely positive in their identification. The skin later became badly discolored and much darker than in life and the features, especially the lips, became swollen with clotted blood, but even in that condition, the head was easy to recognize. It was as certainly the head of Joaquin Murrieta as the head on my shoulders is that of Harry Love."

After Murrieta's death there was never such digging for buried treasure since the romantic legend of Cocos Island caught the imagination of the world, or the shores of Long Island were spaded up from one end to the other in the long search for Captain Kidd's pirate gold. Murrieta, who undoubtedly stole a large fortune during his career as a bandit, was believed to have buried much of his plunder in money, jewels and gold dust in various places. This tradition has persisted through the years and faith in it is strong even to-day. Every once in a while with burros packed with picks and shovels, blankets and provisions, men steal out secretly on the hunt for the outlaw's buried treasure and dig holes in lonely valleys or at the foot of some oddly blazed live oak or near some outstanding landmark in the hills.

Maps, musty and yellow with age, have appeared from mysterious places from time to time, marked with crosses to indicate the exact spots at which the treasure was buried. Always there was an intriguing story that these old charts had been drawn by Murrieta himself, or by Three Fingered Jack or some other captain of the outlaw band. They had been treasured, it was said, by some old Spanish family into whose keeping they had been entrusted, or had been accidentally discovered among the archives of some of the old Missions. The favorite haunts of the treasure seekers have been the Arroya Cantova, which is near the modern town of Coalinga and is now known as Cantua Arroya; Bear mountain near Angel's Camp, where a summit is still called Joaquin's Lookout and where the outlaws had a refuge in what is known as Joaquin's Cave; Priest's Valley and Pacheco Pass in the Coast Range; the Santa Cruz mountains; the hills around Hornitos and Mariposa; and the country in the neighborhood of Carmel and San Buenaventura Missions.

An old Mexican who was a stranger in that part of the country, camped in Priest's Valley for several weeks in 1883. He gave it out that he was a prospector and, though no gold was ever found in the region, he did much digging in the neighboring hills. According to an old tale, Murrieta and Three Fingered Jack had buried $100,000 in varying sums in several places in that locality. This was done with the consent of the band, though only Murrieta and Three Fingered Jack knew where the money was planted. The plan of the outlaw leader was to hoard the loot of his marauding campaigns until enough had been accumulated to allow each of his followers $20,000. But he and Three Fingered Jack were killed before the necessary amount had been acquired.

Soon after the old Mexican had gone away as mysteriously as he had come, a venerable padre, who had been supposed to be sleeping in his grave, returned to the Coast Range after an absence of thirty years.

"A short time before his death," said the padre, "Three Fingered Jack drew a map showing the spots in which the money had been buried and wrote out directions as to how it might be found. Knowing I would never betray his confidence, he gave the chart and instructions to me and asked me, in case he and Murrieta were killed, to deliver them to his family in Mexico, and he left enough money to pay my expenses on such a trip. After he and Murrieta were slain, I went to Mexico and carried out his request. His family was very poor and worked hard for a bare living and I doubted whether any member could afford the money or the time to make the long trip to California. I have lived in the Mexican capital ever since and I lost track of the family many years ago. I do not know whether they ever made any effort to recover the treasure."

In view of the priest's story, the old Mexican who had dug so industriously in Priest's Valley was believed to be one of Three Fingered Jack's kinsmen. But whether he unearthed any treasure was never known.

Several years after Murrieta had been killed, three Mexicans came from Mexico to Hornitos and dug for several days in the garden of a house once occupied by the outlaw. But apparently their labor went unrewarded. According to William Howard, whose ranch was close by, Major Baldwin, an Englishman, while mining near

Hornitos, unearthed a chest containing ten thousand dollars which Murrieta was supposed to have buried. This treasure, it was thought, was what the three Mexicans had been searching for.

For many years a hermit lived in a lonely cabin in the hills back of Santa Cruz. When some men, out on a buried treasure hunt, called at the cabin one day they were surprised to find lying dead on a rude cot a woman dressed in an elaborate gown of silk and lace with a costly necklace about her throat and jeweled rings on her fingers. She was recognized as the hermit. In a gold locket on her necklace was a picture of herself as a beautiful girl and opposite it a picture of Joaquin Murrieta. The woman was believed to have been one of the outlaw's former sweethearts, but who she was was never ascertained. As death approached she had laid aside the rough masculine garments of a hermit and put on the jewels and silken finery of the happy days of her early romance and, adorned as a bride for her husband, had gone to keep tryst with her dead lover.

James H. Wall, an Englishman, who arrived in California in 1851 from Australia, carried constantly on his person, concealed in a belt beneath his clothes, $20,000 worth of diamonds and other jewels. While drunk in a saloon in Hornitos, he boasted of his treasure belt and Murrieta and Abelardo Mendoza heard him. Next day the two outlaws rode into Wall's camp.

"What luck are you having here?" asked Murrieta.

"Bad luck," Wall replied. "I'll never get rich in these diggings."

"Listen," said the outlaw. "I know a place where nuggets as big as hen's eggs are lying around on top of the ground. If we sink a hole there, we ought to take out a fortune. My partner and I are green hands but, if you will help us do the mining, we will split the gold share and share alike."

"Mucho oro, señor," said Mendoza enthusiastically. *"Mucho oro."*

Wall, unaware of the identity of the two villains, innocently accepted the proposition. His horse was soon packed and he and his guides rode several miles until they came to a deep cañon. There they dismounted and made their way on foot down the steep hills that walled the gorge. Murrieta dropped behind the Englishman. A pistol shot echoed among the hills and Wall fell dead. A few weeks later Murrieta and Mendoza buried somewhere in the neighborhood of Santa Barbara the gems that they had found strapped around Wall's body.

"You are one of the few men in my band," said the outlaw chief to Mendoza, "that I have ever allowed to share the secret of any of my buried riches. If you ever lift this treasure or betray its hiding place, I will pull out your tongue by the roots and cast you into the sea to be eaten by sharks. If I should happen to die before I kill you, I will come back from hell and haunt you night and day in the shape of a devil."

When Wall was slain, David Wall, his young son, was employed in the household of the Garcia family in Santa Cruz. Soon after the murder, Murrieta and Mendoza visited the Garcias and for more than a week were domiciled beneath their roof. The Garcias were cousins of Murrieta, and the bandit was in love with Dolores Garcia, a beautiful girl of seventeen. When Murrieta and Mendoza prepared to take their departure, Dolores clung about her lover's neck in a paroxysm of weeping.

"It is our last farewell," she cried. "I have a presentiment I shall never see you again."

Her presentiment came true and, after the outlaw's death, Dolores, who could have had her pick of many rich young gallants, vowed she would never marry and kept her word. She died in 1880.

To solace the girl, Murrieta drew a small package from his pocket and gave it to her.

"Here, Dolores," young Wall heard him say, "is a chart that will guide you to the spot where I have buried $20,000 worth of diamonds and other jewels. If I should be killed, the treasure is yours."

Wall, who had learned of his father's death in the mountains at the hands of two Mexican outlaws, became convinced that Murrieta and Mendoza had murdered him for his jewels. A few nights later, Wall stole the map and disappeared. While in Santa Barbara studying the chart and planning to go in search of the treasure, he saw Mendoza, who he believed had trailed him to murder him and recover the document. In panic at the prospect of sharing the fate of his father, the lad fled to Santa Fe, New Mexico, where the news of Murrieta's death reached him. Still in terror of Mendoza, he dared not return to California. While in Santa Fe, an old Mexican showed him a letter from Mendoza in which the outlaw said he had been unable to find the buried jewels without the map and had spent $3,000 in traveling about the country in an effort to find Wall, who he did not doubt still had the chart in his possession. Mendoza was the last survivor of Murrieta's band of outlaws. He was killed in 1884 while resisting arrest by a constable in San Luis Obispo.

Wall returned to the Pacific coast in 1886 and went to work as a gardener in Santa Barbara. Being unfamiliar with the country, he showed the map to his employer and asked his aid in locating the treasure. The two men drove into the mountains and pitched camp in Rincon creek where they began their search. According to the chart, the jewels were buried at the foot of a live oak marked with a cross and standing near a spring at the end of a row of three trees. Leading toward the spot was a clearly drawn line indicating a trail. But hunting for a tree with a cross on it in a wilderness of mountains was like looking for a needle in a haystack, and they could find nothing remotely resembling a trail. At last by accident they stumbled upon what might once have been a deer path but was now overgrown with brambles and hardly traceable. They managed, however, to follow it to the summit of a ridge. Across a gorge they saw another ridge on top of which stood three white stones plainly visible. Crossing the second ridge they found themselves at the head of Padre Juan cañon in an amphitheater set with live oaks. From the base of a cliff, a spring of clear water was bubbling. Not far away three live oaks stood in line twenty feet apart. On the tree nearest the spring was an almost obliterated blaze; on the second tree, another. They rushed to the third tree. Their hearts gave a leap. There was the cross.

They dug furiously. At a depth of three feet, their spade rang against metal. An iron chest emerged from the earth, tightly locked and encrusted with rust. They knocked off the lid with a hammer. Treasure trove! Their eyes were dazzled by a glitter of diamonds, sapphires and emeralds overspreading a mass of gold nuggets. Wall identified some of the gems as those brought by his father from Australia. The value of the treasure was estimated at between $13,000 and $14,000.

So the red legend of the outlaw chief of California's Age of Gold draws to a close. All the actors in the lurid drama have faded into the shadows of oblivion. Three Fingered Jack, Claudio, Gonzalez, Vulvia, Valenzuela and the rest are dim ghosts of the distant past. Rosita, Carmelita, Ana Benites, Mariquita and La Molinera, who rode with them through purple romance, are half-forgotten names. Farms and homes, towns and cities, crowd the scenes of their wild adventures. The terrible Joaquin Murrieta of old days has become a tale told in the twilight or a song sung to a guitar.

END